DISAFFECTION FROM SCHOOL

ISSUES AND INTERAGENCY RESPONSES

An annotated bibliography and literature review on absenteeism and disruption and on the responses of schools and other agencies to these and allied issues.

Bibliography compiled by Alison Skinner with Hilary Platts and Brian Hill.

Literature Review by Alison Skinner.

ACKNOWLEDGEMENTS

Many people have helped to make this Bibliography possible, but thanks are due in particular to the following:

Individuals, LEAs, social services departments and police forces that made unpublished reports available to us, in response to requests for information, and in some cases wrote at length about policy in their area.

Researchers and practitioners within the field who read and made comments on early drafts of the Literature Review, but who should not be held responsible for its shortcomings. In particular our thanks to Rob Grunsell, Daphne Johnson and Jean Lawrence, who commented on the whole of the Review, and Ros Gill, Henri Giller, R P Gregory, Rod Ling, Ann MacLean, Tim Pickles, Ken Reid, J K H Rose and David Ward, who commented on specific chapters.

Jim Thomas of NYB for editorial assistance on the Bibliography and critical assessment of the Review, including collaboration on Chapter V.

Typeset by Overload Design and Print, 61 Princess Road West, Leicester LE1 6TR and by James Preston at the National Youth Bureau
Cover design by Neil Beesley
Printed by AB Printers Ltd, 33 Cannock Street, Leicester LE4 7HR
Published by the National Youth Bureau, 17-23 Albion Street, Leicester LE1 6GD
ISBN 0 86155 073 0   November 1983
Price £3.95

Contents

INDEXES

Introduction

Children who find themselves in trouble at school, or who cause concern to the authorities because of their absence from school, disruptive behaviour, or educational and social needs, are the focus of considerable attention at present.

A substantial literature has grown up over the last ten to 15 years which analyses the nature, extent and possible causes of these difficulties, as well as describing policy measures and practical initiatives undertaken by local education authorities, schools and other agencies, either separately or co-operatively, to address these issues. Many different points of view on the origins of school-related problems can be found within these publications, including those of pupils, teachers, social workers and academics. Similarly, the policies and practices described reflect the wide variation in attitudes about the most appropriate and productive measures to be adopted with regard to these children.

The Bibliography seeks to draw together a representative collection of this literature, reflecting the range of attitudes and practice and the variety of sources. Its scope and subject coverage are also based on a view that many seemingly diverse aspects of policy and provision for these young people, which are usually treated separately, need to be understood in relation to each other. The accompanying Literature Review is more selective than the Bibliography, both in the issues covered and the perspectives highlighted. It examines five major subject areas of current interest or concern and provides a guide to the key literature on these subjects; on certain topics it summarises and compares the findings or points of view of the principal writers.

This work was originally intended to cover the twin subjects of interagency responses to children in trouble at school and of school involvement, along with other welfare agencies, in responding to children at risk or in trouble in other settings. In the event, it proved difficult to trace sufficient literature on the second subject to maintain this dual emphasis and it remains a minor theme within this work.

This relative scarcity of written material seems to mirror the situation in the field. Trouble at school is dealt with almost entirely by the schools and related LEA services; trouble in the community is mainly tackled by a different set of agencies such as Social Services, Probation, Police, law centres, youth work and child care agencies. The personal or social problems of children who are not found troublesome may be taken on by either or both types of agency, but often in isolated or fragmented ways.

One concern in compiling this Bibliography was to draw attention to the relationship between these problems, as experienced by young people, and to the need for greater clarity about the roles of different agencies and greater understanding about their interface. This concern will be apparent, especially in parts of the Literature Review, but it is only a secondary dimension. The main thrust of the work, corresponding to the existing literature, is directed towards school-based problems such as absenteeism and disruption, and school and interagency responses to them.

The work is intended as a resource for practitioners, administrators, researchers and academics within the education and allied fields who have an interest in and concern for young people in trouble at school and the provision that is made for them. It should also be of interest to those who are involved in work with young people in trouble outside school and are concerned about the role of the school in the lives of these young people.

The Bibliography: Structure, Scope and Contents

The literature in the Bibliography is divided into three main sections and then classified according to subject. The major divisions are between: individual or collective opinions on the causes of school-related problems; research findings on the subject; and accounts of policy, provision and practice. The Contents page provides a guide to the sub-sections within these divisions.

The Bibliography is principally concerned with children of secondary school age, although literature has been included which combines findings from both primary and secondary schools. Documents have been included from England and Wales, Scotland and Northern Ireland, but it should be noted that particular features of the educational system in Scotland and Northern Ireland have not been adequately reflected in the literature available. No foreign material has been included, apart from one bibliography on provision for disruptive children, which also contains literature from the United States. The cut-off point for the inclusion of new material was Autumn 1982. The majority of the works cited were published in the '70s but some literature from the '60s has also been included.

A wide variety of sources have been drawn on, including books, articles, pamphlets, legislation, reports from Government, LEAs, local agencies and projects, conference proceedings, dissertations and unpublished papers. (The reports from LEAs comprise only those which have been made available to the compilers; documents from other LEAs have been cited in works included in this Bibliography but it has not been possible to obtain these.)

The Bibliography did not set out to be a comprehensive guide to the literature on disaffection from school, and, of necessity, its coverage in some areas is more selective than in others, citing only the major works. Areas covered in some depth include:

— the nature, extent and causes of both absenteeism and disruption in school;
— the range of policies, provision and practice for 'dealing with' these children, and the roles of schools, other LEA services and other agencies, including alternative education units, the courts, and intermediate treatment providers.

The Bibliography is more selective, if not thin, on such areas as:

— aspects of the school system that affect large numbers of pupils and are not specific to the disaffected minority, such as curriculum reform, out of school projects, the pastoral care system, or home-school links;
— responses of the education system to special educational needs or to problems that do not manifest themselves in truancy or disruption, such as school refusal, special education, and many of the concerns of the Educational Welfare Service, the School Psychological Service or Child Guidance.

On liaison between LEAs and non-LEA agencies about young people in trouble with school or in the community, the Bibliography has sought to be fairly comprehensive in its coverage, but it is difficult to know how far this has been achieved. In any case, it does not cover educational provision in residential institutions such as community home schools and Prison Service establishments.

Within the policy, provision and practice section, certain agencies such as Social Services are reasonably well represented while others, particularly the Probation Service, the Youth Service and the Health Service appear scarcely, if at all. It seems probable that suitable material is to be found in the Health Service literature, but there was insufficient time to track this down. It is less likely that substantial, accessible literature on Probation or the Youth Service has been missed.

The Literature Review: Scope, Purposes and Style

The Review is organised around five broad subject headings which are given separate chapters and cover topics of current concern and controversy within the field. It is worth noting however, that there may be a time lag between the emergence of an issue in the field and its appearance as a talking point in the literature. The Review is selective in its coverage and does not systematically discuss all the items contained in the Bibliography.

It has to be acknowledged that the choice of subjects within the Review and the way in which they are handled are influenced by certain value perspectives on the position of young people in society and the attitudes and practices which are commonly adopted in relation to them. The Review takes an explicitly anti-labelling stance and emphasises research findings which focus on socio-environmental interpretations of behaviour and on initiatives which address the organisational factors within institutions that can precipitate trouble with school. It also attempts to highlight particular perspectives, including the views of young people, the needs and rights of disaffected pupils and their parents, and ways in which agencies and welfare professionals can direct their energies towards changing their own practices as an alternative to trying to change children and families. In line with the latter point, it is sometimes critical of the current practices of schools and welfare agencies and identifies problematic aspects of their relationship.

The Review, therefore, has two main functions in relation to the literature. It summarises the principal points of view or research findings of contributors in the Bibliography — a traditional function of this kind of resource. It also goes beyond this and draws on the literature to pay particular attention to some issues, given the perspectives noted above. Consequently, different styles of handling the literature will be apparent throughout the Review.

When using the traditional, summarising approach of a review, the treatment of a topic will vary according to its perceived importance to the central subjects covered in this work. Some topics, like school refusal, are dealt with briefly, usually by a listing of the main authors on the subject, with little or no discussion. By contrast, the topic of off-site units receives much more attention, including summaries of research findings and reports and fairly extensive discussion of the issues raised.

To emphasise particular issues or perspectives, the Review may:
— provide a more detailed exposition of statistics or procedures, for instance on care proceedings for truancy;
— gather together research findings from a variety of sources on a subject not hitherto discussed to any extent, such as young people's reasons for non-attendance at school;
— provide a framework for organising issues and findings on topics that have received little attention from reviewers, as in parts of Chapter V.

These different styles of review merge into each other, but no review can be totally neutral and it is hoped that the user, aware of the author's concerns, can pick his or her way accordingly.

Using the Bibliography and Literature Review

The Contents page provides an overview of the main subject covered, separately for the Review and the Bibliography, and a guide to their location. The Subject Index refers to the pages of the Review or sections of the Bibliography that deal particularly with a specified topic, and it also gathers together any other references scattered through the Bibliography and not cited in the relevant part of the Review. The Author Index refers to all items in the Bibliography by a given author and, in some cases, to papers covered, separately for the Review and the Bibliography, and a individuals, not agencies, as authors.

An additional means of access to the literature in the Bibliography is provided by the Index of Areas, Agencies, Projects and Sources: this covers agencies and periodicals cited as sources, the names of projects and agencies described in the literature, and their geographical location. Where the source of a particular document is obscure or is the individual author, additional information may be available in the Address List at the back.

Chapter I
Disaffection from School

I.1 INTRODUCTION

During the early to mid '70s, something of the dimensions of a moral panic seized certain parts of the education world about the numbers of children and young people who were reported to be regularly missing school or disrupting classes.

Some of the agitation reflected the concern of the teachers' unions for the well-being of their members, who were reported to be dealing with intolerably difficult children in the classroom and, in some cases, facing physical threats. Some commentators felt that this kind of behaviour in schools mirrored declining standards in society as a whole (NAS/UWT, A13, A14; Liverpool Teachers Advisory Committee, C24), while others questioned the relevance of the educational experience on offer to the needs of the children behaving in such ways (Midwinter, A22; Roberts, A23).

Feeling themselves under some pressure, local education authorities set up working parties to study the issues of disruption and non-attendance (C15, C16, C18, C19, C22–C31). In the wake of these, some, although by no means all, LEAs made special provision for disruptive or absentee pupils in the shape of on-and off-site units.

A notable initiative was undertaken by ILEA in 1978/9 when £1.5 million was made available under its Disruptive Pupils Programme. Following applications by primary and secondary schools, voluntary organisations and IT projects, a total of 2,280 places were created in off-site units, on-site nurture groups and other forms of provision for disruptive and absentee pupils (Tattum, B105).

The literature on ~~the problem~~ ... ~~reflects~~ fluctuations of concern ... mid '70s the focus was on truancy and ~~subsequently it was~~ the issue of disruption in ... ~~commentators~~ and researchers, givi... ~~subject~~ ... the subject.

From an historic ... ~~truant~~ from school or being ... a new phenomenon. Hump... class education between 1889 and ... of the repressive nature of schooling in those early days and the widespread resistance it provoked in the shape of truancy, classroom unrest, refusal to learn and school strikes.

Within and outside the school setting, pupils may behave in a variety of ways which indicate stress, disturbance or disaffection from the values and practices of the institution. To varying degrees they may also be experiencing difficulties in maintaining progress with their school work. Schools are now expected to diagnose these symptoms of distress among their pupils and make appropriate use of a range of resources and personnel to meet their individual needs.

A continuing theme of this chapter and the review generally will be that, while most schools undoubtedly undertake excellent work with distressed or disturbed children, some find it difficult to acknowledge the possibility that pupil behaviour may express a legitimate criticism of aspects of school organisation or individual teacher practices. The way such pupils are handled within school and the explanations put forward for their conduct all point to the urge to deploy psychological explanations about the individual and the family, and to devise treatment strategies designed to reconcile pupils to the existing demands of the institution.

This approach was supported by many early researchers into school refusal, truancy and disruption, who regarded such behaviour as an interesting symptom of underlying individual and family malfunctioning requiring analysis and treatment

(Hersov, B19, B90; Tyerman, B79, B80; Chazan, B85).

A more recent emphasis in research, however, is to regard absenteeism and disruption as a warning signal of stresses and strains within the education system which should act as a stimulus to action. Sharp (A6), Bird et al (B99), Galloway et al (B101), Tattum (B105) and Grunsell (C178) recognise certain kinds of behaviour as dissent on the part of the pupils, although it may not always be explicitly defined as such by the children themselves, and as an implicit challenge to the legitimacy of school authority. Sharp (A6) notes that dissent is a persistent and important communication from pupils, and Bird et al (B99) and Tattum (B105) highlight the role of the pupils who, by their actions and outbursts, draw attention to features of school life which their less demonstrative peers also find frustrating, distressing or unjust.

Disruption and absenteeism are the most extreme and noticeable forms of disaffection from school. Until now they have, for the most part, received separate attention from researchers and commentators as manifestations of personal and family difficulties, but these two types of behaviour have some common features, in terms of the individual children concerned and their experiences of school processes. Some absentee pupils withdraw from their classes without creating any trouble and some disruptive pupils are regular attenders, but other pupils who are a disruptive influence attend only intermittently, often to the unconcealed relief of their teachers (Bird et al, B99).

The following sections will review separately the literature on the nature and incidence of first absenteeism (I.2) and then disruption (I.3), paying particular attention to the views of pupils on the causes of this behaviour. The rest of the chapter (I.4) will focus on the specific factors and experiences within the school setting which have been highlighted by pupils and researchers as potential contributory causes of disaffection.

I.2 ABSENTEEISM

I.2.a Extent of Absenteeism

Attendance at school for all children between the age of five and the prescribed school leaving age has been partially compulsory since 1880 and entirely so since 1918. The Education Act of 1944 requires LEAs and schools to provide an education appropriate to a child's age, ability and aptitude and expects parents to ensure that their children receive a full-time education (Taylor and Saunders, C11). This is underwritten by legal sanctions which can be brought against both parents and children.

Non-attendance became a problem as soon as the first Act came into force. Humphries (A3) suggests that in Britain as a whole the average attendance rate rose from approximately 60% in the 1880s to over 80% from 1906, but that this was only achieved after a prolonged struggle to overcome the resistance of working class children and their parents.

Attempts were made in the early to mid '70s to measure the rate of attendance at school and a number of reports were produced showing attendance during a day (DES, B42; ILEA 1976, 1980, 1981, B44–B46); a week (NACEWO, B29; SEO, B39; ISTD, B73); a term (Fogelman et al, B14; Sheffield Education Dept, B49); and a school year (Baum, B40; Billington, B41; ILEA 1981, B47; White and Peddie, B50). Findings from these surveys show an average attendance rate varying between 85% and 92%.

The ILEA Research and Statistics Division (B23) has produced a useful review of the research findings on school non-attendance, which includes discussion of the methodological problems involved in compiling attendance figures. Baum (B40)

and a WHERE article (B38) have noted some of these and their comments are reinforced by the Welsh HMI report (B43), which points out that the casual weekly absenteeism of pupils who are ostensibly preparing for examinations creates a considerable problem of continuity for teachers, which may be concealed by gross percentage figures. Baum (B40), Billington (B41), the ILEA 1981 survey (B47) and White and Peddie (B50) have studied patterns of attendance, which show a marked reduction during the course of the day, week, term and school year.

I.2.b Types of Absenteeism

The terms 'absenteeism' and 'school non-attendance' have been used in recent research to denote all types of absence except for that justified by illness. Certain distinct categories of absence have been studied in some detail in recent years. These include 'truancy', defined as unjustifiable absence without parental knowledge or consent, and 'school refusal' or 'school phobia', which has a variety of definitions in current usage, but includes cases of severe emotional upset on the part of pupils when faced with the prospect of going to school.

Truancy rates have been estimated by Caven and Harbison (B9), Fogelman et al (B14), Galloway (B15, B16), NACEWO (B29), the DES survey (B42) and the Pack Report (C5), and the figures vary between two and 12%. School phobia is a much smaller problem and Berg (B82) estimates that, by his definition of the term, its prevalence in early adolescence is about one per cent.

An additional category which is receiving increased attention is parentally condoned absence, ie absence that parents are aware of and consent to, either actively or passively. Galloway's (B15, B16) research in Sheffield suggests that this can amount to as much as half of the total reasons for unjustified absence, and Caven and Harbison's (B9) study in Belfast, using the same categories, assigned three quarters of the absence rate to this category.

I.2.c Causes of Absenteeism

Although certain commentators may have no hesitation in hypothesising causes for truancy, most researchers are more cautious and would claim only that certain factors are associated with truancy or with absenteeism in general.

These factors cluster around three main areas: individual and family characteristics and circumstances; socio-environmental and cultural factors; and school characteristics. Up to the mid '70s it was customary to look for explanations of absenteeism within the home and the family, but increasingly researchers are examining the influence that school curricula, organisational structures and general ethos can have on individual pupils. Since these school factors are a main focus of this chapter, discussed in more detail in a later section (I.4), the research on other factors will be summarised here.

Fogelman et al (B14), Reid (B31, B35) and an ILEA report (B47) examine the influence of individual, family, neighbourhood and school factors on all categories of non-attendance. Butler and Dunn (B7) provide an overview. Eaton and Houghton (B11), Eaton (B12), Harbison et al (B18), Jackson (B24), Mitchell and Shepherd (B27) and Reid (B31, B35) analyse the individual and personality characteristics which are associated with absenteeism. Caven and Harbison (B9), Galloway (B15, B16), Mitchell (B28), Phillips (B30) and an ILEA report (B47) look at additional socio-environmental factors in families and neighbourhoods. A reiterated finding of these researchers into persistent absenteeism is the presence of family and home circumstances of multiple deprivation.

Truancy as a specific category has received attention from Billington (B70), Farrington (B71), ISTD (B73), Mawby (B75), Tibbenham (B77) and Tyerman (B79, B80), who present data on the individual, family and environmental factors associated with this form of absenteeism. The contrasting individual and family characteristics of pupils exhibiting truancy and school phobia are considered by Barker (B6), Denney (B10) and Hersov (B19).

There has for a long time been considerable concern about the possible association between truancy and delinquency.

Tennent (B36) reviews research findings up to 1971 and concludes that the evidence shows a significant correlation between the two. Farrington's (B71) analysis from the longitudinal Cambridge Study in Delinquent Development found that secondary school truancy was significantly related to juvenile delinquency, but suggests that these are two symptoms of the same underlying problem and the one does not cause the other. In comparing delinquent and non-delinquent truants he concludes that the delinquent truants had similar individual and family features to the others but in a more extreme form. May's (B26) research in Aberdeen found that only a minority of irregular attenders appeared in court and only a minority of delinquents were also absentees or truants. A 1975 survey of head teachers by the Lincolnshire Education Committee (B25) found that although some considered that ROSLA had contributed to absenteeism in some schools, the general opinion was that there had been no attendant increase in juvenile crime.

There is considerable literature analysing the causes and treatment of school refusal or school phobia, however defined. Kahn et al (B91) provide an overview of research findings. Baker and Wills (B81), Berg (B82), Chazan (B85), Cooper (B86), Davidson (B87) and Hersov (B90) review causes and characteristics; Blagg (B83), Framrose (B88), Hamilton (B89) and Rock (B92) discuss treatment strategies; and Boreham (B84) provides some follow-up data on the subsequent careers of young people who had received treatment for school refusal.

There is as yet no systematic research on the reasons for parentally condoned absence, although Phillips (B30) reports some informal discussions with parents on the south London estate she studied.

Evidence of the influence of school factors on absenteeism is provided by Reynolds (B57–B65), Galloway (B15, B16), Rutter et al (B66) and Bird et al (B99), and is discussed in a later section.

I.2.d Pupil Explanations of Absenteeism

Much of the research already cited has used sources and data such as demographic variables, standardised tests and the judgment of teachers and education welfare officers, to build up a picture of the characteristics and motivation of absentee pupils. It is only comparatively recently that researchers have asked young people directly what reasons they would give for staying away from school. Reid (B31, B35) has provided a series of categories for classifying the answers given, which is similar to a framework used in a survey conducted by the ILEA Research and Statistics Division (B47). The following table uses Reid's framework and notes the supporting evidence from researchers and commentators who have questioned young people and recorded their views on their reasons for absenteeism.

The evidence cited does not come solely from truants, but includes the views of pupils who could be classified as other kinds of absentee according to the definitions already given. It includes sample surveys of pupils in the school setting (Reid, B31, B35; ILEA, B47), interviews with young people at an off-site unit and List 'D' school (Buist, A1; Anderson, C185), and unstructured conversations with self-confessed truants on the streets (Seabrook, A5; Sullivan and Riches, A8; Phillips, B30).

Absenteeism: reasons given by young people

Personal factors

Lateness, oversleeping, dislike of long school journey (Reid, B31, B35; ILEA, B47)

Social factors

Influence of peers (Buist, A1; Reid, B31, B35; ILEA, B47; Pack, C5)
Attraction of alternative entertainment (Reid, B31, B35; ILEA, B47)
Attraction of alternative employment for own benefit or to help family income (Phillips, B30; Reid, B31, B35; ILEA, B47; Green, B72)

Family factors

Care for younger brothers and sisters (Phillips, B30; Reid, B31, B35; Pack, C5)
Illness of parent creating anxiety and requiring support (Reid, B31, B35; ILEA, B47; Green, B72)
Preferring home to school (ILEA, B47)

School factors

School transfer (Reid, B31, B35)
Curriculum and exams: creating boredom or anxiety, perceived as irrelevant (Buist, A1; Seabrook, A5; Sullivan and Riches, A8; Reid, B31, B35; ILEA, B47; Green, B72; Anderson, C185; Reynolds, C205; Beresford and Croft, C259)
Bullying, difficult peer relationships, noise and disorder at school (Sullivan and Riches, A8; Reid, B31, B35; ILEA, B47; Pack, C5)
School rules and punishments: pettiness and inconsistency (Buist, A1; Seabrook, A5; Reid, B31, B35; Reynolds, C205; Beresford and Croft, C259)
Relationship with teachers (Buist, A1; Seabrook, A5; Sullivan and Riches, A8; Reid, B31, B35; ILEA, B47; Pack, C5; Anderson, C185; Reynolds, C205)
Reaction to absence: sarcasm from teachers and peers on return from previous absence (Reid, B31, B35; ILEA, B47; Green, B72)

As noted above, the family and home circumstances of persistent absentees are frequently characterised by multiple deprivation, and the reasons for absenteeism given by pupils reveal the interaction of family and social factors with school experiences. Absenteeism can be seen in one sense as the reconciliation of conflicting demands, in which family responsibilities and anxieties take precedence over the demands of school. It may also be a withdrawal from personally distressing experiences at school, such as failure with school work, conflict with a particular teacher or bullying from peers. In a third sense, absenteeism may be a positive expression of disaffection from school, where pupils opt out, sometimes in groups, in search of more attractive and remunerative ways of spending their time.

I.3 DISRUPTION IN SCHOOLS

Disruption, as a concept, is more complex than absenteeism since it presupposes a context of classroom and school rules and the interaction of teachers and pupils within these. Within schools, it can be viewed either as irritating and undesirable misbehaviour by pupils in general, or as the special form of behaviour displayed by a particular type of child known as the 'disruptive pupil'. The identification of disruptive behaviour or the disruptive pupil is an extremely subjective process and depends very much on the expectations and tolerance levels of the individual teacher.

The definitions given by three researchers in the field illustrate the range of interpretations which are possible.

Lawrence et al's (B104) definition, which is an adaptation of the one used by Lowenstein (B97), encapsulates a common educationalist view which interprets disruption in terms of its consequences for the institution: 'Behaviour which seriously interferes with the teaching process and/or seriously upsets the normal running of the school. It is more than ordinary misbehaviour . . . and includes physical attacks and malicious destruction of property.'

Galloway et al (B101) emphasise the importance of the teacher's perception of the problem: 'Disruptive behaviour is any behaviour which appears problematic, inappropriate and disturbing to teachers.'

Tattum (B105) stresses the context in which the behaviour takes place: 'Disruptive behaviour is rule-breaking behaviour in the form of conscious action or inaction, which brings about an interruption or curtailment of a classroom or school activity and damages interpersonal relationships.'

Lawrence et al's (B104) study of teacher responses to disruptive behaviour provides the following list of some of the types of pupil behaviour regarded as unacceptably disruptive: 'Blank defiance, rejection of reasoning, unacceptable noise levels, physical violence between pupils, threats to teachers or pupils, theft, extortion, graffiti and vandalism, verbal abuse, lack of concentration, boisterousness, lack of consideration to others.'

I.3.a Extent of Disruption

Galloway et al (B101) provide an historical review of the prevalence of disruption under the heading of 'An increasing problem — or just increasing provision?'. Attempts to quantify the amount of disruptive behaviour in schools have encountered various problems, such as the difficulty of actually defining the behaviour in a way that is widely acceptable. In addition, schools are often reluctant to admit to having problems of this kind unless they feel they have something to gain from the disclosure, such as additional resources.

Lowenstein's (B97) 1975 survey of secondary schools on behalf of the National Association of Schoolmasters had a relatively low response rate but found that there were four and a half disruptive incidents per 100 pupils over a two month period. It seems likely, however, that schools differed in their interpretation of disruptive behaviour. Laslett (B96) reviews the findings from surveys by the DES (B93), Lowenstein (B97) and others, and Dunn (in Dunn et al, C241) provides a brief overview.

A recent survey of teachers by Dierenfield (B94) found that over half of them reported a problem with disruptive behaviour but only a very small proportion regarded it as serious. Similarly, the HMI's (B5) 1979 survey of secondary schools found very few schools reporting a considerable problem of indiscipline.

I.3.b Causes and Types of Disruption

The types of explanation which are advanced for disruption in schools will depend on whether the focus of attention is on the behaviour itself and the context in which it takes place, or on the individual child.

The 1974 NAS pamphlet, 'Discipline in schools' (A12), listed 26 possible causes of indiscipline, ranging from weakness of parents, permissiveness in society, pop culture and 'do-good' attitudes of social workers, through to inappropriate curriculum, overcrowding and the poor quality of a minority of teachers.

Docking (B109) summarises the range of psychological theories which have been advanced to account for children's behaviour, including psychodynamic, cognitive-developmental and social learning theories, the incompatibility of working class and middle class values, sub-cultural and labelling theories. He notes that the strategies recommended to deal with disruptive behaviour will depend on the particular explanation favoured and concludes that in our present state of knowledge there seem to be no grounds for adopting one approach to the exclusion of others.

The teachers questioned by Lawrence et al (B104) put forward the following explanations for disruptive behaviour: 'Lack of intelligence/reasoning ability, home problems, unsatisfied needs, boisterousness as a reaction to being controlled, unfamiliarity with the teacher, tense and inexperienced teachers, incompatible teachers and children, and physical intervention by staff, leading to violence.'

Tattum (B105) notes that many disruptive children are socially inept, without the skills to handle an escalating situation. They are verbally abusive when disciplined, where other children remain silent, and feel the need to defend themselves, save face and preserve self-esteem.

Because of the subjectivity of the judgments required, there is as yet no real agreement on either the special characteristics of the disruptive child or the possible existence of different categories of disruptive children. Some informal attempts have been made to distinguish certain types (Jones-Davies and Cave, B111), while Bird et al (B99) and Grunsell (C178) provide some case studies which illustrate the ways in which certain personal and family factors can interact with school experiences to produce disruptive behaviour. The following passage describes different types of family backgrounds which may affect children in certain ways.

Some children, through force of circumstance, acquire adult responsibilities and experiences and are given adult status by their families. School life, by comparison, can appear petty and restricting, and attempts to impose a subordinate pupil status on them meet with resistance and often withdrawal (Bird et al, B99; Grunsell, C178). Jones (in Jones-Davies and Cave, B111) identifies this group as 'the mature' and shows some sympathy for their situation.

Secondly, there are children who are well integrated into families which are markedly anti-school and anti-authority in attitude. In many cases this is backed up by a neighbourhood culture which places a low value on schooling and seems able to provide a viable alternative in terms of identity and employment (Phillips, B30; Grunsell, C178). From the point of view of the child this can provide a justification for absence and disruptive behaviour if school experiences are adverse.

There are also children who come from families which might have similar material disadvantages to the others described but are marked by additional tensions in family relationships. Adult relationships may be changeable and violent, sibling relationships difficult, and parent-child relationships neglectful, punitive, overdemanding or rejecting. Children from these families may experience difficulties in relating to adults at school, particularly when parental authority has been exercised harshly (Seabrook, A5; Bird et al, B99; Grunsell, C178).

A fourth category distinguished by Reynolds (B57, B61), Bird et al (B99), Jones (in B111) and Lawrence et al (B104) embraces pupils who, for whatever reason, no longer have any formal interest in school but continue to use its facilities for their own social purposes. It is these pupils' capacity to subvert any orderly classroom regime which necessitates the establishment of truces or deals between individual teachers and pupils to guarantee good behaviour, particularly in the final school year.

I.3.c Pupil Explanations of Disruption

Pupil explanations of disruptive behaviour are uncommon in the literature and Tattum (B105) is a valuable source of data on this aspect. On the basis of information supplied by pupils placed in a special unit for disruptive behaviour, he puts forward five headings which summarise the major reasons cited by these young people. These are listed below together with the explanatory details provided by Tattum. Where a particular reason is confirmed by other research findings, this is included.

'It was the teacher's fault'
Research findings reviewed by Docking (B109) show that there is widespread agreement among pupils on what constitutes a 'good' teacher, who is expected to be relatively strict but fair, approachable, and to show an interest in pupils. Teachers who are regarded as soft, ineffective, rigid, harsh or uncaring or who incite physical confrontations, can provoke deep resentment which leads to indiscipline and disruption. It is agreed by most commentators that very few children are universally disruptive and most have a good relationship with at least one teacher.

Not being treated with respect
There is resentment of behaviour by teachers which undermines the self-respect of pupils. Adolescence is generally recognised as a time when young people are aspiring to adult status and are especially sensitive to threats to their self-image.

Inconsistency of rule application
The need to manage large groups of children and establish crowd control is sometimes incompatible with strict notions of justice and individual responsibility, and pupils may be unfairly singled out for actions they did not commit. The resulting resentment and resistance can lead to more serious incidents at the time or later on.

Having a laugh
A degree of pupil subversion of the normal routine is an accepted, if not overtly condoned, part of school life. For some pupils, however, creating a diversion is their main claim to status within their group and they have a need to go beyond the routine

misbehaviour of their classmates. Sharp (A6) examines the relationship of the disruptive pupil to the rest of the class. Longworth-Dames (C180) suggests that such a pupil may be conforming precisely to the requirements of his group, and can become trapped in the role and unable to change his behaviour without losing face.

The school system
Pupils point to long difficult lessons at the end of a school day, when teachers and children may be both irritable and tired and minor incidents can escalate into major confrontations. Researchers who have analysed disruptive incidents identify peaks of activity when teachers and pupils are furthest removed from natural breaks in their relationship. These are during the midweek period, particularly Wednesday (Lawrence et al, B104), the middle of the term and the middle of the school year, particularly November, February and March (Galloway et al, B101; York et al, C184).

I.4 SCHOOL FACTORS

The role of the school, as a contributory factor in absenteeism and disruption, is receiving increased attention from researchers at present. This can take the form of either an examination of the nature of pupil experiences in individual schools, or an analysis of the way in which certain practices may differ among a number of schools, with possible repercussions for the pupil population in each. This section examines findings on the nature of these school factors, drawing on two main types of source.

The first comprises the researchers who have established that considerable differences exist between schools in their rates of suspension and referrals to outside services, and in delinquency among their pupils. Others in this group have analysed aspects of school ethos and organisation which are associated with differing rates of pupil absenteeism and delinquency.

The second type of source comprises the explanations given by pupils for absenteeism and disruptive behaviour set out earlier in this chapter. Certain aspects of school life have been identified by them as potential precipitating factors in their behaviour. These will be examined in turn, along with the school processes involved, drawing on evidence from other researchers on the subject.

I.4.a School Differences, Ethos and Organisation

Power (B55), in an important pioneer research study, provided the first indication that schools might be exerting an independent effect on pupil behaviour by demonstrating that schools in Tower Hamlets differed considerably in the delinquency rate of boys attending them. Gath et al (C138), in a later study of schools in Croydon, also found independent variations in juvenile delinquency rates, which were associated with rates of referral to Child Guidance. Galloway et al (B101, C175, C176) and Grunsell (C178) both found marked differences between schools in their rate of suspension of pupils. The former studies confirmed, in addition, that these differences were unrelated to variations in the catchment areas. Both findings are further discussed in Chapter III.2.c.

Bird et al (B99) found that schools differed in their use of off-site units, and this reflected different practices within the school regarding the handling of difficult pupils. Some referred pupils early at the first sign of disaffection, while others referred late as a last resort after exhausting school resources. These practices are further discussed in Chapter IV.

While some research findings have demonstrated that idiosyncratic differences between schools do exist, other studies have attempted to analyse what aspects of school ethos and organisation are associated with particular forms of behaviour on the part of pupils.

The effect that school ethos can have on individual pupils was underlined by Clegg and Megson (A18) back in 1968 in an influential work. They were particularly concerned with the way in which school practices can divide the slow children from the bright, reinforcing the disadvantages of the weaker children.

Reynolds (B57–B65), investigating comprehensive schools in South Wales, found that those with comparable intakes varied considerably in the amount of school non-attendance they experienced. He found that high attendance schools were characterised by small size, lower institutional control, less rigorous enforcement of certain key rules on pupil behaviour, higher co-option of pupils as prefects and closer parent-school relationships. The high truancy schools appeared to be narrowly custodial in orientation, with high levels of control, harsh and strict rule enforcement and an isolation of the formal staff organisation of the school from potential sources of support amongst both pupils and parents.

Rutter et al's (B66) research has confirmed the importance of school ethos with the findings that in the schools he found most successful there was a prompt start to lessons, strong emphasis on academic progress and attainments, generally low frequency of punishment and a high rate of recognition for positive achievements, well cared for buildings and a feeling by pupils that they could approach teachers for help with a personal problem. The HMI (B53) report on ten good schools confirms this overall approach as good practice.

Reynolds (B57, B61, B63) suggests that schools with low rates of absenteeism and delinquency establish a 'truce' with working class pupils in which certain rules are not enforced stringently in exchange for cooperation in other aspects of school life. This is seen as a way in which schools as institutions can accommodate themselves to pupils who do not share their dominant values.

Bird et al (B99) report a similar phenomenon from London schools but are critical of the practice, seeing it as a way in which schools can avoid acknowledging the existence of pupil disaffection. Practices include ignoring pupil absence, excluding pupils from lessons and bartering for good behaviour which, in effect, allow individual pupils to opt out of the mainstream and follow an individualised programme.

I.4.b Pupils' School Experiences

Aspects of school life which have been highlighted by pupils as particularly problematic are teacher-pupil relationships, experience of the curriculum and school rules. In some cases these difficulties may reflect problems inherent in the nature of classroom teaching, while in others they illustrate particular types of school ethos.

Teacher-pupil relationships
When pupils claim that their relationship with a teacher is a major reason for staying away from school or disrupting lessons, some of the practices they cite are — being picked on unfairly, not being treated with respect or being dealt with excessively strictly (Buist, A1; Tattum, B105). Teachers themselves, however, can also experience stress when faced with aggression from pupils and a continual undercurrent of noise, disorder and lack of attention in class. In some cases they too may feel the need to withdraw from the situation, using sick leave for the purpose (Dunham in Wedell, B113).

Both sets of experiences reflect circumstances in which the ritual strategies adopted by both teachers and pupils to keep their relationship fairly evenly balanced have been taken to excess. These strategies can be analysed in terms of the type of approach adopted, the underlying reasons for it and its ultimate effect on the recipients.

Teachers develop strategies which are primarily aimed at anticipating and preventing possible challenges to their authority, and Hargreaves (B52) and Leach (in Wedell, B113) demonstrate how this can take the form of stereotyping individual pupils according to their capacity to create trouble. Information is pooled within the staff room so that even the newest recruit is fully informed about potential troublemakers. Teachers vary considerably in the strictness of the regime they maintain within their classes, with some evidently feeling the need to respond verbally or physically to the first hint of a challenge to their authority (Hargreaves, B52).

The issue of control and the preservation of authority is central to the teaching profession for a number of personal and professional reasons. Teaching makes substantial demands on the resources of its practitioners and places them in a particularly vulnerable position vis-à-vis pupils who may be disillusioned and disaffected in their final years at school (Jones in Hersov and Berg, B20; Dunham in Wedell, B113). In addition, certain subjects may need to be taught to a tight schedule requiring the maximum order and attention from pupils and any interruption of this through disruption or absenteeism can create considerable problems.

A possible consequence for pupils of certain of the teaching practices mentioned is that once a reputation is gained for troublemaking, staff are continually on the alert for any fresh outbreaks and new teachers are warned in advance about certain pupils, which prevents a natural relationship being formed with them. In many cases it becomes very difficult for the pupil to demonstrate that a genuine improvement in conduct has taken place, and to have this believed and accepted (Buist, A1; Bird et al, B99). Authority which is exercised excessively strictly can provoke reaction and Shostak (A7) reports some research on pupil attitudes to teachers in a northern school, which indicates how deeply they resent being called names, physically manhandled, never allowed to act on their own initiative and continually supervised.

Pupil strategies have been examined by Corrigan (A2), Marsh et al (A4), Willis (A9) and Hargreaves (B51, B52), who have started to uncover some of the rules and norms which govern the behaviour of working class boys at school. They describe two major forms of universally accepted behaviour — testing out teachers and 'messing about'.

All pupils test out teachers — respected educationalists often nostalgically recall teachers from their own school days whose lives they helped to make a misery — and this can be seen as a necessary way of establishing each teacher's particular idiosyncracies and tolerance levels. 'Messing about' takes the form of a moderately disruptive subversion of the orderly school routine, which is generally regarded by pupils as a natural reaction to boredom and constraint.

Most teachers can take these challenges in their stride, but those who have difficulty maintaining control, or have to teach unpopular subjects, may find the noise and disturbance levels in their classes rising above tolerable limits. This creates stress in the teacher who may then react strongly to an individual incident — which at other times might be overlooked or merit only a mild response — with potentially serious consequences for the pupil concerned (Lawrence et al, B104). Most teachers and pupils find reasonably satisfactory ways of coexisting but the pressures which are built in to the relationship do have the potential to create stressful situations from which both parties may feel the need to withdraw.

Experience of the curriculum
Bird et al (B99) identified four main ways in which pupils' experience of the curriculum could be adverse: if they found it irrelevant, if they could not relate to its academic slant, if they could not meet the demands it made, and if it left them with a sense of failure. These findings are also reinforced by pupil comments on the curriculum, given as part of their explanations of absenteeism (I.2.d above). Although pupils may not experience many formal methods of assessment within school before the fifth year, it is clear that they receive informal messages about their ability by observing the success of others, teachers' reactions to them in class and the degree of help they receive. Tattum (B105) quotes a boy as saying: 'School is for learning, but all it learned me is that I'm no good for anything.'

Fogelman (B13), Galloway et al (B101), Lawrence et al (B104), Varlaam (B106) and York et al (C184) are agreed that absentee and disruptive children often have serious learning difficulties with the curriculum, are backward at school and underachieve. A key finding in most studies has been that the children are generally bright enough to know they are not matching up to the school's demands. Teachers may underestimate the genuine difficulty some children have in understanding what is required of them. Sharp (A6) quotes a pupil comment: 'Some teachers don't explain what they want you to do and then get mad when you can't do it,' and Anderson

(C185) reports similar pupil difficulties with work they felt was insufficiently explained to them.

Pupil comments recorded by Buist (A1) and Anderson (C185) among others suggest that in the early secondary school years children are sensitive to school assessments of their ability and conduct and will miss specific lessons to avoid conflict with teachers and the experience of failure. They may also disrupt lessons to distract attention from their difficulties. As they get older, however, the school's assessments of their work and general competence as individuals may assume less significance in the light of the confidence gained from successful experiences in other areas of their life, such as part-time employment, family responsibilities and peer groups (Bird et al, B99).

School rules

Infringement of school rules may be the first stage in the process that, in the eyes of a teacher, marks out a pupil as a potential troublemaker, leading eventually to more serious confrontations. Pupil comments indicate that some rules may be infringed through no fault of their own, eg family circumstances, some may be resented as an injustifiable imposition in the light of their developing adult status, while others may be enforced inconsistently by teachers.

Virtually all schools have general proscriptive rules concerning dress, personal decoration and interpersonal behaviour, which are traditional battlegrounds in the secondary school; but there is also an additional set of rules governing pupil behaviour in the classroom which is more complex and variable. Hargreaves (B52) and Tattum (B105) have analysed the different types of rules which are normally in force in the classroom, constraining movement, talk and behaviour, and have also recorded the occasions which these may be relaxed. Hargreaves (B52) further notes that teachers may be either moralistic or pragmatic in their attitude to classroom rules — either enforcing them stringently or assessing the benefits of enforcement against likely costs in each situation.

By observing children through the school day, Hargreaves (B52) demonstrates the level of sophistication required of pupils to adapt their behaviour to the nature of the classroom task, the demands of the subject and the individual requirements of the teacher, all of which may change radically at 40 minute intervals throughout the day. Pupils may find themselves in trouble with one teacher for behaviour which is tolerated by another, or lack the social skills to adapt to the changing demands made on them.

Reynolds' (B57–B61, B64) research findings from schools in South Wales suggest that the degree of stringency with which schools enforced two key behavioural rules against smoking and chewing gum was positively associated with levels of pupil absenteeism and delinquency. As described earlier, certain schools, in effect, made a truce with pupils allowing them greater freedom in their personal behaviour in return for cooperation with other aspects of school life.

Where pupils feel rejected by the traditional values of the school on both an academic and cultural level, they may set up their own counter-school culture, which becomes an alternative source of esteem and status (Marsh et al, A4; Willis, A9; Hargreaves, B51).

I.5 CONCLUSION

The most recent research is now suggesting that trouble with school is a complex interaction of individual, family, sub-cultural and school factors which cannot be explained adequately by concentrating on any one factor in isolation. While the explanations for pupil disaffection have to take account of this complexity, the solutions have to be sought in the areas which are most amenable to change. Educational authorities and schools have not found it easy to 'treat' children successfully, let alone change family patterns or class attitudes but it should be in their power to make changes in schools.

The critical attention being given to the school factor may be regarded by educationalists as yet another imposition on a system already attempting to do the impossible in the face of conflicting demands from society. The message from Reynolds (B58) and Rutter et al (B66), however, is an encouraging one — that schools do make a difference, and the practices they choose to adopt can make a substantial contribution to the level of disaffected behaviour manifested and to the quality of the educational experience of the children in their charge.

Chapter II
Education System Responses to Disquieting Pupil Behaviour

II.1 INTRODUCTION

The best schools have always been able to provide a compensatory environment for children beset with all kinds of difficulties. They can sometimes be the first to alert other welfare agencies to the existence of problems, and through their own pastoral care resources and other initiatives can often provide the right kind of sympathetic support and practical help. The Schools Council Working Paper (A24) provides case studies of children exhibiting learning or behavioural difficulties who were helped in this way. Clegg and Megson (A18) put forward a powerful case for schools to make a positive effort to alleviate the plight of children in distress, and FitzHerbert (C34) reinforces the importance of teachers as front line workers, who need to be aware of the range of services available to help children they have identified as being in need.

Most schools will readily mobilise their resources to help children who are obviously withdrawn, unhappy and underachieving. More of an effort is required to do the same for children who have become disaffected from school and whose behaviour creates all kinds of problems for the teacher and the institution, although their home circumstances may be equally stressful. In some cases, efforts to help are hindered by the inadequacy of existing links between home and school, or misunderstandings between parents and teachers.

The first instinct of most schools is to seek ways of reconciling pupils to the existing regime, first through routine school sanctions and then through a variety of special initiatives providing remedial education, compensatory social and learning experiences and individual support. Always available in reserve, however, are the more drastic options of court proceedings and suspension. Schools will vary considerably in the level and type of resources available to them, the order in which they deploy them and the speed at which punitive sanctions replace the more welfare-oriented ones. This idiosyncratic approach was noted from research findings in the previous chapter (I.4.a) and reveals itself in such measures as the difference in suspension rates between schools with similar intakes.

This chapter falls into five sections. There is a brief discussion of LEA and school policies on pupil disaffection (II.2), followed by three main sections on: the process of identifying and categorising problem pupils in schools (II.3); the range of responses that may be employed by schools from their own resources (II.4); and referral to outside support agencies (II.5). A short fifth section looks at the use of outside resources to help schools and teachers to cope and change (II.6). Recourse to suspension or court proceedings is dealt with in the next chapter, and the use of separate educational provision, whether on-site or off-site, is covered in Chapter IV.

II.2 LEA AND SCHOOL POLICIES

LEAs and schools have considerable discretion in deciding what policy they adopt on issues such as absenteeism and disruption. Young et al (C32, C33), reviewing the evidence from LEA working party reports and policy documents, found that a growing number now have a policy on disruptive behaviour. This takes different forms, however, according to whether disruption is seen as behaviour that large numbers of children could exhibit partly because of school practices, or whether disruptive pupils are equated exclusively with suspended and pre-suspension pupils. If the former view is taken, preventive strategies such as the modification of the curriculum or the appointment of a school counsellor may be adopted. If the latter view is seen as more relevant, the establishment of an off-site unit may be seen as a priority. Frequently, however, a dual policy may be operated.

There seems to have been rather less attention by LEAs to developing a policy on school non-attendance, but the reports which exist have stressed the need to improve inter-departmental communication, improve school practices in recording and identifying persistent non-attendance and strengthen the Education Welfare Service (Strathclyde, C29; West Glamorgan, C31).

The above has outlined some of the factors which may influence LEA policy on disruption and absenteeism and some of the forms this can take. However, it in no way covers the array of LEA policy issues which are closely related to the above or must underpin it. There is, for instance, the fairly fundamental issue of how far the LEA sees its schools as a broadly preventive front line welfare service or how far schools are expected to concentrate on teaching, leaving welfare functions largely to other services.

In any case, the LEA has policy options as regards, for example, the balance between schools and external support services as the main location for responding to various needs and problems; the relative importance attached to the different support services such as Education Welfare, Child Guidance, the School Psychological Service or special education; the relative support and encouragement given to different types of school initiative, such as developing pastoral care systems, remedial education, special curricula or organisational change. LEAs have to take decisions on these kinds of issues, for example, in choices about how they allocate resources. However, policy discussion of such issues does not figure prominently in the literature contained in this bibliography, and relevant LEA policy documents have proved difficult to trace.

Within their LEA framework of policy, individual schools may differ according to the use they make of the resources available to them. Gath et al (C138) note that schools in Croydon varied in their rate of referral to Child Guidance and special education. Bird et al (B99) have described the differential referral by schools to an off-site unit, and other evidence from Staffordshire (C28), Gillham (C121), Davis (C174) and Grunsell (C178), where welfare agencies have described their relationships with schools, confirms these individual differences.

The patterns of use by schools of outside resources and school relationships with external agencies are described more fully in Chapters IV and V.

II.3 IDENTIFICATION, ASSESSMENT AND REFERRAL OF PUPILS PRESENTING PROBLEMS

Millham (C203) makes a somewhat caustic comment: 'If you are difficult with worried parents, you go through child guidance, maladjusted schools and later to adolescent units. If, however, you are just a deprived and delinquent child with indifferent parents, you are processed through local authority care into the penal system.' Although the evidence to back this statement is not yet extensive, it underlines the concern felt by many commentators about the different routes that can be taken by pupils according to the decisions made about them by schools and welfare professionals.

This section provides an overview of the ways in which children are identified and then dealt with as non-attenders or disruptive pupils. The literature tends to treat these separately as distinct groups of pupils with little overlap, although it is known that some children behave in both ways. In both cases the behaviour will be viewed and handled differently according to the age of the child and the stage he has reached in his school career, with a common breaking point usually occurring in the fifth year (Bird et al, B99; Milner, C222).

II.3.a Identifying and Responding to Absenteeism

The speed at which schools and education welfare officers identify significant cases of absenteeism is a good indication of the quality of liaison between the two services and the effectiveness of the school pastoral care system. In some schools, such problems may be identified at an early stage if the pastoral care system is particularly sensitive. In others, if the pattern of absence is sufficiently irregular and spasmodic, the behaviour may be allowed to continue unchecked (Bird et al, B99).

The degree of seniority of staff who are assigned responsibility for dealing with incidents of truancy may be of some significance. Reynolds and Murgatroyd (B60) present findings from an unpublished study of 76 schools, comparing those that acknowleged they had a truancy problem with those that felt they did not. The former tended to make more use of the most senior staff and of middle management (defined as heads of year, heads of house and counselling staff) to coordinate information on absenteeism and liaise with education welfare officers. Furthermore, those schools where the growth of middle management posts was accompanied by a decline in the responsibility of the form tutor for dealing with truancy had a number of associated problems, including poor rates of attendance and high rates of cautions for delinquency.

During the first two to three years in the secondary school there may be more intensive initiatives to reinforce attendance and to minimise the educational damage to the pupil (Milner, C222). Referral to Child Guidance or the School Psychological Service may be an option in cases of suspected school refusal; this is more common in the primary school, although cases are reported from secondary schools (Galloway, B15, B16). A short-term placement in an on-site or off-site unit may be an option in the second or third year to establish habits of attendance and provide remedial education (Palfrey, C98; Taylor et al, C103). Court proceedings may also be used as a strategy (Galloway et al, C194). Most of these strategies, however, assume that the causes of absenteeism are to be found within the child or in his or her family and home circumstances. There will be little systematic investigation of the contribution of school factors to the behaviour.

By the fifth year, if the school-based initiatives have been unsuccessful, a pattern of behaviour will have been established which may be exceedingly difficult to break. Various outcomes are possible for different groups of absentee pupils. Some may evade all official checks on their behaviour until they reach school leaving age, often with the passive collusion of their school (Sullivan and Riches, A8; Bird et al, B99). A select few may spend their last year in an on-site unit, officially still within the main school setting, but in reality completely separate from its demands and routine (Jones and Forrest, C170). Some may end up in court and be put on a care or supervision order (see Chapter III.3), especially perhaps those who combine truancy with delinquency (May, B26). A selection of these children together with those formally suspended by the school will finish their education in off-site units of various kinds (Ball and Ball, C86; BIOSS, C87; Grunsell, C91; Robinson, C99).

II.3.b Identifying and Responding to Disruption

Children who are disruptive pose more of an immediate management problem to schools. The pupil will be identified as a potential problem much earlier and there may be more urgency in the attempts to find a solution, particularly one which will effectively remove such challenges to the existing school system.

The post-war period has seen a spectacular growth in the range of provision for children with special needs and in the amount of research and investigation devoted to analysing the nature and origins of their educational and behavioural problems (Galloway and Goodwin, C39; see also Chapter IV.3.a). A present day school, therefore, faced with a disturbing child, has theoretically more resources to draw on in the shape of knowledge, support and remedial teaching techniques than a pre-war establishment. There is also the possibility of detecting early signs of potential behaviour problems through the use of predictive psychological tests.

The existence of these possibilities requires teachers and senior staff to make judgments about the right course to follow with a pupil at certain points in his school career, and provides them with the significant option of deciding his needs cannot be met within mainstream education. They may then judge it necessary to refer him for assessment by an educational psychologist with the ultimate aim of transferring him to special education (Galloway et al, B101).

By the end of the second year there will be some consensus within the school about the children who are giving cause for concern because of their failure to learn, underachievement and extreme behaviour in the classroom (Bird et al, B99). Some of these may include children who appear to have fulfilled teacher expectations that they will be a disruptive influence, based on their record at primary school, family or sibling reputation, and the teacher's own assessment of their character (Hargreaves, B52; Leach in Wedell, B113). In the majority of cases it will have proved almost impossible to separate the learning difficulties from the behavioural problems and to assess how far the one precipitates the other. In making their initial assessment, schools will be trying to find out the underlying causes of the learning problems and discover whether the behavioural difficulties have their origin in individual psychological disturbance or social factors within the family and neighbourhood (Galloway, C146).

Statements from teachers and educationalists recorded by Lawrence et al (B103, B104) and in LEA reports (Isle of Wight, C23; Liverpool Teachers Advisory Committee, C24) reveal that some are quick to assign an 'ESN' or 'maladjusted' label to pupils, using a vocabulary derived from the categories in use, pre-Warnock (C13), to classify children in need of special education.

Prior to the 1981 Education Act (C3) pupils could be categorised as possessing various handicaps, the majority of which were physical in origin. Two categories related to educational, behavioural and emotional handicaps — 'educationally subnormal' (ESN) and 'maladjusted' pupils. After the Education (Handicapped Children) Act of 1970, the ESN category was split informally between ESN (M), or moderately mentally handicapped, and ESN (S) for severely mentally handicapped (Galloway and Goodwin, C39). These authors further reviewed the way in which these groups were identified and assessed, and found that while there was some agreement on the level of IQ which defined the ESN (M) children, the identification of conduct which could be described as 'maladjusted' was fraught with difficulty.

Even before the Warnock Report (C13) appeared, the category of 'maladjusted' was increasingly being regarded by educational psychologists as a meaningless concept, whose use was justified only as a way to obtain a special education place (Galloway et al, B101). The 1981 Education Act (C3) has abolished the old categories and replaced them with the Warnock-derived concept of children with special needs, but the bulk of the literature in the bibliography refers to the situation existing prior to this.

Because of their psychological interpretation of children's behaviour, certain schools and teachers may be predisposed to recommend that the majority of disruptive children should be educated outside the mainstream, and make their referrals to the educational psychologist accordingly (Liverpool Teachers Advisory Committee, C24; Galloway and Goodwin, C39). An even more pressing reason for referring a pupil to Child Guidance or an educational psychologist, however, can be a strong desire by some schools to remove the child from the institution and make him somebody else's responsibility. The differing rate of referral by schools of children to Child Guidance has already been noted (Gath et al, C138), and Galloway et al (B101) include some evidence revealing differences between local authority areas and regions in the numbers of children ascertained as maladjusted or awaiting placement in special schools. It is clear that the general availability of special education places within an authority will have a major influence on the numbers of children diagnosed as being in need of such provision, and it may also influence the type of initial assessments made by schools.

Educational psychologists have the ultimate responsibility for assessing the child and making any recommendations for special education, but increasingly they are resisting pressure from schools to provide an instant diagnosis and cure for the problem. Instead, many are suggesting that attention is paid to the interaction of the child, parent and teacher, which may be a contributing factor to the problem (Galloway and Goodwin, C39; Gillham, C121; Loxley, C123, C124).

If after the first referral a special education recommendation is not made and the school is required to continue to deal with the difficult child, there are a variety of remedial teaching initiatives which can be taken to provide for his educational needs. In some cases these may also help to overcome the behavioural problems. Galloway (C146) provides some sample case studies of these kinds of activity and many more exist which are not covered in detail in this bibliography.

Children whose behavioural problems are assigned to social causes may be subject to a combination of routine school sanctions and pastoral care initiatives, which might include referral on a short-term basis to an on-site or off-site centre (Bird et al, B99; Grunsell, C178).

As the child gets older and physically stronger in the third and fourth years, the educational and behavioural problems may become more pronounced, or exacerbated by a sudden family crisis. Further assessment by the school and the educational psychologist may decide in some cases that a special education placement is now appropriate. For other disruptive pupils the parallel process may be a continuing series of incidents within the school, a hardening of teacher attitudes towards them and a series of short-term exclusions (Bird et al, B99; Grunsell, C178).

By the fifth year, schools may well have reached the end of the line with certain pupils who have exhausted the school resources and become exceptionally difficult to contain. In some cases suspension will be used as a technique for obliging the LEA to take some action. Referral to special education may again be one of the options, although the special schools are usually most reluctant to accept children at this stage. For other pupils the options may be continued containment within the school on the basis of truces or bartering arrangements for good behaviour, or suspension with or without the possibility of placement in an off-site unit (Bird et al, B99; Galloway et al, B101; Grunsell, C178).

The following section brings together some of the special initiatives which can be taken in school time, although not exclusively in the school setting, by teachers, volunteers and other welfare professionals, to provide individual support and a range of compensatory experiences for pupils who are causing concern through their absenteeism and disruptive behaviour. These do not include the specialist remedial teaching initiatives which occur in many schools.

Approaches that are covered include school pastoral care systems, the use of specialist staff such as counsellors, social workers and group workers, various forms of curriculum innovation, and the use of volunteers as befrienders of individual pupils. The use of intermediate treatment within the school setting is also reviewed here. On-site units may also be viewed as a special school initiative, but many commentators would regard their objectives as falling more towards the control end of the spectrum than the largely welfare measures discussed here. They are considered in more detail in Chapter IV.

II.4 SCHOOL-SPONSORED INITIATIVES

II.4.a Pastoral Care and Counselling

The pastoral care system can be defined as the functions of guidance, support, discipline and administration that schools perform in relation to pupils. Schools differ in the way in which they organise their pastoral care systems, and in the range of staff who may be involved such as class teachers, specialist pastoral care staff or trained counsellors. Each school works out its own individual blend of emphasis and approach depending on the educational philosophy held by the head or other key staff. Its value lies in providing a framework within which the individual

teacher is able to act when faced with pupils who have special needs or problems, experience learning difficulties or cause trouble (Bird et al, B99; Johnson et al, C220).

Much of the literature concentrates on the guidance and support functions, making suggestions on how these should be carried out or giving examples of practice from case studies. The literature is deficient in systematic evaluations of the effectiveness of pastoral care systems and school counselling in meeting the needs of pupils or changing their behaviour. Best et al (C144) have noted that there is considerable imprecision about the way in which terms such as 'pastoral care', 'counselling' and 'guidance' are used and in the meanings assigned to them. Blackham (C145), Hamblin (C147, C148), Marland (C149), Jones (C158), Lytton and Craft (C160) and Moore (C161) discuss possible structures for pastoral care systems within schools, their role and function in relation to pupils, and their implications for staffing and relationships within the institution. The writers on counselling — including Galloway (C146), McGuiness (C150), Hamblin (C153, C154), Holden (C155, C156) and Lewis and Murgatroyd (C159) — examine the role of the counsellor within schools and the nature of counselling as it is practised within the school-setting.

Best et al (C144) and the Teachers' Action Collective (C151) present a more critical view of pastoral care, suggesting that in practice schools place more emphasis on the disciplinary and administrative functions. It is further hypothesised that pastoral care can be a mechanism for the imposition of tighter discipline on disaffected pupils and become a euphemism for the administration periods which are necessary to enable a school of over 1,500 to run smoothly and efficiently.

Studies of pastoral care in action, though few and far between, reveal differences in the effectiveness of certain systems in monitoring pupil well-being and providing a satisfactory support structure for teachers. Bird et al (B99) found differences between schools in the latitude which was allowed to pupils to express dissent and the firmness with which disaffected behaviour was identified and followed up with disciplinary or remedial action by pastoral care staff. At one end of the spectrum pupil behaviour was systematically monitored and action taken at the first sign of disturbance. At the other end a more informal system existed which tended only to register the most overt symptoms of distress or dissent. Johnson et al (C220) describe the pastoral care practice within the schools they studied and note that most teachers felt the system was able to cope with the conflicting demands made upon it, although a minority of staff felt that disciplinary or administrative procedures were incompatible with the caring functions.

Galloway et al (B101) include some comments from teachers in their study of practice in Sheffield schools and report that some pastoral care systems appeared to succeed in allowing class teachers to consult with colleagues informally and receive advice on how to handle difficult pupils, thus helping to defuse potentially explosive situations. Other systems, which require teachers to refer pupils to specialist head of year staff, often divert the problem from its source and carry the danger of turning a minor incident into a major confrontation, thus increasing the possibility of suspension at the end of it.

Pupil comments on their experiences of pastoral care systems are not common. Murgatroyd (C162) reports on a study which suggested that pupils in one school did not see counsellors as a major source of help with personal problems but as senior teachers with considerable administrative duties. This view is challenged by Hooper (C157), who found otherwise in another school but, along with Murgatroyd, he underlines the importance of the orientation of the individual counsellor, who has to choose between being an institutional or client-centred agent.

Johnson et al (C220) report from their study that most pupils regarded the school counsellors as approachable, and built up close relationships with individual teachers who might or might not have pastoral responsibility for them. Nevertheless, these pupils did not regard the school pastoral care system as impinging in any significant way on their problems outside school. It was also recorded in passing that some pupils considered there were too many people in the school interested in finding out what their problems were.

Lewis and Murgatroyd (C159) make the general point that

schools setting up a middle management pastoral care system have de-emphasised the role of the school as an organisation in generating its own problems and diminished the role of the form teacher in pastoral care. The possible implications of this as outlined by Reynolds and Murgatroyd (B60) have already been discussed (II.3.a).

II.4.b Referral to Other School-based Welfare Staff

Some schools have a specialist welfare worker, such as a school-based social worker, instead of or in addition to a school counsellor. This person may be on the school staff, or a Social Services worker attached to the school, or perhaps part of an experimental team project. In such cases, referral to this worker is an option when it is decided that pupils need individual help with their problems, or support for difficult family and home circumstances.

Bond (C236) describes in some detail the way in which a school social worker can interrelate with the existing pastoral care system. Harvey et al (C246), Marshall and Rose (C250), Rose and Marshall (C255) and Wolstenholme and Kolvin (C257) report on experimental research projects which introduced social workers into schools to provide counselling support to teachers and pupils. A variety of models exist for locating social workers in schools, whether part- or full-time (Dinnage, C240; Johnston, C247), in the combined role of teacher-social worker (Morris, C251), in a new role as liaison-teacher (Francis, C244), or as an extra teacher performing a social work role (Firth, C243).

Such workers can provide specialist counselling skills and form links with families, which are invaluable in providing a more complete picture of the needs of the child. From the literature it is clear that considerable care needs to be taken in working out the relative responsibilities of pastoral care staff, social workers, counsellors and education welfare officers, and most projects report some initial hostility and friction from one or more of those workers which needed to be overcome.

In some cases schools may appoint a new kind of worker. Austin (C52) reports on the group workers placed in four Belfast schools, who were able to set up social education programmes for fifth year pupils as well as providing some social work support. Their position also enabled them to challenge the accepted school verdict on the pupils. Llewelyn-Davies (C55) describes the home-school liaison officer initiative in Birmingham.

Harding (C245) regrets the division between the teacher/counsellor/pastoral care staff who deal with the child in the school context, and the social worker/liaison officer who is concerned with the child's home environment and the network of external agencies. He proposes a role for a school-based worker who would be a combination of school counsellor, liaison officer and family therapist and thus provide a unified service for pupils. A joint education/social services initiative is represented by the schemes reported by Derrick (C239) and McGrath (in Dunn, C242), in which teams of workers consisting of a school counsellor, an education welfare officer and a social worker were attached to schools and were able to provide specialist help to pupils and teachers.

II.4.c Social Education and One-to-One Befriending Schemes

The educational world has increasingly recognised the necessity for some collective provision for older, non-examination pupils which acknowledges their need for a positive, alternative learning experience to the traditional school curriculum. Many such programmes were initiated in the wake of ROSLA (raising of the school leaving age) and are outside the scope of this bibliography. The schemes mentioned below have a mixture of aims. Some are provided on a universal basis as part of the educational provision for this age group, with the additional passing hope that improved attendance and behaviour may occur as a spin-off. Others are specifically designed for individually referred children.

Examples of the universal provision include a weekly community education placement outside school (White and Brockington, C166), an opportunity to tutor younger children at another school (Drinkwater, C165), and social education courses within the school setting which bring together workers from other agencies such as social workers, education welfare officers and intermediate treatment officers (Bedford Social Services Dept, C228; Padmore, C231; Pritchard, C232).

Other initiatives use resources from outside school to provide support for individual children as part of their school experience. Plouviez (C307) describes a school-sponsored scheme in which volunteers were recruited to act as counsellors to disturbed children who were underachieving, and spent one session a week with them building up a supportive relationship. Marshall (C306) describes an initiative whereby fourth year pupils with learning difficulties and associated personality and behaviour problems were linked with a volunteer 'tutor mother' who shared her home activities with the pupil for one day a week over a term. This was intended to provide opportunities for a close relationship to develop and demonstrate good models of home and family care.

A different kind of group experience, usually involving the cooperation of schools with Social Services staff, is provided by the intermediate treatment group which meets in school time, either on or off the premises, as an agreed part of the curriculum for pupils who may be referred for behavioural or attendance problems. This usually has a varied programme including discussion, group exercises and activities, offering the pupils a chance to articulate their problems and enjoy a range of compensatory experiences. Bietzk (C279), Pitts (C287) and Staines et al (C288) provide examples of the usual type of programme. The scheme reported by Hutchings et al (C283) is unusual in having a programme explicitly designed to modify pupil relationships with teachers, parents and other adults in the community.

A feature of such groups is the informality of the relationships between staff and pupils, and teachers who take part in them frequently find it a stimulating experience. An initial concern is often whether children will react adversely to them or whether it will affect their in-school relationships, but these fears are usually groundless. There may be additional benefits from increased contact with fellow professionals.

These issues of teacher involvement in IT groups are examined by Pritchard (C232), Groves (C282), Mulholland et al (C286) and Ward and Pearce (C289), mainly in the context of after-school and evening IT groups, discussed in the next section.

II.5 REFERRAL TO OUTSIDE AGENCIES

The Education Welfare Service, School Psychological Service, Child Guidance and Social Services may all be consulted at some time in connection with absentee and disruptive pupils, generally with the school objectives of reinforcing attendance, obtaining some positive information and guidance on how to handle the pupil, or in the hope that the child will be placed elsewhere. FitzHerbert (C34) and Johnson et al (C220) provide an overview of these services and the place of the school in what is termed the 'welfare network'.

II.5.a Education Welfare Service

The Education Welfare Service is part of the LEA, although there has been a continuing debate as to whether it might more logically form part of the social services department: this is taken up in Chapter V.2. The Ralphs Report (C6) is the major statement on its overall philosophy and desirable future. MacMillan (C112) reviews the strategy and functions of the service, and from a national survey identifies the core functions provided by Education Welfare as court proceedings for school non-attendance, checking on child employment, investigating neglect and advising on clothing and free meals. Davis (C107) reviews patterns of organisation in the service and Milner (C113) describes the role of individual EWOs and their training needs.

The EWO will be the first point of referral in cases of school non-attendance although the precise method will vary between authorities. In some cases teachers themselves will make referrals. Where school counsellors have been appointed they have usually taken over responsibility for liaising with EWOs (Johnson et al,

C220), and in other cases the EWOs will study school registers themselves to identify particular patterns of non-attendance (Wood in Dunn, B1).

Through home visits, EWOs are expected to uncover the underlying reasons for non-attendance and effect improvements though a variety of strategies, applied where appropriate to the individual circumstances, including exhortation, welfare work, direct action, summons to appear before school attendance committees or court proceedings as a last resort. Gregory (C111) provides some research findings which question whether home visits in themselves achieve any improvement in attendance. Webb (C116) and Wood (C118) describe types of welfare work undertaken by EWOs, and Pedley (C114) notes the contradictions which are inherent in their dual care and control role. Their part in bringing court proceedings for non-attendance will be discussed in Chapter III and their relationships with other professional groups are reviewed in Chapter V.

II.5.b School Psychological Service

The School Psychological Service varies in its organisation and composition across the country but is commonly staffed by educational psychologists, who receive referrals from schools and may undertake cognitive and personality assessment of a child's educational and emotional needs. On the basis of their own results and observations, coupled with reports from other professionals, they will make recommendations concerning the future handling or placement of the child.

The Summerfield Report (C10) describes the functions, training and activities of educational psychologists, and Wedell and Lambourne (C130) provide an overview of the services currently provided in England and Wales. Topping (C128) supplies a literature review on the development of educational psychology as a profession.

A feature of the current scene is a questioning of the educational psychologist's traditional role as dispenser of IQ and personality tests, and new ideas are circulating about ways of working more directly with schools in general and individual teachers in particular. Gillham (C121) edited an influential book of readings which sums up current thinking in the field, Hargreaves (C122) suggests that educational psychologists need more understanding of classroom processes, and Loxley (C123, C124) describes possible new directions in community psychology.

Relationships between teachers and educational psychologists are not always characterised by complete mutual understanding and appreciation of each other's difficulties and professional expertise. Topping (C129) and Wright and Payne (C132) report findings from consumer surveys of the School Psychological Service which highlight both positive and adverse experiences. There is further discussion of interagency and interprofessional relationships in Chapter V.

II.5.c Child Guidance Service

The Child Guidance Service is normally staffed by an interdisciplinary team comprising psychiatrists, psychiatric social workers, non-medical psychotherapists, and educational psychologists. It provides a service of diagnosis and treatment to disturbed children and their families and may be particularly concerned with treating cases of school refusal. It would appear that the majority of its clients are younger, primary school age children, but there are substantial differences in practice between different Services in various parts of the country.

The extent of its relationship with schools appears to vary considerably, with little effective contact in some areas and close links in others. It has been extensively criticised in the literature for remoteness, irrelevance and ineffective functioning through understaffing (Fawcett, C137; Rehin, C140; Sampson, C141; Tizard, C142), and as vigorously defended by practitioners (Barnes, C133; Davie et al, C135; Mead and Mead, C139; Whittam, C143). In the absence of any national survey of its functions it is difficult to obtain a comprehensive picture of its role as a support service for schools, Reports of the operation of two different services are provided by Central Regional Council

(C134) and BIOSS (C136). Gath et al (C138) note from a survey in Croydon that schools vary considerably in their rate of referral to child guidance. Further comments on school experiences of the Child Guidance Service are recorded in Chapter V.

II.5.d Social Services Departments

Schools may refer pupils to the social services department either because aspects of their personal and home circumstances seem to require special attention from social workers, or because the department provides special facilities which schools think are of particular benefit to pupils whom they are just starting to see as a problem. On the former, there seems to be a dearth of substantial literature, except in relation to school-based social workers, discussed above (II.4.b; see also V.2.b).

A good example of the latter kind of provision is the after-school or evening IT group that caters exclusively for young people referred by schools. Groves (C282), Leeds Social Services Department (C284), Mulholland et al (C286), Weiss (C290) and Westley (C291) describe projects of varying length which have a similar programme to the school-based IT groups such as discussion, group exercises and activities, although the evening groups appear to offer more opportunities for outings. Such groups often involve EWOs as a source of referrals and may develop out of relationships built up between local schools and specialist IT workers based in area social services offices.

Pupils with school-related problems may also be referred to evening IT groups which have a more varied membership including young offenders. Crutcher (C281) describes an intensive evening programme at an IT centre in which pupils referred for school non-attendance participated alongside children on care and supervision orders.

Kenny's (C262) survey of IT practice in London boroughs reveals that problems with school attendance and behaviour are often a major selection criterion for acceptance on to projects. This concern may prompt agencies other than Social Services to offer similar opportunities, from an IT or a youth work perspective. Burley (C280) describes an initiative by a voluntary agency in setting up a social education group for non-attenders and inviting school referrals.

II.6 OUTSIDE INITIATIVES SUPPORTING SCHOOLS AND TEACHERS

School-sponsored responses to disaffected pupil behaviour will tend to locate the source of the problem within the child and most of the initiatives will be directed towards reconciling the pupil to the needs and demands of the institution. Attendance enforcement techniques will do this most overtly but Best et al (C144) suggest that this attitude is an underlying feature of all pastoral care approaches.

Research demonstrating the contribution that school processes and ethos can make to overall pupil conduct has helped to renew interest in initiatives within schools that can assist teachers in managing difficult behaviour. Lawrence et al's (B103, B104) research has helped to identify certain flash points within the school organisation, and Gillham (B110) brings together a set of papers on analysing and changing schools systems. Another study by Lawrence (B117) provides practical guidelines for teachers to enable them to analyse and cope with disruptive behaviour in schools.

Some LEAs sponsor schemes which provide special in-school support for teachers. Barnsley Special Education Team (C53), Coulby (C54) and Sterne (C56) all report on the peripatetic team approach in which a group of teachers are assigned to a school to provide help, usually with pupils exhibiting behavioural and learning difficulties. In some cases the intervention will be directly with the class teacher providing help and advice on classroom management techniques. Further information on these techniques is provided by Upton and Gobell (B112).

This kind of approach is also being advocated by educational psychologists, and Topping (C129) reports on one such worker who spent the majority of his time on intensive in-service training and curriculum development work with schools. Wolfendale

(C131) describes ways in which educational psychologists can work with teachers on early identification of pupil difficulties, and Ravenette (C127) describes techniques whereby teachers can be helped to broaden their understanding of the origins of pupil behaviour. HMIs and consultancy services may be another source of analysis and advice to schools on aspects of their structure, organisation, ethos and rules.

II.7 CONCLUSION

Although there is an impressive range of initiatives for dealing with problematic behaviour potentially available to schools, it must be remembered that resources for implementing them are unevenly distributed across the country. Some pupils may experience very little in the way of sympathetic and remedial handling of their problems before resort to punitive action, while others with similar difficulties may be matched to a range of highly imaginative approaches under the auspices of specially qualified and skilled workers.

This patchiness in provision is further underlined by the relative absence in the literature of works which provide a critical analysis and evaluation of the range of strategies available to schools and LEAs, touched on in this review, which would enable comparisons to be made on various criteria.

Chapter III

Formal Sanctions: Suspension and Court Proceedings

III.1 INTRODUCTION

When all the school-based initiatives have finally been exhausted, head teachers and LEAs may reach a stage when they have to take action which states publicly that their resources are insufficient to cope with certain pupil behaviour, and additional pressure and help from external agencies are required.

This action can take the form of court proceedings against absentee pupils or their parents and the suspension of pupils who are disruptive, although some children may also be suspended for school non-attendance. Both of these formal sanctions have aroused controversy and there are signs that LEAs are becoming increasingly sensitive about their use, particularly suspension. This chapter reviews the literature on each in turn (III.2, III.3), and adds a further section on school involvement in the juvenile justice system generally (III.4).

III.2 SUSPENSION AND EXCLUSION

When schools are faced with exceptionally severe breaches of conduct by pupils, they have three sanctions at their disposal – expulsion, suspension or exclusion. Expulsion, as the permanent debarment of a pupil from a particular school, remains the ultimate sanction, although Jennings (C179) reports that there is still a divergence between those local authorities that accept the legality of expulsion from state schools and write provisions for it into their Articles or Notes of Government for schools, and those that say it cannot be done. Galloway et al (B101) state that although it is theoretically possible in law, few LEAs allow head teachers to expel pupils as their names are then removed from the school roll, creating administrative problems in later admitting them to short-term alternative education.

Suspension is a right conferred on schools by their Articles of Government, subject to the safeguard contained in the 1959 Schools Regulations that 'a pupil shall not be refused admission to or excluded from a school on other than reasonable grounds' (Taylor, C183). It has the same effect as expulsion, although the pupil remains on the school roll, and it implies that the head teacher sees no immediate possibility of re-admitting the pupil. Formal action has to be taken to notify parents, the chief education officer and school governors and, in some cases, appeal procedures are available (ACE, C173).

Exclusion, known in some authorities as short-term suspension, allows a head teacher to debar a pupil on a temporary basis. This may be on health grounds under the 1944 Education Act or the 1936 Public Health Act, or as a cooling-off period following an incident at school. A standard length of time is three days, although a survey by the Advisory Centre for Education (C173) has found that longer periods occur in some authorities. It is usually regarded as an informal measure not requiring any formal notification of the LEA and school governors and not subject to appeal.

III.2.a Statistics on Suspension and Exclusion

It is difficult to establish a national picture of the total numbers of pupils affected by suspension and exclusion (Galloway et al, B101). Detailed examination, particularly by Grunsell (C177, C178), has cast substantial doubt on the reliability of suspension statistics originating from LEAs. There is sometimes considerable imprecision in distinguishing between suspension and exclusion; cases may go unreported and figures may vary drastically from year to year following a tightening up of procedures.

The Advisory Centre for Education (C173) carried out a survey of suspension statistics in LEAs and obtained complete figures from 42 authorities for the year 1979/80. However, they advise caution in interpreting the statistics for the reasons just mentioned.

Galloway et al (B101, C175) present statistics on children suspended and excluded for at least three weeks from Sheffield schools in the period 1975 to 1979. This particular LEA had an established procedure for recording suspension and exclusion and the figures show that in the peak year of 1977/78 the number of pupils affected was never more than 0.38% of the total on the roll in any age group. Of the total, two thirds were boys and a third girls.

Grunsell (C178) provides figures for one London borough between 1975 and 1978. After remedying the under-reporting and various inaccuracies, he reports that in the peak year, also 1977/78, suspensions and exclusions amounted to 0.73% of the secondary school population. York et al's (C184) figures for Edinburgh in 1967–69 were equivalent to 0.023% of the total school population, as discussed by Galloway et al (B101).

III.2.b Reasons for Suspension and Exclusion

All schools would agree that actual assaults on teachers and pupils and serious cases of vandalism against school property are acts meriting instant suspension. Reports such as the one from Staffordshire LEA (C28), which provides lists of reasons for suspension, confirm that such incidents do happen in schools. Media reports and articles by other commentators, however, may give a distorted impression of their frequency. Galloway et al's (B101) and Grunsell's (C178) figures reveal that violence towards teachers is a very small proportion of the total, amounting to 12 cases out of 266 in the four year aggregated Sheffield figures and five cases out of 85 in Grunsell's 1977 statistics. Acts of bullying and violence towards other pupils are more frequent, but Galloway et al's figures show that even after combining all the violence and vandalism incidents together, they still only account for between one eighth and one quarter of the total. Abuse and insolence to teachers, refusal to keep school rules and accept school discipline, disobedience and disruption of lessons, usually over a long period of time, are the major reasons for suspension.

However infrequent, acts of violence towards teachers naturally provoke strong feelings. Teachers' union publications (A10–A12, A16) provide guidance on teachers' legal rights and the sources of support available to them in taking court proceedings against pupils for assault once they have been suspended, if this is felt to be justified. A report by the Assistant Masters Association (A10) says that assaulted teachers should not be obliged to receive the pupils back into their classes without their consent.

As Galloway et al's (B101) study and the Advisory Council for Education (C173) survey reveal, exclusion and suspension are not just penalties and warning actions exercised against pupils, but may also be used as ploys by head teachers to elicit certain desirable reactions from LEAs, parents and outside agencies.

Exclusion is particularly used as a way of demonstrating the seriousness of a situation to parents and inviting their cooperation. It may also be intended to involve the Education Welfare Service and child guidance staff in the case (ACE, C173). Galloway et al (B101) asked head teachers to state their aims in suspending pupils and found that just over a third of the reasons given were concerned with maintaining the safety of staff and other pupils. Just under a third intended the action to make other pupils aware that certain behaviour would not be tolerated. The remainder regarded the act of suspension as a way of making the Education Committee or the chief education officer provide some alternative form of education. Davis (C174) notes a tendency for some schools to be over ready to suspend children living in local authority children's homes on the assumption that alternative arrangements can readily be made for them by Social Services.

III.2.c Individual, Family and School Characteristics

In seeking explanations for the behaviour of children suspended for disruptive behaviour, most research has looked first at family and personal factors. Galloway et al (B101, C176), Longworth-Dames (C180) and York et al (C184) have studied the family circumstances and individual personality of children suspended from school. York et al (C184) found that 41 children suspended from schools in Edinburgh were intellectually dull, seriously backward and came from family environments characterised by low socio-economic status, marital discord and personality disorder. Longworth-Dames (C180) compared the personalities of a small group of excluded children with peers who had not been excluded and found no difference in personality between them although behaviour differed. She suggests that excluded children may be well integrated into an adolescent culture and may be behaving in a very socially precise way to maintain their position within it. There was some evidence of behaviour change when pupils moved to a new school.

Galloway et al (B101, C176) investigated 58 pupils under long-term suspension from school and found that both pupils and parents had histories of illness, and that the children were likely to have been in care, to have low IQs and to be seriously backward in reading. Unlike school non-attendance, neither social class nor socio-economic disadvantage was a reliable predictor of suspension rates.

Although Galloway et al (B101, C175) and Grunsell (C178) have both confirmed differences between schools in their suspension rates, it is still unclear what exactly the distinguishing characteristics are. Other idiosyncratic differences between schools in their attitude to and handling of pupil misbehaviour have been revealed by researchers into 'school factors', whose findings were reviewed in Chapter I.4.a. One particular line of investigation undertaken by Reynolds (B57–B65) and Rutter et al (B66) has examined the relationship between pupil behaviour and types of school ethos, although neither researcher has used suspension rates as a specific measure. Galloway et al (B101, C175) and Grunsell (C178), however, have both noted a slight trend for schools with the highest suspension rates to be comprehensives which had incorporated an existing grammar school on reorganisation, and which might well, as a result, be attempting to maintain a certain standard of behaviour.

School factors may contribute to the accumulation of disruptive incidents which eventually culminates in suspension, as Galloway (C175) notes in a study of suspended pupils. A third of them reported a long-standing personality clash between the pupil and a particular teacher. There was a tendency for small acts of indiscipline to escalate into major disciplinary confrontations, particularly when head teachers felt the need to support actions of class teachers, or when the pastoral care system did not allow the class teacher scope to deal with the incident at source.

Galloway concludes that, for whatever reasons, some schools suspend pupils for behaviour which others seem able to cope with. He suggests that the findings imply that a pupil's chances of being excluded or suspended are influenced at least as much and probably more by which school he attends, as by any stress in the family or constitutional factors within the pupil himself.

III.2.d Legal Status and Rights

For pupils and parents, suspension and exclusion can raise fundamental issues of natural justice.

When a pupil is sent home under suspension there will be an indeterminate period of time before the head teacher convenes a meeting with the school governors and any outside agencies. There may possibly be an appeals procedure against the suspension decision at this stage and then finally some attempt to provide an alternative placement for the pupil. During this period, as the ACE (C173) survey notes, a child under suspension is still registered as a pupil at the school as the law requires, but is not receiving the efficient, full-time, suitable education that the law intends.

There are no reports in this literature of LEAs being held liable for failing to provide education, but parents, under a neat 'Catch 22' clause, can be held responsible for the non-attendance of children who have been suspended or excluded from school. This could apply in cases where the pupil had failed to conform to a simple school rule such as school uniform or refused to accept a routine punishment. A child's absence in these circumstances is considered voluntary and the parents prosecutable (Jennings, C179).

Felicity Taylor (C183) provides some guidelines for parents on the law concerning suspension and steps that they can take to ensure the fullest and fairest review of the situation. The ACE (C173) survey, however, reveals the possible obstacles in the way of this in the shape of authorities with no appeals procedures, and those where the procedures would make it very difficult to challenge the combined authority of the head teacher and the Board of Governors. The report judges that many authorities fell far short of principles of natural justice in the appeal process adopted. Ideally the process, exemplified in a few authorities, would enable parents to bring representatives to the proceedings, enable all parties to question those making statements, and require the head teacher to withdraw while decisions are being made. The importance of an independent element in the appeals panel, apart from the school governors and head teacher, is also stressed.

Galloway et al (B101) state explicitly that appeals against suspension are extremely rare and that an appeal to the governors is likely to be a distressing experience for the parents, with very little chance of success. They suggest that most LEA employees, such as education officers or educational psychologists, will try to dissuade parents from appealing. They give three reasons for this: firstly, parents of suspended pupils are usually less articulate than teachers and unskilled in putting their case persuasively; secondly, they have little independent evidence on which to challenge the teacher's version of events; thirdly, most governing bodies see their job as supporting the head teacher.

III.2.e What Happens to Suspended Pupils?

A pupil who has been suspended is in limbo until some decision is made about his education. Grunsell (C178) describes some of the realities of this period: the pupil has no chance to work, unless he risks working illegally, and has to get through the school day without most of his age group for company. During this period he is increasingly at risk of committing offences.

One possible form of educational provision which can be available to pupils at this time is 'home tuition' – a maximum of ten hours a week of one teacher's time, spent either at the pupil's home or the tutor's home. This was originally intended to meet the needs of pupils temporarily out of school for health reasons and has developed as a stop-gap measure by which LEAs attempt to meet their obligations under the 1944 Education Act. Grunsell (C178) notes that, in his sample of suspended pupils, among those who left school without any full-time educational provision being found for them, about half received home tuition, either individually or as part of a group. Galloway et al's (B101) sample of suspended and excluded pupils showed that 12% were referred to the home tuition service.

The amount of delay before a decision on the pupil's future is taken will vary in different parts of the country. Galloway et al (B101) report that about 70% of their sample of suspended and excluded pupils had returned to their original school or were receiving some alternative form of education within eight weeks of their exclusion or suspension. In London, Grunsell (C178) found that for the children permanently suspended in 1977, the average delay before any kind of part-time or full-time provision could be found was three to four months. For just under a quarter of the cases, no provision of any kind was found for six months or longer.

The information provided by Galloway and Grunsell reveals not only the range of options available for suspended children but also the numbers who may be left without any provision at all. In Grunsell's sample of permanently suspended pupils, nearly a half were not found any full-time educational provision before they reached school leaving age. This group constituted the largest single category of outcome. In Galloway's study, which also covered pupils excluded from school for at least three weeks, this category was the second largest, with 18% of the sample. His largest group, about a quarter of the total, were re-admitted to their original school. Following these, the most common outcomes of both sets of figures were transfer to another secondary school, then transfer to special school, followed by a placement in a centre for disruptive pupils.

Galloway and Grunsell both note that the older the pupil, the more difficult it is to place him in any mainstream educational setting; an off-site centre might be an alternative, but places are limited. For many of these pupils, the realities come down to a few hours of home tuition and waiting until they reach school leaving age.

In certain cases permanent suspension is a protective measure for the school and the need for it is manifestly obvious. In other cases however, pupils are suspended, in effect permanently, for persistent challenges to school authority, which may be symptomatic of underachievement, disaffection and feelings of rejection from the school community.

An additional perspective suggests that children may ultimately be the victims of processes originating outside the school. Newsam (C182), writing while Education Officer at ILEA, suggests that rising suspension rates may be an expression of the pressures that schools are under in the wake of falling rolls. The continued survival of an individual school may be dependent on the reputation it acquires among parents in the neighbourhood, which in turn may depend on the public behaviour of pupils. Those who do not conform to acceptable standards may find themselves at greater risk of suspension because the school can no longer tolerate behaviour which puts the institution at risk. According to Beresford and Croft (C259), the existence of this kind of outlook was confirmed by staff in an IT day centre, who found themselves with the task of educating some of the children who had been excluded or suspended from mainstream education.

III.3 COURT PROCEEDINGS FOR NON-ATTENDANCE

III.3.a Current Legislation in the UK

Since throughout the UK school attendance is compulsory, children who fail to attend school without a justifiable reason can be held to be breaking the law and both they and their parents may be brought to court. In England and Wales the Education Welfare Service usually has the responsibility for bringing court proceedings for school non-attendance (West Glamorgan Council, C31; Galloway et al, C195).

Education welfare officers will be alerted by schools or their own examination of attendance registers to cases of persistent non-attendance and will first visit the home of the child in question to discuss the matter with the parents. There will be a continuing series of initiatives to try and encourage better attendance, until eventually court proceedings may be brought against either the parent or the child, although not usually both simultaneously. If the parents are the main target of intervention, this may be preceded in certain circumstances by the serving of a school attendance order on them.

In England and Wales (Taylor and Saunders, C11), the LEA can prosecute parents under Section 39 of the 1944 Education Act for failing to ensure their child's attendance at school, or under Section 37 for failure to comply with a school attendance order. On conviction, Section 40 of the Act permits magistrates to fine (or on third conviction, imprison) the parent. They may also, or instead, direct the LEA to bring the child before the juvenile court under Section 1 of the 1969 Children and Young Persons Act (C2).

LEAs can also bring independent proceedings under Section 1(2)e of the 1969 Act, which permits the juvenile court to make a case order or supervision order on the child if 'he is of compulsory school age within the meaning of the 1944 Education Act and is not receiving efficient full-time education, suitable to his age, ability and aptitude . . . and if he is also in need of care and control which he is unlikely to receive unless the Court makes an order' (C2). The LEA has sole responsibility for initiating care proceedings in respect of school non-attendance, but will in practice liaise closely with the social services department, which has responsibility for initiating care proceedings on other grounds.

Scotland has a different legal system, although there is similar provision for separate action against parents and children. Section 35(1) of the Education (Scotland) Act of 1962 states that 'where a child of school age who has attended a public school on one or more occasions fails without reasonable excuse to attend regularly at the said school, then, unless the education authority have consented to the withdrawal of the child from school . . . his parents shall be guilty of an offence against this section' (cited in Strathclyde Education Dept, C29). For the purposes of prosecution, a certificate by the head teacher of the school is considered sufficient evidence of the child's record of attendance, which effectively throws the onus of establishing a reasonable excuse on to the parent. Other sections of the Act involving the serving of attendance orders on parents can also be invoked (C29).

Whether or not the parent is convicted, the Sheriff may refer the child to the Reporter to the Children's Panel with the expectation that this will result in an appearance before the Children's Hearing, which has functions similar to those of the English juvenile court. The Education Authority can also independently refer the child to the Reporter under the 1968 Social Work (Scotland) Act (C9) — Section 32 states: 'A child may be in need of compulsory measures of care within the meaning of the Act' (which may be residential care or supervision in the community) 'if he has failed to attend school regularly without reasonable excuse.' The Reporter has independent powers of assessment and at this stage can decide that no further action is required, although the majority of cases are referred to the Hearing.

Northern Ireland currently has broadly similar juvenile legislation to England and Wales, but the review of legislation and services relating to children and young people carried out by the Black Committee in 1979 (C1) has recommended a new juvenile court model with the separation of care and criminal proceedings. Voluntary supervision by an education welfare officer should be the first stage in cases of school non-attendance and if this proved unsuccessful, a supervision order could be requested from the juvenile court under care proceedings, with the nominated supervisor usually the EWO. School non-attendance would not of itself be grounds for seeking a care order, although the breakdown of a supervision order would be.

III.3.b Attitudes to Court Proceedings

While the procedures exist to bring parents and children to court for pupil absenteeism, there is a considerable divergence of views among the professionals involved and other commentators as to the desirability of actually exercising these powers.

The evidence that exists of school attitudes to court proceedings for non-attendance indicates that a section of the teaching profession welcomes the availability of legal sanctions for truancy and is only concerned that these do not appear to operate as swiftly and effectively as they would wish. Criticisms are made of the delays involved in bringing cases, the inadequacy of the fines imposed on parents, the reluctance of social workers on occasion to cooperate in taking children to court and their ineffectiveness in ensuring that children under their supervision attend regularly (Pack, C5; Liverpool Education Committee, C24, C25; Staffordshire LEA, C28; Strathclyde Dept. of Education, C29; W. Glamorgan Council, C31).

The ambiguous attitude of social workers in this process has been noted and both teachers and education welfare officers accuse them of not regarding absenteeism as a serious problem (Liverpool Education Committee, C24, C25; Johnson et al, C220). Galloway et al (C195) record that some social workers were sceptical of the effectiveness of court proceedings for non-attendance, but Giller and Morris (C198) make it clear that other influences are at work in forming their attitudes (see III.4.a below).

Academic commentators on juvenile justice issues are taking a stand on the natural justice aspects of the process, where there is a possibility of children being placed in residential care for long periods of time for behaviour which is a status offence, ie one which only carries a penalty for a juvenile. Taylor et al (C207) sum up a common view, that there is an injustice implicit in judging individuals in truancy cases as being in need of care and protection when there is no investigation by the court of overall truancy rates from the schools concerned. Evidence concerning the quality of the education received, as a justification for truancy, is also not admissable.

Research on various aspects of the juvenile justice system (not covered in this bibliography) has highlighted that official intervention with children often has unintended and unwanted consequences, and some academic commentators are cautious about saying when official action is better than doing nothing.

The Education Welfare Service should have the most clear cut views on the use of court proceedings, but here also, as the next section reveals, there are differences of opinion leading to variations in practice.

III.3.c Education Welfare Discretion in Bringing Court Proceedings

This section refers only to Education Welfare practice in England and Wales. The Service is organised differently in Scotland and also differs in the procedures adopted in the case of school non-attendance.

Persistent school non-attendance does not carry an automatic penalty of court proceedings for either parents or children. Although there has not apparently been any national research carried out on this, it is clear that considerable discretion can be exercised by education welfare officers in deciding which cases are taken to court, and research in West Glamorgan (C31) and by Galloway et al (C195, C197) in Sheffield has revealed substantial differences in judgment between individual EWOs.

Galloway et al (C194) consider some underlying principles of prosecution which an LEA might adopt, which would vary the target of intervention on pragmatic grounds. Prosecution may be aimed at parents if it is felt they would be receptive to a court appearance and have sufficient influence over the child. Care proceedings may be brought against the pupil if it is judged that the parent would be unresponsive to prosecution and has effectively lost control of the child. Galloway et al's (C195, C197) Sheffield study attempted to uncover the principles adopted by EWOs in taking some parents and children to court, recommending some to attend an intermediate body called the School Attendance Section of the LEA, and taking no action in other cases. They concluded that there appeared to be no clear and consistent principles governing the selection of cases for formal action. The individual judgment of EWOs, their own attitudes towards legal and administrative sanctions, the nature of the schools and catchment areas they served, together with pressure from within the Education Welfare Service, were more accurate explanations of their actions.

Further research by the same team (C196) suggests that legal action against both pupils and parents was more likely if the child had committed offences. This view is confirmed by Taylor et al (C207) who found, on the basis of evidence from an unpublished study, that children reported by LEAs for truancy were more likely to be those who had attended irregularly and created 'trouble' than those who had absented themselves over a long period of time.

Green (B72) suggests that EWOs have various strategies for dealing with non-attendance, which are designed to reduce the amount of truancy that receives official recognition, and avoid swamping the alternative provision available, such as residential schools, alternative education units and home tuition. She highlights the range of devices and strategems which all parties can use in order to ensure continuing delay or inaction, with the result that a high proportion of children can routinely absent themselves from school with relative impunity.

Similar discretion is exercised by social workers and police in relation to the various other routes for bringing children before the juvenile court. Increasing attention is being given to the question of limiting this discretion, at least for social workers, by, for example, setting criteria in order to reduce both unnecessary referrals and inappropriate recommendations to the court. It seems possible that similar pressures will arise to specify criteria for taking parents or children to court for non-attendance.

III.3.d Prosecution Statistics

National statistics show that in 1980 there were around 4,000 prosecutions of parents in England and Wales under the Education Act (Thomas, C210). The Galloway team (C195) present local figures from Sheffield showing that 87 parents were prosecuted during the school year 1976/77. In 1980, 2,230 children in England and Wales were brought before the juvenile court on care proceedings under Section 1(2)(e) of the 1969 Children and Young Persons Act, on the grounds of non-attendance at school. This accounted for one per cent of all juvenile court cases, the vast majority of which were criminal prosecutions (Thomas, C210).

Galloway et al (C195) cite statistics from Tyerman (B80), Berg et al (C188) and Tennent (C209) on the number of prosecutions of parents and children in the mid '60s and early '70s. Berg et al (C188) found that the number of children brought before the juvenile court in Leeds during the school year 1972/73 amounted to roughly 0.014% of the total school roll. Galloway et al (C195) indicate that prosecutions in 1976/77 involving both parents and children represented about 0.15% of all pupils on the rolls of Sheffield schools.

Statistics on formal action for truancy in Scotland are provided by Martin et al's (C202) authoritative study of the Children's Hearing system. They report that in 1979 there were over 2,500 cases referred to the Reporter on the grounds of truancy — mainly by the education authorities. These constituted ten per cent of all referrals, for all grounds including offences. In a sample study they found that Reporters dealt with 15% of the cases themselves and referred 85% to the Children's Hearings. The latter were therefore dealing with about the same number of truancy cases as juvenile courts throughout England and Wales, which cover a population ten times greater.

The authors do not report what percentage of school rolls these cases represent, but it is clear that, for whatever reasons, the proportion is a great deal higher than in England and Wales. The differences are even more striking when it emerges that, because a lower proportion of offence cases were referred to the Hearing, truancy alone accounted for about one in six cases brought before the Hearing, compared to around one in 100 juvenile court cases in England and Wales. It is beyond the scope of this paper to provide reasons for the difference in approach of authorities in Scotland, England and Wales, but it is further evidence of the differential response to the phenomenon of non-attendance on the part of individual schools and LEAs.

III.3.e Outcomes

Of the 4,000 parents prosecuted under the Education Act in 1980, 3,670 were found guilty, and of these, 83% were fined and 15% received absolute or conditional discharges (Thomas, C210). Galloway et al (C194) report that 78% of parents appearing in magistrates' courts in Sheffield during 1976–78 were fined and eight per cent were conditionally discharged. In certain cases the outcome for the parent was combined with a direction that the child be brought before the juvenile court.

Out of the 2,230 juvenile court truancy cases in England and Wales in 1980, the magistrates made no order in 15% of the cases; of the remaining 1900, around half received supervision orders and half care orders (Thomas, C210). Galloway et al (C194) report the final outcomes of 126 juvenile court truancy cases in Sheffield during 1976 to 1978, which show that 11% of cases were withdrawn or dismissed, and a further 14% were adjourned sine die; 51% received supervision orders and 24% received care orders.

In Scotland, Martin et al (C202) found that in their study sample, the Children's Hearing discharged just under a quarter of the truancy cases, made supervision orders in 70% of cases, and orders requiring residential care for six per cent. When comparing Scotland to the rest of Britain on a measure such as the lower use of residential care as a court outcome for truancy, the differing proportions of truancy cases and their comparative rarity in the English juvenile court system should be borne in mind.

A court disposal which has received a considerable amount of attention is the adjourned case. Under this procedure, the case is adjourned every time the child comes to court, with the aim of seeing if school attendance will improve. Berg et al's (C188) initial study of the subsequent attendance of Leeds children who had been dealt with under this procedure, in comparison with those placed under supervision, found that the former group attended more frequently than the latter.

In a subsequent study by Berg et al (C189), Leeds magistrates agreed to allocate children randomly to adjournment or supervision outcomes without making this known to the parents and children or to the other professional workers involved in the case, such as social workers or EWOs. Subsequent investigation found that children whose cases were adjourned attended school more frequently and committed fewer criminal offences than those supervised. Reynolds (C205) reports on the disquiet aroused among social work staff by the eventual revelation of this experiment, and the concern that court disposals applied arbitrarily, without consideration for the individual features of a case, may have made certain situations worse. Galloway et al (C196) suggest that the technique is expensive in terms of magistrates' time and in the demands it makes on social services departments' time and resources when children whose cases are adjourned are placed on interim care orders.

Their own study (C196) looked at the subsequent school attendance of various groups of pupils in Sheffield following legal or other kinds of action against the children or their parents. One group consisted of children whose parents had appeared before the School Attendance Section, while in the second group the parents had been brought before the magistrates' court. Both groups showed substantial immediate improvement in attendance. The third group comprised children who had been taken to the juvenile court, and they showed a minor improvement. When attendance was monitored for a complete term following intervention, it was found that the first two groups maintained their improvement, while the juvenile court group's attendance declined to below the original level recorded prior to intervention. The attendance of children with whom no formal intervention was made improved steadily over the same period, and while it did not achieve the levels of the first two groups, it was discernibly better than that of the juvenile court group. An additional finding revealed improved attendance following transfer to another school.

While there is no information in this bibliography on the consequences of supervision orders specifically for truancy, there is data on care orders made in care proceedings on these grounds. Thomas (C210) notes that while 973 care orders (about half for males) were made in 1980, there were on a given day 4,700 children in the care of local authorities (not necessarily in residential care) on grounds of truancy. Of those leaving care in the previous year — mainly because they had reached the age of 18 — half had been in care for three years or longer, and 93% for more than a year.

This particular court disposal currently inspires considerable controversy because of its capacity to remove children from home and place them in residential settings for considerable periods of time. Casburn (C191) challenges the appropriateness of care orders as a court disposal for girls involved in truancy cases, which was the usual practice in the juvenile court she studied, and suggests that the order is an expression of the repressively protective and surveillant attitudes of juvenile courts towards female behaviour which diverges from the acceptable norm.

III.4   SCHOOL INVOLVEMENT IN THE JUVENILE JUSTICE SYSTEM

A considerable amount of critical attention is currently being given to the operation of the English juvenile justice system and it is gradually being realised that the part played by schools in this process is a potentially far reaching one which has, up to now, been neglected by commentators and researchers. In many respects this section can only raise issues and note that they have not yet received any substantial discussion, but it will make reference to the literature where this exists. In this connection Giller (C199) and Rathbone (C204) provide an introduction to the points of concern in the general relationship of schools to courts.

III.4.a Consultation before Court Proceedings

Schools are usually aware of proceedings which are likely to be taken against children for non-attendance, but from the little evidence available it is unclear how far they are kept informed or are aware of court proceedings pending against their pupils for other reasons, like criminal charges, until or unless they receive a formal request for a report for the court. An obvious time for liaison between schools and welfare agencies would be during the pre-court period when the Police may be deciding whether to prosecute the child and when social workers and probation officers are marshalling their information on the case. However, there is no real evidence from the literature on how widespread this practice is as a general rule.

The Liverpool Education Committee (C25) and the West Glamorgan (C31) reports both make reference to the House of Commons Report from the Expenditure Committee on the operation of the Children and Young Persons Act 1969 (1975, HMSO), which recommended that school heads should be informed, as of right, of every child who comes to the attention of the Police or local authority. The Liverpool Education Committee report records that the government response to this proposal, which is contained in their 'Observations on the Eleventh Report from the Expenditure Committee' (1976, Cmd 6494), was that a statutory requirement on the Police to notify head teachers would represent a considerable burden of work and that locally agreed procedures would better meet the objectives of the Committee.

Davie (C192) considers that schools could have a key role in the pre-court consultation period and recommends that Police should send enquiry forms to schools as well as Social Services. The West Glamorgan (C31) report records that this recommendation was carried out by the South Wales Constabulary but the form used proved inappropriate and the procedure lapsed, leaving the issue unresolved. In the Liverpool Education Committee report (C25) an appendix from the Merseyside Police notes that juvenile liaison officers will discuss each case with the head teacher of the school in offence cases. The North Wales Police report (C296) records a similar link by their Juvenile Liaison scheme.

A study by Giller and Morris (C198) of how social workers make decisions suggests that they will give differing emphasis to the child's school record according to the classification they have made of the essential nature of a case involving offences. This finding emerged from an examination of the cases of 79 children made the subject of a care order on offence grounds in 13 social services departments in inner London boroughs. Through interviews with their social workers, the researchers were able to outline the basis on which these cases were categorised and subsequent placements decided. Depending on whether the offence was seen as the major cause for concern or a symptom of other problems in the home, cases were usually divided into 'delinquency' or 'care' categories. Typical outcomes were home placement for 'care' cases and removal from home for 'delinquency' cases. Truancy, where it existed as a further factor in the situation, could be viewed either as an additional symptom of difficulties within the home, but not necessarily important in its own right, or as the precipitating factor in the child's offence. Since social workers may also be critical of a school's regime and regard it as a contributing factor to the behaviour, it is clear that there are grounds for considerable variation in the amount of liaison which may take place between schools and social workers.

III.4.b Court Reports

The school authorities are usually asked to provide a report for the court on the attendance and behaviour of the child, and recent research has demonstrated that these reports may be more influential than many commentators had previously realised. Millham (C203) suggests somewhat sardonically that the school report carries greater weight with magistrates than social work reports, because it is written in a language they understand, is spelt correctly and is rather less justifying in its analysis of the child's behaviour.

Ball (C186) first noted, unexpectedly, in an analysis of magistrates' reasons for making a care order, that the unsatisfactory nature of the child's school record, as revealed in the school report, was a primary factor influencing the court's decision. In contrast to the practice with social work reports, the content of school reports was usually not made known to the defendant. Further investigation (C187) of the prevalence of this practice revealed that in a survey of 444 juvenile court panels, 59% of school reports were not shown to defendants and 41% were. Choice of practice within any court depended on idiosyncratic factors such as the individual preference of the court clerk, initiatives taken by magistrates, and the relationship between local head teachers and the juvenile bench. Magistrates' rules require that the substance of information concerning the character or conduct of a child should be revealed to him, but this is subject to wide variations of interpretation. Ball (C187) concludes that the amount of discretion allowed to head teachers and the degree of collusion that exists between some juvenile benches and schools could amount, in some cases, to the administration of secret justice.

Martin et al (C202) confirm that similar attention is paid by panel members in the Children's Hearing to the child's conduct and progress at school, and this often constituted a considerable proportion of the total discussion. Despite similar Hearing rules on revealing the contents of the reports, two Hearings in every five did not mention the school reports although they had been received. The remainder alluded to comments contained within them, without revealing detailed content. The researchers were able to analyse the content of some school reports, which they characterised as negative and incomplete, noting only the child's record of attendance, level of educational ability and attainment, and standards of general behaviour. The quality of the child's relationship with teachers and other pupils was not mentioned unless it was unsatisfactory.

Ball's earlier study (C186) of the English juvenile court found that head teachers were often unwilling to provide full reports if they were to be read out to the offenders and their families. However, where arrangements about confidentiality had been reached with the court they were less restrained and she quotes several extracts from school reports, characterised as pejorative and damaging allegations about conduct and character, which had influenced the judgment of the bench but had not been put in detail to the offender.

There is no information on how schools see their role in supplying reports to the court or on what basis they are compiled but this is likely to come under more scrutiny in the future.

III.5 CONCLUSION

As forms of action, court proceedings and suspension have certain similarities and contrasts in terms of their overall effect and underlying philosophy.

The most obvious contrast is that suspension seeks to remove a child from school, while proceedings for truancy are intended to get her/him to attend. Another difference is that suspension is entirely at the discretion of the school system, while truancy is a matter for the courts to decide. In terms of similarities, in both cases there is considerable discretion, at times verging on arbitrariness, as to whether any action is initiated at all. Both approaches are marked by a mixture of caring and punitive intentions and both tend to individualise the problem, assigning ultimate responsibility and blame to parents and children, for whom the action may have serious consequences, raising issues of natural justice.

While certain kinds of conduct would undoubtedly lead to suspension in virtually all schools, the differences in rates recorded by Galloway (C176) and Grunsell (C178) underline the extent to which this sanction can be used by schools to reflect their own individual standards and expectations. Where off-site units have been established by LEAs, the demand for places greatly exceeds the supply, and it seems likely that the existence of this form of provision may act as an additional incentive for some schools to suspend large numbers of pupils despite the relative scarcity of such places. The pros and cons of off-site education are discussed in Chapter IV.2.c.

A strong impression emerging from the literature is that the idiosyncratic practices of schools, in relation to suspension, have their parallel in the judgments and recommendations made by professional welfare workers dealing with truancy and possible court proceedings. In this case, the discretionary element appears to be exercised on the basis of intuitive hunches, departmental policy and external pressure following delinquent episodes. While this may at times be exercised in favour of children and their parents, at other times it can be distinctly unproductive for them.

The section on the relationship of schools to the juvenile justice system underlines the fact that, although they appear to be detached from many of the processes, they may nevertheless be exerting a significant influence (through their reports to courts) on the subsequent careers in care or custody of a minority of their pupils.

Chapter IV
Special Provision for the Disturbing and Absentee Pupil: Integration or Segregation?

IV.1 INTRODUCTION

When schools decide that certain pupils are not responding to initiatives designed to help with their behavioural and educational difficulties, they may decide that more specialised measures are needed. As noted in Chapter II.3.b, a blurred distinction is made by professionals within the education field between children whose learning and behavioural difficulties are assigned mainly to psychological and constitutional factors, and those whose behaviour is held to reflect social and environmental deprivation, compounded by individual bloody mindedness.

For the first group — children with special needs — there has been a limited historical tradition of provision, and more recently, attention from legislation. The second group — the disruptive pupils — has only recently been added to the lexicon of educational categories, exemplified by the few brief references to them in the Warnock Report (C13), and their characteristics, motivation and treatment are currently open to wide interpretation and provision unhindered by legislative guidelines.

A number of issues are currently under debate concerning provision for these children. One major controversy has centred around whether they need specialist facilities away from the ordinary classroom and their fellow pupils, and if so, where and how this should be provided. The terms 'integration' and 'segregation' have been used to describe various approaches to this question but, as will be shown later, they may refer to a reality more complex than just catering for pupils on or away from the school campus.

This chapter is organised around this debate. The first half reviews the issues in educational policy and philosophy (IV.2): after an overview of recent trends in policy and provision (IV.2.a), it examines the kinds of policy choices to be made by LEAs and schools (IV.2.b), and considers the arguments for and against off-site provision (IV.2.c) and on-site units (IV.2.d). The second half discusses the literature on what has been happening in practice (IV.3): provision for children with special needs (IV.3.a), off-site education centres (IV.3.b), IT day centres (IV.3.c), and on-site units (IV.3.d), plus the evidence of reintegration into mainstream schooling (IV.3.e).

In this chapter, the term 'special units' will be used to refer to distinct, specialised facilities, whether on or away from the school campus, catering primarily for young people whose behaviour is considered a problem, ie disruption, sometimes truancy, and (in the case of IT centres) delinquency. Those facilities which are organisationally part of a particular mainstream school are here called 'on-site units': usually they are physically located on the school campus, but are sometimes geographically separate. Those run by the LEA, but which are physically and organisationally separate from any one school, are called 'off-site units'. As a slightly broader term, 'off-site education centres' is used to embrace not only these LEA off-site units but also similar special units run by voluntary agencies and IT day care centres.

IV.2 ISSUES IN POLICY AND PHILOSOPHY

IV.2.a Trends in Policy and Provision

Prior to the 1944 Education Act, the vast majority of children with educational and behavioural difficulties managed as best they could within ordinary schools. During the 19th and early 20th centuries some specialist schools were established for the 'feeble-minded', but provision was never widespread, and it was only in 1944 that the Education Act placed a duty on LEAs to provide special education for maladjusted and educationally subnormal children along with other handicapped pupils (Galloway and Goodwin, C39; see also Chapter II.3.b).

The variety of provision which existed at the time of the Warnock Report (C13) in 1978 is an indication of the diversity of views within the education field about the best ways of meeting the needs of these pupils. A survey by Wilson and Evans (C51) provides an overview of the range of placements available. Some children continued to be taught within ordinary classrooms without any separate or specialist provision being made for them. A greatly expanded 'special education' sector made places available in a variety of facilities, under an assortment of somewhat loosely assigned names, such as residential boarding schools, day schools, day units, tutorial centres, remedial centres and educational guidance centres.

The Warnock Report (C13), subsequently backed by legislation (C3), recommended that special categories of handicap should be abolished and replaced by the concept of children with special needs. Furthermore, children assessed as having special needs should, wherever possible, receive their education through integrated provision in ordinary schools. As a further refinement of the term, 'integration' was not to be regarded solely as specialist provision on the school campus, isolated from the rest of the school population, but would entail some genuine sharing of programmes and resources. LEAs now have a clear duty towards these children and some practice guidelines.

In the case of disruptive pupils, identification of the group as such has sometimes been unclear. Provision for them has consequently been discretionary on the part of LEAs.

In the mid '70s there was strong pressure on LEAs for specialist placements for disruptive pupils to be made available away from the classroom. Young et al (C32, C33) suggest that the 1974 local government reorganisation was instrumental in creating a framework within which LEAs felt able to examine the issue in some detail and formulate a comprehensive strategy. In the majority of cases the provision of off-site units was seen as the most appropriate response, although a substantial number of on-site units were also established. In many cases however pupils continued to be managed within the school setting along traditional lines.

There was not the same degree of pressure for special units for absentee pupils, but once units of various kinds had been established, many LEAs felt that they could be used with advantage for a wide range of pupils including absentees.

The development of LEA units of various kinds was haphazard, but by 1979 the Liverpool Education Committee (C25) was quoting reports from some local authorities that were already opting for on-site, in preference to off-site, units to overcome perceived problems of stigma and reintegration.

The whole development of special units represents a very considerable innovation in educational practice, involving a substantial investment in buildings, staff and pupil placements. Even though its growth has been discretionary and haphazard, without official guidelines, this kind of provision has the capacity to cater for at least 5,800 pupils in England and Wales according to recent, incomplete figures (ACE, C73).

The HMI (C74) survey of behavioural units on- and off-site provided the first detailed statistics of the growth of this new form of provision. In 1977, 239 units were recorded of which 70% were off-site. Although the first unit had been established in 1960, over three quarters were established between 1973 and 1977, with 1974 as the peak period for new units. The ACE (C73) survey of LEAs in 1980 confirmed, though from incomplete returns, the existence of 386 units. Of these, 226 were accounted for by the ILEA Disruptive Pupils Programme which, by offering places to 3,800 pupils, was providing nearly the same number of places in 1980 as the whole of England and Wales could muster in 1977. The remaining LEAs that responded to the survey accounted for 160 units providing 2,057 places.

Statistics on the ILEA programme are provided by the Research and Statistics Division (C78) in its first annual report on the monitoring study of the support centres programme. It reports the average number of pupils which each type of unit planned to cater for and gives a figure of 17 for off-site units and eleven for on-site secondary school units. The figures further reveal that 18 voluntary centres and eleven IT schemes were taking part in the Disruptive Pupils Programme.

IV.2.b LEA and School Policies

The formulation of an LEA policy for dealing with absentee and disruptive behaviour in schools requires choices to be made between alternative strategies. Essentially, these revolve around whether the pupils concerned need to be segregated from their peers for a short or long period of time, or remain integrated within the school setting. The main options can be seen in terms of:

- preventive pastoral care vs specialist provision on- or off-site;
- on-site specialist provision vs off-site specialist provision;
- short-term vs long-term provision (whether on- or off-site).

Arguments can be made supporting these various options on educational and pragmatic grounds, but the experience of other LEAs and the current climate of opinion may be important influences. Young et al (C32, C33), outlining the reasons why a particular kind of policy may be adopted by LEAs, suggest that LEA perceptions of the nature of disruption have been a prime influence (see Chapter II.2).

LEAs may formulate the overall policy on how these pupils should be handled and what resources will be made available to meet their needs, but within each authority schools may differ in how they implement the policy and make use of the resources. Where off-site units have been provided, schools can vary in the extent to which they make use of the unit and at what stage (Bird et al, B99). Where the LEA policy is primarily a preventive one, schools nevertheless may continue to suspend large numbers of pupils or refer them to special education. Galloway and Goodwin (C39) refer to the need for a reciprocal relationship between schools and LEAs on this issue: the LEA administration may insist on a child's return to school following suspension, but compelling an unwilling school to keep a disturbing child is not the best way of ensuring that his needs are fully met.

The choices that LEAs make between the various strategies outlined earlier will determine whether their policy may be regarded as one of segregation or integration. There are however additional refinements within this classification, some of which arise out of school practices, and these will now be noted.

Segregation — long term
Very few LEAs have made this an overt policy, although the Isle of Wight Education Committee (C23) specifically recommends the establishment of a no-return unit for disruptive pupils. Reports from off-site education centres, however, confirm that long-term segregation does occur in practice when schools refer pupils to off-site education, take little further interest in their progress and discourage attempts to return them to school. This can create problems in the relationship between centres and schools, especially when the former are still attempting to pursue a reintegration policy and find their efforts blocked or undermined (Ball and Ball, C86; Grunsell, C91; White, C106; Beresford and Croft, C259; Vincent, C277).

Segregation — short term
This policy on the part of LEAs and schools assumes a general commitment to mainstream education for all, but recognises that there may be a need for certain children to be withdrawn from school on a temporary basis to provide relief for teachers and special remedial help for pupils. Special units will be provided either on- or off-site and there is usually stress on the

early identification of children who could benefit from this facility and their eventual reintegration into the classroom. School and units that operate on this basis appear to have a more positive relationship with each other. This approach to off-site provision forms the basis of the ILEA Disruptive Pupil Programme (ILEA, C75–C79; Wright, C72) and has been adopted by other LEAs (Cleveland, C15). On-site units of this kind are described by Tattum (B105) and Hunkin and Alhadeff (C169).

Integration — locational
The Warnock Report (C13) refers to 'locational integration' when describing self-contained special education units in ordinary schools. The point is made that being self-contained, they are in practice as far removed from school activities as an off-site unit would be. The equivalent facility for disruptive pupils would be an on-site unit which was self-contained within the school and did not practise reintegration. Jones and Forrest (C170) describe one such unit, which provides an alternative education for pupils during the last year of schooling. Some existing on-site units found themselves operating on a similar basis during their early days because pupils were referred to them at a late stage in their school careers. They made a conscious decision however only to accept short-term referrals and attempt to ensure reintegration (Hunkin and Alhadeff, C169).

Integration — functional
The Warnock Report's (C13) definition of 'functional integration' is where handicapped children share the same educational programme as their fellow pupils. A minority of LEAs have decided against on- or off-site provision and have put their efforts into preventive policies and practices which can defuse potentially explosive situations and retain all but the most disturbed pupils within the classroom (Hampshire, C21; North Yorkshire Teachers Panel, C26).

IV.2.c Off-site Education: Support and Criticism

There is currently a fierce debate in the literature concerning the desirability of off-site education. For LEAs there are certain administrative advantages and disadvantages which may sometimes override the social and educational benefits and drawbacks for the pupil. For academic commentators there are wider issues concerning the function of education in society and the treatment by schools of their non-conforming elements. The views of workers within centres vary considerably according to their perception of the value of the experience to the child and their relationship with referring schools.

Supporting views
For LEAs, off-site units provide a ready solution to the placement problems posed by suspended pupils who are unacceptable to schools. The supply may not match the demand, but their establishment is a way of demonstrating that the authority has taken a serious view of the situation. Some may use units as a last resort prior to suspension or court proceedings for non-attendance, while for others they represent a diversified form of provision within the school system (Young et al, C32, C33).

The majority of workers in long-term off-site provision would justify the existence of such centres by pointing to the potential benefits for young people. These include the creation of an environment in which children can be helped to achieve success after years of failure at school and the provision of compensatory social and educational programmes. The favourable staff/ student ratios are also seen as enabling young people to benefit from the increased attention and develop non-authoritarian relationships with adults. For workers, the existence of the centre creates a unique opportunity to experiment with elements of regime and curriculum and explore the extent to which democracy and participation can be built into the programme (Ball and Ball, C86; Grunsell, C91; White, C106; Beresford and Croft, C259; Leggett, C265).

In those short-term off-site centres where pupil reintegration is regularly (if by no means always) achieved, the workers concerned usually see the centre as providing pupils with a chance to catch up on interrupted school work in a non-threatening environment, have their special needs attended to, and generally receive a second chance to finish their school careers (Wright, C72; Dain, C88; Swailes, C102).

Critical views

For LEAs there are certain policy and administrative disadvantages with off-site units which need to be taken into account. There are costs involved in establishing and maintaining the units, particularly given the low pupil/teacher ratios; their existence runs counter to established policy on comprehensive schooling; and their ultimate effectiveness has yet to be convincingly demonstrated (Young et al, C33).

The main criticisms of these units by outside commentators focus on their stigmatising effects on young people, their effect on mainstream education, and the quality of the education they provide.

A major concern is the issue of stigma and the labelling of pupils. The separation of groups of young people from their peers which involves them being officially labelled as disruptive or maladjusted is seen as undesirable and unacceptable. In particular, there have been fears that a covert form of racial discrimination may be at work because of the large numbers of West Indian children to be found in off-site education centres. The Rampton Report (C7) acknowledges the concern but was unable to find any direct evidence of over-representation. The National Association for Multi-racial Education (NAME, C67, C68) expresses concern about the lack of information on numbers of children from ethnic minorities being placed in off-site units and reports some evidence from Birmingham where ethnic monitoring is carried out. Grunsell (C178) found that to some degree West Indians appeared to be over-represented in his suspension statistics for 1977. Butler (C61) suggests that Black children are more at risk of being described as disruptive when their manifestations of class consciousness, ethnic pride, or minority group identity are categorised by teachers as, at best, youthful non-conformity, but more often as symptoms of alienation and delinquency.

Schools are criticised for being over ready to use the units as a first resort when faced with disaffected pupils instead of reviewing their curriculum and pastoral care procedures. There is a general feeling that the removal of non-conformist elements from the school, whether pupils or teachers, lessens the stimulus for change (ACE/NAME, C57; White, C106).

There is concern that these centres have a narrow curriculum, that many operate from substandard accommodation, and that some focus more on treatment than education. The professional isolation of staff is also seen as a drawback. There are disadvantages for pupils and parents in that there is usually no appeal against referral to a unit if this is deemed necessary and units are not usually accountable to any groups outside their sponsoring agency (Galloway and Goodwin, C39; ACE/NAME, C57; Basini, C59, C60; Francis, C63; Golby, C64; Lloyd-Smith, C66; NAME, C67, C68; Newell, C69). Even where it can be demonstrated that a centre is providing a beneficial experience for pupils, the small numbers involved in relation to the potential demand is held to underline the essential futility of the exercise (Beresford and Croft, C259).

Where off-site education centres are providing short-term provision for pupils in close association with schools, there is criticism that this may involve the use of reward systems which train the child to adapt to the demands of the institution without reforming school practices (Kenny, C262). Where IT centres are involved there may be concern that this represents too great a subordination of the centre objectives to the needs of LEAs, although there may not be any objection to long-term provision of this kind (McCarrick, C268). However, critics of IT involvement on a long-term basis can be found (Pickles, C274). The restriction of exam opportunities for pupils in long-term off-site provision is also viewed with disquiet (ACE/NAME, C57).

IV.2.d On-site Units: Support and Criticism

On-site units have received far less attention than their off-site counterparts. Thus the literature discussing their advantages and disadvantages is less extensive. There tends to be less discussion of the merits of on-site units as an alternative to retaining the pupil within the classroom, and more concentration on their advantages in comparison to off-site centres.

A comprehensive list of advantages of on-site units put forward by Tattum (B105) includes the following: the reduction of stigma; opportunities for teachers to exchange knowledge and ideas about methods and practice; a reduction of the problems associated with reintegration; greater ease of organising part-time attendance; availability of a wider range of resources; greater access to external exams for pupils; less isolation of unit teachers; and the possibility of self-referral on the part of pupils.

There have been very few critical examinations of on-site provision but Galloway et al (B101) investigated the establishment of special groups in Sheffield and make the following observations. Special groups on-site may be fairly cheap to run but are expensive to staff, as teachers in charge need to have seniority and authority in order to negotiate with other class teachers regarding pupils. Despite the theoretical ease of reintegration, in practice this proved difficult to achieve in the schools investigated. They did not prove effective in reducing school suspension rates.

IV.3 INTEGRATION OR SEGREGATION IN PRACTICE

IV.3.a Provision for Children with Special Needs

The following is a very brief overview of some of the literature on provision for children with special needs. It is included here because many of the issues discussed, such as assessment, reduction of stigma and relationships with mainstream education, have direct relevance to the provision of segregated education for disaffected pupils.

Galloway and Goodwin (C39) provide a comprehensive discussion of these issues in the light of the Warnock recommendations, and include a section on the provision of off-site units for disruptive pupils. Dawson (C38) and Wilson and Evans (C51) provide information from a national survey on the practice of special education in different settings. Adams (C36), Mongon (C48) and Williams (C50) describe initiatives organised by the School Psychological Service in the form of the remedial education service, the educational guidance centre and the tutorial class. Examples of different kinds of day schools and classes, on- and off-site, are provided by Jones (C41–C43), Lane and Millar (C46), Lansdown (C47) and Rodway (C49). Kolvin et al (C45) describe a research project in which social workers worked with teachers and parents to try and help children with adjustment problems, as part of a carefully controlled research programme to identify maladjusted children in ordinary schools and to evaluate the effectiveness of different treatment approaches applied to them.

IV.3.b Off-Site Education Centres

This section describes practice in LEA off-site units and similar centres run by voluntary agencies, but excludes IT day care, which is discussed in the next section. These centres for children who are persistently absent from school or disruptive in class have taken their place alongside other off-site provision, such as IT day centres and special education day units. There is also a parallel off-site tradition in the free school movement, which flourished in the '60s, and of which a few examples still survive. Free schools can be regarded as the pioneers of off-site education centres, since they initiated what is now regarded as good practice in these settings — good pupil/staff ratios, innovative curricula and individual care and learning.

Grunsell (C65) provides an overview of the development of off-site education in London and notes how there has been a cross-fertilisation of ideas between staff and different centres. Neustatter (C81), Rock and Taylor (C83) and St-John Brooks (C84) summarise the issues involved and document the aims and objectives of different kinds of centres. These aims and objectives, and hence the programmes, are extremely varied. Topping and Quelch (C85) conducted an early survey of LEA policy and practice concerning special units and classes of all kinds for children with behavioural problems. They found that the only aim with which there was widespread agreement among those responding, was to return the child to ordinary schooling. Only a few were prepared to state that their ultimate objective was to provide alternative education for uncontainable pupils. The later, HMI survey (C74) also notes the differing philosophies which underpinned the units, including social adjustment, remedial work in basic skills and general enrichment for deprived pupils. A few were seen as punitive institutions or just concerned with containment.

Pupils arrive at off-site education centres by a variety of routes. The majority of centres use admission panels to vet referrals. These panels generally originated as a means of self-preservation following nightmarish early experiences, when schools in their catchment area referred all their most difficult pupils at the same time (HMI, C74). The HMI (C74) survey notes that suspended pupils accounted for just over a quarter of all the pupils in the units visited. Schools may refer pupils prior to suspension (Dain, C88), and educational psychologists, education welfare officers, Child Guidance, social workers and even self-referrals are additional sources (Ball and Ball, C86; Rowan, C100; Taylor et al, C103). Centres may also act as staging posts for children en route between courts, community homes with education, observation and assessment centres, and special education placements.

There appears to be considerable variation in the previous record of pupils referred to off-site education. Some may have confined their activities to persistent absenteeism and disruptive behaviour in class, while others may in addition have many court appearances to their name (Tattum, B105; Taylor et al, C103). Many centres cater specifically for pupils referred for disruptive behaviour, some provide for a range of pupil needs, and others are concerned specifically with school non-attenders (Grunsell, C91; Palfrey, C98; Robinson, C99; Taylor et al, C103).

The HMI (C74) report notes that overall emphasis within the programmes varied between remedial work and social training. English and maths were taught in virtually all units but history, geography and science were less frequent and modern languages and music were only available in a small minority. A recent survey by Alhadeff et al (C58) found that two thirds of the 213 units contacted used groupwork to discuss personal issues and intragroup relationships and just over half claimed to be using behaviour modification techniques.

A basic difference between centres is whether they expect to reintegrate pupils back into school after short periods or assume responsibility for them up to school leaving age.

The off-site education centres which act as short-term placements endeavour to build up close relationships with schools and use devices such as regular meetings with teachers, pupil registration at school or attendance there for one day a week to ensure that the links are preserved. Timetables may be more structured and there is often an emphasis on helping children with behaviour which creates difficulties for them in relating to teachers and other children. In these settings reward systems are often employed, loosely referred to as behaviour modification techniques, although few of them would conform to a strict psychological definition of behaviour modification. An exception to this model is reported by Swailes (C102) at the Parkhead Centre, which has a flexible curriculum and considerable emphasis on outdoor activities. For the possibility of reintegration to exist, many centres have had to concentrate on the younger age group of 11–13 year olds and this has sometimes entailed a shift of policy from their original objectives (Tattum, B105; Dain, C88; Davies, C89; Mack, C95; Palfrey, C98; Spencer, C101; Vernon, C105).

Centres in which reintegration back into school does not assume such importance may concentrate on different aims in relation to pupils and permit such behaviour as smoking and swearing (Ball and Ball, C86), which in other off-site centres might result in the loss of precious behaviour points (Spencer, C101). Such centres are usually catering for the older, 14 plus age group with long histories of disaffection, and have often found difficulty in building satisfactory relationships with their local schools. In many cases this experience is the precipitating factor in the development of a philosophy which is more critical of main-stream education and concerned to develop a viable alternative in the smaller centre for children who have been unable to cope with ordinary schooling (Grunsell, C91; White, C106).

Apart from time devoted to core subjects, timetables may be more flexible or individualised and particularly oriented towards survival outside the centre and work experience. Where it seems appropriate pupils may return to school but not necessarily full-time. Ball and Ball (C86) describe a 'stepping stones' procedure in which children attend school for particular lessons. Centres with a long-stay policy may cater for both disruptive and absentee pupils (Ball and Ball, C86; BIOSS, C87; Grunsell, C91; Robinson, C99; Taylor et al, C103; White, C106).

Pupils' opinions of off-site centres have not been recorded to any great extent, but evidence from Ball and Ball (C86), Galway (C90), Grunsell (C91) and White (C106) indicates that they welcomed the freedom and trust they experienced in the centre, the escape from the size, noise and continual changes of their previous schools, the chance to work at their own pace and develop new interests, and the quality of the relationships they were able to develop with staff. These comments have mainly been drawn from experiences in long-stay centres. Very little has yet emerged of children's views of short-stay centres.

IV.3.c IT Day Care Centres

Social Services are increasingly setting up IT day care centres, as a way of meeting their responsibilities for children subject to court orders, and especially as a way of developing alternatives to care or custody. These centres often have evening as well as day programmes and cater for a wide range of children. An educational programme is a key component of day care and the education department may cooperate with Social Services by providing teaching staff, and in some cases by jointly funding the scheme as a whole. Locke (C266) provides a brief overview of such provision drawing on data from a survey. The relationship and relative responsibilities of the two agencies may well be problematic, and this is taken up in Chapter V. The focus at this point is on the implications for young people of this segregated form of education provision.

When IT programmes are planned as an alternative to care or custody, the decision to set up a day programme may be based less on the educational needs of the participants than on the need for intensive intervention with the young person — or for credibility with the courts in this respect. Such projects may have precise referral criteria, expressed in terms of delinquency or of risk of removal from home by the court. Others work with many different kinds of children, and problems at school or truancy may be just one consideration or the major criterion for referrals. The difference in target group is important. For young people in serious trouble, IT day care is less segregating than the alternative it seeks to replace, removal to an institution; but for young people whose problem is with school, the IT programme is more segregating than the ordinary classroom.

In practice, young offenders are likely to have school problems. Kenny's (C262) survey of IT practice in London boroughs reveals that education welfare officers along with probation officers and the Police were the second most frequent source of referrals. Irregular or non-attendance at school and behaviour problems at school were the commonest features mentioned in connection with the selection criteria of children's behaviour, attitudes and family background. The day care projects in London tended to operate for children at most risk of going into institutional care, where problems with school attendance and attainment were combined with persistent delinquent activity.

Evidence from project reports suggests that, in relation to school referrals, IT centres show a similar division to that of other off-site centres. Pickles (C274) categorically states that intermediate treatment should not be an alternative to school on any long-term basis. Certain centres provide short-term placements for children in a similar way to LEA off-site units and ensure that close links are retained with the school to facilitate reintegration. In several cases they have also concentrated on the younger age group. The curriculum and programme adopted are very similar to other short-term centres, comprising basic education, crafts, outdoor trips and activities, although there seems to be less emphasis on reward systems (Hammersmith Teenage Project, C260; Harbridge, C261; Kensington and Chelsea Social Services Dept, C263; McAulay and Cunningham, C267; Mid Glamorgan Education Authority, C272; Vincent, C277).

Despite the existence of these kinds of IT schemes, the evidence suggests that IT centres cater predominantly for older (14 plus) pupils on a long-term basis (Beresford and Croft, C259; Taylor, C276). Kenny (C262) reports this factor as one of the main criticisms of LEA policy by IT staff, who find themselves receiving children nearing the end of their school career who can no longer be contained in school. The programme within these centres is similar to that in other long-term off-site education centres, comprising basic education with counselling, groupwork and discussions, and work preparation.

A series of reports on the Wandsworth day care programme (Leggett, C265; Addison, C258; Beresford and Croft, C259) highlights the dilemmas and opportunities of this kind of provision. In many cases staff are able to report positive achievements by the children, who attended regularly after years of absenteeism and made substantial progress. There is some ambivalence expressed about the lack of interest displayed by schools after the referral and the impossibility of exerting any effective influence on their practices (Beresford and Croft, C259). Leggett's (C265) earlier report, however, indicated the possibility of part-time attendance being negotiated with some schools.

Although it should no longer be strictly regarded as IT, the Markhouse Centre (C269) can be seen as a form of practice which attempts to meet a wide variety of educational needs and to build up a close and influential relationship with its referring schools. As regards pupils' views of their experiences in IT day care, no substantial literature has been found for inclusion in this bibliography.

IV.3.d. On-Site Units

Most schools contain some kind of cooling-off facility for disruptive pupils, which may simply be a room with a teacher in attendance. Some go further and establish a more substantial on-site resource with specialist teachers and an individually-tailored curriculum. These may sometimes overlap and be confused with remedial education units and classes. Despite its existence as an approach from early days, the on-site unit has received less attention than off-site centres.

While less numerous than their off-site counterparts, the number of on-site units is increasing. The HMI (C74) survey in 1977 found a total of 70 on-site units and by 1980 the numbers had risen to 136 (ACE, C73). Since the later survey received returns from only half the LEAs in England and Wales the overall number may well be higher.

Holman and Libretto (C168) discuss some of the issues raised by this kind of provision and Galloway et al (B101), Tattum (B105), Hunkin and Alhadeff (C169), Jones and Forrest (C170), Leavold (C171) and Witter and Postlethwaite (C172) provide descriptions of the work of existing units. Dain (C167) provides some guidance notes for teachers. The on-site unit is established to perform a similar function to the off-site unit – it is a place where children whom teachers wish to remove from class can receive sustained attention and treatment along with others exhibiting a range of behavioural and perhaps learning problems.

As with all special units, the type of philosophy adopted is of paramount importance in determining whether the facility is regarded as a punitive/containment disposal, or a place for positive help and counselling. Many of the reports reveal a sensitivity about whether the unit will be regarded as a sin bin or a sanctuary, with deliberate avoidance of extreme practices which might have connotations of either. In some cases it might be part of the main school physically as well as organisationally (Galloway et al, B101; Tattum, B105). In others it might be a different building some miles away but still organisationally part of the school (Jones and Forrest, C170).

The HMI (C74) survey describes the admission policies adopted by on-site units; these were normally decided through a committee of senior staff. Tattum (B105) notes the spin-off benefits of this arrangement, where teachers are pooling their knowledge about problematic pupils and acknowledging difficulties in a situation that does not threaten their professional standing. However, Galloway et al's (B101) findings suggest that in some schools control over admission procedures was vested in a few senior staff to avoid teachers channelling too many pupils into the special groups.

A familiar division emerges between units. There are those that adopt a structured programme catering for younger pupils, in some cases faithfully reflecting the main school ethos (Tattum, B105; Hunkin and Alhadeff, C169), and achieving a regular reintegration in class, and there are those that provide an alternative education for the final years comprising remedial education, community service placements and work experience courses (Jones and Forrest, C170). Witter and Postlethwaite (C172) describe a flexible individualised programme which achieves regular reintegration of pupils. The special experimental groups studied by Galloway et al (B101) set out to attain reintegration but met with a more variable response and they note that various procedural devices which kept the class teacher in touch with the pupil appeared to help in the process. Without this safeguard, it was clear that referral to an on-site unit removed a pupil as effectively from the concern and responsibility of his original teacher as referral outside the school would have done.

IV.3.e Rates of Reintegration

Where LEAs are justifying special provision on the grounds that it is a short-term placement, the success or otherwise of units in reintegrating pupils into school assumes some importance. The HMI (C74) survey makes a general observation that procedures for returning pupils to school were often less well developed than those for referral to units; more often, cases of successful return to normal schooling seemed to have involved pupils under the age of 14 and have taken place in situations of good liaison and cooperation between teachers in school and units.

The Research and Statistics Division Report (C78) on the progress of the ILEA Programme describes the outcomes for 579 pupils. It reveals that 27% of pupils left the various kinds of off-site education centres to return to their parent schools and 52% when they reached school leaving age or moved out of the district. Other types of destination included entering another centre, a special school or local authority care, although these proportions were all very small. A higher rate of reintegration was achieved for on-site secondary school units, 75% of pupils returning to their parent school. The figures further reveal that while 72% of 11–13 year olds returned to school from both on- and off-site centres combined, only 18% of 14–16 year olds achieved the same target.

A number of project reports discuss the process of reintegration, from which it is clear that regular contact needs to be maintained with the referring school and that the phased re-entry of the pupil may be helpful. In some cases pupils are only accepted on condition that they will be received back by their school after placement (Webb, C71; Dain, C88; Grunsell, C91; Palfrey, C98; Spencer, C101; Swailes, C102; Kensington and Chelsea Social Services Dept, C263). Tattum (B105) puts forward some extended guidelines on the processes which are needed in school to achieve successful reintegration.

Where placements back in the school are unsuccessful, Galloway et al (B101) provide some possible explanations based on a study of special on-site groups set up in Sheffield schools. Unreceptive attitudes on the part of class teachers were seen as one contributory factor and this problem is also confirmed by Mack (C95).

IV.4 CONCLUSION

In the choice between preventive pastoral care and specialist provision for disturbing and absentee pupils the majority of LEAs appear to have opted for the specialist units. In choosing between on- and off-site units, the latter predominates by two to one (ACE, C73). Much of the debate has now shifted to the patterns of how schools use off-site centres and the most appropriate location and content of the education provided for 14–16 year olds. Some LEAs, however, reserve the option of turning a blind eye and not acknowledging that problems exist.

The literature reveals two distinct forms of practice. One is the close cooperation of on- and off-site education centres and schools in identifying, working with, and reintegrating pupils in the 11–13 age group. The other is the existence of substantial numbers of 14–16 year olds completing their education in on- and off-site educational centres following a total breakdown in the pupil/school relationship, often preceded by years of tension and strain.

Supporters of the first practice point to its advantages for pupils and schools but as yet there is no evidence to show whether the reconciliation lasts until school-leaving age. Some teachers are also concerned that children may be labelled prematurely under this process, and are reluctant to have to concede that the school can no longer manage the pupil. Supporters of the second practice highlight the special opportunities for young people in the individualised programme which can be devised for them and the more relaxed atmosphere and relationships which characterise the long-term unit. Critics reply that it should not be necessary for adolescents to have to be separated from their peers and labelled as disruptive in order to receive an education appropriate to their needs and circumstances, and to be treated with a modicum of respect and consideration.

The key issues which are now emerging are — whether early identification of potential flash points in the first two years of schooling may prevent trouble later on, whether attention to aspects of school organisation and teacher management techniques may prevent undesirable confrontations arising, and what type of curriculum and school ethos needs to be provided in order to retain young people in schools productively.

Some commentators are hopeful that the full implementation of the Warnock philosophy may lead to a radical change in attitudes, on the grounds that it is inconsistent to integrate one group of children and segregate another. All have special needs and all should be accommodated within the school system.

Golby (C64) and White (C106) make the point that, whether supported or criticised, alternative education is a fact of life and that it is building up a body of knowledge and experience concerning the most difficult and disturbing children from the school system. The ultimate purpose of alternative education may be to analyse the shortcomings of mainstream schooling, as revealed by the pupils referred, and feed back knowledge on curriculum innovation and methods of handling and teaching such children which can be applied in the school setting.

There are signs that, in a limited way, this process is already starting to happen. Some initiatives aimed at helping schools to change their practices and helping teachers to cope with problematic classroom situations were reviewed in Chapter II.6. One promising but underdeveloped strategy is getting staff based in special units to spend time with teachers in mainstream schools helping them work with their most difficult pupils (Coulby, C54). More generally, the growth of staff in special units has led to the creation of a new professional association, the National Organisation for Initiatives in Social Education (NOISE, C97), which sees one of its aims as being 'to encourage a continuing dialogue and the formation of practical links between centres, mainstream schooling and other relevant agencies'.

Chapter V
Interagency and Interprofessional Relations

V.1 INTRODUCTION

Previous chapters have largely been about pupils whom schools identify as a problem, either by their absence or their disturbing behaviour. Other agencies have been brought in, mainly in their capacity to help schools with the young person – especially the LEA support services. (The exception was the section on school involvement in the juvenile justice system, Chapter III.4.) But many young people may come to the attention of other agencies because of problems, needs or troublesome behaviour which are not directly or initially related to schooling. So various statutory agencies outside the LEA are responding directly to these school-aged young people: the Health Service, the social work agencies, the Police. There are also a host of youth and community organisations, voluntary social welfare agencies, and neighbourhood bodies, all working with young people.

There is an ideal that somehow all these agencies should be able to work together, presumably in the interests of young people and the community in the broader and long-term sense, and given the importance of formal schooling, there is an assumption that cooperation with and on the part of schools is essential, or at least very desirable. There is therefore concern about the level of cooperation between agencies and between workers, which is often thought to be inadequate.

This chapter reviews the interagency and interprofessional literature from three points of view. The first concerns agency roles and interagency relationships (V.2). The assumption here is that agencies have different functions and different priorities, and hence differing interests. Whatever their shared interest in the welfare of young people, in the short term they may be concerned with different groups of young people, different facets of their lives or different time scales. These differences may become institutionalised into a concern to defend bureaucratic interests. How easily agencies may cooperate will depend on the degree to which each agency, in pursuit of its own goals, can provide the other with the kind of service and support that the recipient agency feels it needs and has a right to expect.

Much of the literature is not about clashes between agencies, but is pitched at the more personal level of differences between workers in different professions. While some of these may genuinely be due to professional differences, such as in values or socialisation of new members, much is simply due to the effects of working in agencies with different functions. To these inevitable differences may be added problems of poor communication, ignorance or unrealistic expectations about the other's role, and stereotyping. The middle section of the chapter (V.3) reviews this literature on how members of different professions see each other, and on general problems of cooperation between them, especially teachers and social workers.

The final main section (V.4) reviews the literature on various attempts to overcome some of these problems, through better liaison, cooperative initiatives or joint action, either at management or practitioner level. A final concluding section (V.5) draws out a few main issues.

Much of the literature is about Social Services and Education, or social workers and school staff. One reason is simply that, as noted in the introduction to this publication, effectively no material is included on the Health Service or the Youth Service; nor on the variety of voluntary agencies, law centres, counselling agencies, community organisations, and so on, which may be concerned about young people in trouble and what the school can do or indeed is doing. That leaves a limited number of statutory agencies: the Education Service, Social Services, the Probation Service and the Police.

For some purposes the education department as a whole is taken as the relevant unit of organisation, but most of the time the school is treated as an agency in its own right. In any case, the main focus is on school and teacher relations, either with outside agencies and workers of all kinds, or just with non-LEA ones. If in all this there is disproportionate emphasis on schools and Social Services or teachers and social workers, it is a reflection of the accumulated literature on the subject and of the interest and concern of the field.

V.2 AGENCY ROLES AND INTERAGENCY RELATIONS

This section looks at a few topics in the literature about interagency relationships, in the light of the differing functions or priorities of the various agencies.

Chapter II reviewed this area from the school perspective: the school usually turns to outside agencies when it feels there is a problem with an individual pupil, like disturbing behaviour or absence, which it cannot deal with alone. It looks outside for diagnosis, advice, support, amelioration of the problem, treatment, the imposition of external sanctions, and, in the last resort, removal from school to an alternative placement. Generally, the school will be looking for a speedy response that will enable it to get on with its main explicit function, children's cognitive development. Sometimes, when school resources are exhausted or a crisis has developed, it will want urgent action, which it may see as the responsibility of another agency.

These other agencies fall into two groups. The first comprises services within the LEA which exist largely to assist the school system: the Education Welfare Service, the School Psychological Service and, to some extent, Child Guidance. These services may largely accept this role, within the constraints of their resources, but differences in emphasis may still emerge. One example is the schools' demand on the School Psychological Service for individual assessments, while the SPS itself may be moving to a more preventive view of its functions (Gillham, C121; Topping, C129). Another, taken up below, is the balance between social work and other tasks in the EWS. The second group includes Social Services, Probation and the Police. These are independent of the LEA and have their own distinctive functions and priorities. Even if there are no real conflicts of interest, cooperative arrangements have to be negotiated. The issues in this section concern school or LEA relations with this kind of independent agency.

V.2.a Police and Schools

The main functions of the Police regarding juveniles are crime prevention, crime detection, and processing — perhaps prosecuting — those charged with offences. There is a welfare element to some of these. For purposes of crime prevention, including better 'community relations' and getting young people to trust the Police, police forces around the country have, over the last few years, been building closer relations with both primary and secondary schools. They may help run sports and social events and projects, and are regularly given space in the timetable to present programmes to pupils on, for example, road safety, the law, crime, police work, citizenship (McNee in DHSS, C219; Bourne, C292; Merseyside Police, C295; Phillips and Hocking, C297; Schaffer, C300; Shanks, C301). This may be part of longer-term community approaches to policing, and a Home Office Circular (C294) encouraging this gives additional examples of Police-school projects. From this material it appears that schools welcome this contribution, though the trend is not without its critics (Teachers' Action Collective, C303).

Schools may want to call in the Police to deal with particular crimes or vandalism, and the Police may seek information from the school when deciding whether to caution or prosecute — though not everywhere as much as schools would wish (see Chapter III.4.a). A North Wales Police (C296) report mentions an interprofessional dinner club, chaired by a school head and with Police participation, 'to discuss the problems of particular children'.

Police and the LEA (including schools) share a concern about truancy. The Police are concerned about offending by young people when not in school, and in some areas, as a form of preventive policing, they have formed truancy patrols in cooperation with the EWS (McNee in DHSS, C219; North Wales Police, C296; Reynolds, C298; Rowlands, C299); this is commended in the Home Office Circular (C294), which cites other examples, but questions have been asked about Police involvement since truancy is not a crime (Reynolds, C298).

This limited literature suggests that although the functions of Police and schools are very different, each can get the cooperation of the other in pursuing its own purposes. The same cannot be said as clearly about schools and Social Services, though both are welfare agencies.

V.2.b Social Services Departments and the LEA

Broad overviews or discussions of the respective functions of Social Services and Education, as agencies, are few in this bibliography (Seebohm, C8; ADSS, C211; Davie in Kahan, C221; Robinson, C254), and this section is mainly about Social Services and the school. An exception is the issue of agency responsibility for the Education Welfare Service.

The Seebohm (C8) vision of comprehensive personal social services has faded somewhat and various constraints, not least financial, have forced social services departments to concentrate more on specific statutory duties. The first part of this section looks briefly at a few topics, and notes others, on LEA and school involvement in enabling Social Services to carry out these duties. The second part takes a different starting point: what social work services are provided to or through schools, and what agency should be responsible for them.

Statutory social work functions

Robinson (C254) discusses a number of Social Services functions and the boundary issues in relation to schools. Some of these functions derive from mental health and handicap legislation and require links with special education, but mostly they derive from child care legislation, including the 1969 Children and Young Persons Act (C2). Social Services has considerable discretion in how it interprets some of its duties, eg the duty to try and prevent family breakdown and the need to take young people into care. 'Preventive' work of all kinds gives rise to plenty of 'grey' areas between Social Services and the LEA, and the literature on social work and schools is often unclear about the statutory basis of the tasks under discussion.

Two major areas of work can be noted here. Child protection, especially against non-accidental injury, mainly concerns children of primary school age, who are outside our scope, but this issue has considerable influence on general attitudes towards interagency cooperation. Secondly there are the processes leading up to and including an appearance before the juvenile court or Hearing; LEA and school involvement was dealt with in Chapter III.3 and III.4.

A third area concerns Social Services' responsibility for children in its care. A significant issue in Education/Social Services' relationships is education provision in residential facilities — community homes with education (CHEs) and observation and assessment centres — and another is the respective functions of CHEs and boarding special schools, but these are outside the scope of this bibliography.

A lesser issue, though of some concern, is when a child in care changes residence and Social Services has to arrange for education in an ordinary, local school. This arises when a child

goes into residential care (except CHE), and in Davis's (C174) survey of Social Services directors, some reported a reluctance by schools to accept such children, or problems with their subsequent exclusion. It arises more acutely when children are returning home, perhaps 'on trial', from a CHE or (in Scotland) a List 'D' school (McKail et al, C96; Davis, C174; Anderson, C185), perhaps via an IT programme (Scrutton, C226). Comments in a Liverpool Education Committee (C24) report suggest that problems of reintegration arise when schools are sceptical that the return home indicates a real improvement in the child's behaviour and suspect instead that it is an administrative move designed to free a place needed for another child.

Anderson (C185) follows this process through and notes that there are differences in perception between teachers and List 'D' school staff about the degree of progress made by pupils, and schools often reported a lack of communication with the referring institution. Scrutton (C226), in a case study, claims that the delays in reintegration affected the young person's progress; he suggests that outside pressures on the school are making it more difficult for staff to be receptive and to give the time and effort required to reintegrate a pupil who has previously created problems for them.

A fourth area of work is the implementation of supervision orders. Except where IT is involved, there appears to be no substantial literature on links with schools: the subject gets a one-line mention in a lengthy BASW discussion paper on 'Social work in relation to schools' (Andrews, C233) and little attention in Robinson's (C254) book. The Probation Service, in fact, implements about half the supervision orders under the CYP Act 1969. (It also supervises orders under matrimonial and divorce legislation and young people returning from custody.) Yet there appears to be very little literature on its relationship to schools, and only a few incidental references have been included here (Staffordshire LEA, C28; Suffolk LEA, C30). The implication is either that social work agencies do not feel school involvement is needed for this supervision work, or that the relationship is too routine to merit discussion.

Where IT is included in the supervision order, there are at least three issues for the social work agency. If a day care programme is required, how is the education to be provided? Usually the LEA provides the teachers or makes an equivalent contribution, though not always (Kenny, C262; Locke, C266; Vincent, C277). Secondly, the project will usually want the young person to be integrated back into school when the day programme ends (Addison, C258; Kenny, C262; Leggett, C265; Pickles, C274). Thirdly, in any kind of IT project, what action should the workers take vis-à-vis the school in response to participants' anxiety about or disaffection from school — an issue raised in many IT reports, though not explored enough to cite here.

Most IT provision is, in fact, not primarily for young people with IT conditions in their supervision orders, and much of it is a form of 'preventive' work by Social Services. The overlap in provision is considerable, and the issues are similar, with an important addition: should — or to what extent should — Social Services provide IT for young people whose main problem is disaffection from school, whether in alternative day care (Beresford and Croft, C259; Pickles, C274), in evening schemes, or preventive school-based groups. The IT literature is discussed more fully elsewhere (Chapter II.4.c, II.5.d and IV.3.c), and joint IT projects are mentioned in V.4.c below, but on the policy issues, while there are exhortations to cooperation between the two agencies (Carlisle in DHSS, C219), there is a shortage of clear statements by local authority policy makers. The question here is part of the wider issue of social work services to schools, which is taken up next.

Social work services and schools

A number of writers discuss the provision of social work services in, to or through the school (Craft et al, C216; Andrews, C233; Davis, C238; Dunn in Dunn et al, C241; Lyons, C249; Musgrave, C252; Packwood, C253; Robinson, C254; Saltmarsh, C256), sometimes in the context of the wider welfare network (FitzHerbert, C34; Johnson et al, C220). (Ways and projects in which such services are actually provided are reviewed in Chapters II.4 and II.5 and in V.4 below.) Some of this literature appears to refer more to children in primary schools than to older ones; some embraces pastoral care, counselling and educational welfare as well as Social Services work. Among the issues discussed are:

- the nature of the social work function and its differences or similarities to education, in relation to children, families and the wider community (see also V.3.b below on social workers and teachers);
- the range of social work tasks involved;
- the need for a more comprehensive service of assessment and early intervention;
- the functional base for these activities, in the school or the community or some compromise, and the responsibility of Education or Social Services for providing them.

From a Social Services perspective, this literature and other reports on Social Services/Education relations (ADSS, C211; Kahan, C221) give the impression that general issues about working with schools are more salient than particular matters related to the specific statutory tasks covered above. Given its existing remit, issues for Social Services include:

- what resources it can devote to school-related preventive work;
- at what point in the (predicted) process of social breakdown, or for what proportion of the school population, it should provide services;
- to what extent its role is to work with and through the school (or other LEA services) — eg by support, advice, coordination or advocacy — and to what extent directly with children and their families, and at what point it takes over primary responsibility for the case.

Sometimes concern is expressed that schools refer too late; an extreme case (leaving aside fears of child abuse) is when they exclude pupils and then tell Social Services, on the assumption that the latter will deal with the problems (Davis, C174). For Harbert (in ADSS, C211), the issues about Social Services' assumption of responsibility are not just resources, but the interests of the children concerned and the reduction of pressure on education departments to improve their services — in short, the issues of segregation discussed in the previous chapter.

Agency responsibility for the Education Welfare Service

The Education Welfare Service is clearly one of the major ways of providing social work services to or through schools, and increasingly it has been referred to as 'educational social work'. The Seebohm Report (C8) certainly saw its tasks largely in social work terms, as did the Ralphs Report (C6), which recommended a social work training and qualification for EWOs.

This shift has at times led to differences in views about its functions between the EWS itself and the schools (Pedley, C114; Johnson et al, C220). It also led to a debate on whether it should continue to be part of the LEA or should be transferred to Social Services. The Seebohm (C8) recommendations to this effect were never enacted, but stimulated controversy for a period (MacMillan, C112; Andrews, C233; Robinson, C254), including polemical reports from the Association of Directors of Social Services (C234) and the Society of Education Officers (C115) which highlight the different concerns and priorities of the two departments.

In part the issue is how far the EWS is a service to schools and to the LEA and how far it is a social work service to school children and their families. The former is accepted as legitimate by both sides, but the ADSS Report explicitly challenges the emphasis on getting truants to school on the grounds that firstly, this neglects the needs of many school children under stress, and secondly EWOs, perceived perhaps as agents of social control, may not be addressing the underlying problems of truants. The SEO reply, confirming the value of school attendance in itself, sees 'the seeds of a fundamental conflict of purpose' in the ADSS report. If the EWS was transferred, the LEA would have to replace it with a new group of workers to carry out various welfare, attendance and liaison functions on behalf of the schools. (Criticisms about agency priorities could no doubt be reversed:

more recently, Social Services could be said to be limiting itself much more to its statutory responsibilities, with increasing emphasis in adolescent work on dealing with delinquents as a service to the courts.)

The more general issue illustrated by educational social work is the question of boundaries of responsibilities between agencies for needy or problematic young people. It is generally thought desirable for agencies to define as clearly as possible their respective functions, but does this, in the end, miss an important issue — namely that the needs of young people and their families cannot be classified in any simple way, so that to cope with the 'grey areas', field workers have to cooperate in flexible ways, supported by their agency managers (Harbert, Kogan, in ADSS, C211). These issues and the problems involved are taken up in the next section.

V.3 PROFESSIONAL PERCEPTIONS AND INTERPROFESSIONAL RELATIONS

The quality of relations between agencies finds its main expression in the quality of relations between their workers. Since each of the agencies considered has a dominant professional group, issues of interagency relations cannot easily be separated from interprofessional ones, though it is quite possible that differential professional recruitment and initial training account for some of the difference. This section reviews two areas: how workers in different agencies in fact perceive each other; and general issues in interprofessional cooperation and the obstacles to this, with special reference to social workers and teachers.

V.3.a Interprofessional Perceptions

Contact and collaboration between members of different professions can take place at any level, from chief officer to basic grade staff, and in a variety of contexts — formal committees, case conferences, liaison between individual workers, inter-disciplinary teams, and so on. There is little systematic evidence about the actual experiences of interprofessional working in these various contexts, and therefore the perceptions of workers reported in this section should be seen as an extremely limited sampling, which could be unrepresentative.

On the conduct of relations at the most senior levels there appears to be a dearth of literature, which is not entirely unexpected. Interdepartmental groups and committees, of the kinds described in Section V.4.a below, are sometimes set up specifically to remedy problems of poor communication at this level. Price and Briault (C223) and Price (C224) refer to these kinds of difficulty, which were the stimulus for the initiatives they describe.

The bulk of the literature reflects the experiences and opinions of those who need to liaise with other workers about the welfare of individual children: most of it comes from school staff, some from social workers, education welfare officers and educational psychologists. (Teacher/social worker relations are reviewed more fully in a later section.) These views are recorded in working party reports from Cumbria (C16), the Isle of Wight (C23), Liverpool (C24, C25), Staffordshire (C28) and South Glamorgan (Kahan, C221) and in research or survey reports by Topping (C129), Wright and Payne (C132), Davis (C174) and Johnson et al (C220).

How school staff perceive professionals in other agencies

When teachers and school heads express satisfaction or otherwise with other professionals, the reasons are usually of three kinds: the professionalism of the group concerned – their expertise and competence; their style of work and the helpfulness of this to teachers; and their values regarding young people.

Police and probation officers receive the most uncritical comments from school staff. Police were regarded as effective and reliable (Staffordshire, C28; Suffolk, C30); a sample of teachers reported easy liaison with a Juvenile Bureau team, as their role and responsibilities were seen as clear cut (Johnson et al, C220). Probation officers received favourable mentions for helpfulness in the Staffordshire (C28) and Suffolk (C30) reports.

Education welfare officers have a mixed reception: their work is highly valued in the Cumbria (C16) and Suffolk (C30) reports, but more critically regarded by head teachers in the Staffordshire one (C28) as demonstrating insufficient powers or follow-up. Accessibility and speed of response are important to school staff, and EWOs are likely to be the most accessible of outside workers. Coverage, however, varies from place to place, and some Staffordshire schools (C28) reported the service as slow, while Johnson et al (C220) reported teachers as having few contacts with EWOs because of shortage of staff and heavy caseloads.

Educational psychologists traditionally command respect for their expertise, but school staff do not always find them very helpful. The Portsmouth SPS survey (C132) reported some positive comments from teachers on personal contacts and on the help they had received, including practical advice on management techniques. Other reactions were mixed. Some thought they were good at diagnosis, but had little time for treatment (Suffolk, C30) or provided no practical advice, taking no account of the child's behaviour in a group, which was the teacher's main concern (Johnson et al, C220). Heads in Staffordshire (C28) said they were sometimes slow to respond, had little contact with school staff, and tended to confirm what school staff already knew. Liaison with Child Guidance workers did not figure in most of the reports, but Johnson et al (C220) report teachers as finding them reluctant to divulge information, understaffed and slow in responding to referrals.

Social workers attracted the most criticism for their style of work, on the grounds of: poor communication and feedback of information (Staffordshire, C28; Suffolk, C30); being too busy through heavy caseloads to respond effectively (Staffordshire, C28); having a rapid turnover of staff (Suffolk, C30; Johnson et al, C220); and lack of speed in dealing with court cases or lack of effectiveness in supervision (Liverpool, C24, C25; Staffordshire, C28; Suffolk, C30). In the Cumbria report (C16) it was said that they could no longer be regarded as specialist child care officers, with some consequent loss of confidence on the part of teachers.

Professional values are important. A key factor in teacher perceptions of other professional workers is whether they have the same attitude to the difficulties being presented by young people and agree on the proper course of action. This often revolves around the emphasis which is given to particular behaviour, in relation to underlying causes. EWOs, probation officers and police officers appear to be regarded by some teachers as potential allies, who will ensure that the seriousness of truancy and delinquency will be effectively communicated to the child concerned and some form of sanction brought to bear, before other action is taken about individual and family problems.

Educational psychologists may be regarded as inevitably more concerned with underlying causation, but social workers receive sustained criticism for not taking absenteeism seriously enough and being more concerned with the social circumstances of the child and his family (Suffolk, C30; Johnson et al, C220).

How other professionals perceive school staff

Views on teachers and heads from professionals in other agencies are much more limited in this group of references, and will be dealt with briefly; social worker/teacher differences are covered more fully in the next section. These other professionals concentrate their comments on the way they are misunderstood by school staff, in terms of their functions, powers or methods of work.

Thus, reports by both Social Services and Probation to the Staffordshire LEA working party (C28) note difficulties arising from teachers' unrealistic expectations about the discipline and control that social workers exercise over young people. There was a tendancy to expect too much of workers in Social Services, who were often asked to help at a late stage and then expected to respond quickly or deal completely with the problems (Staffordshire, C28; Davis, C174). EWOs have sometimes felt that they were expected to restrict themselves to school non-attendance, at the expense of the social work aspect of their role, or were too much at the beck and call of school heads (MacMillan, C112; Johnson et al, C220). Educational psychologists may feel

constrained by the level of expectations from school staff for individual assessment and treatment, at the expense of preventive approaches (Gillham, C121; Topping, C129).

V.3.b Interprofessional Cooperation and its Problems

Concern about inadequate cooperation between workers of different professions, exhortations to improvement, analyses of the problems, and strategies for change are widespread in the literature. They are offered by central government (DHSS, C219; Home Office, C293), by official committees (Black, C1; Pack, C5; Seebohm, C8; Warnock, C13), by researchers, trainers and advisers (Bastiani and Ward, C213; Davies, C217; Johnson et al, C220; Davie in Kahan, C221; Dunn in Dunn et al, C241), by senior officers (Harbert in ADSS, C211), and by practitioners themselves (Kahan, C221; and the various reports cited above on interprofessional perceptions).

These references are only examples from an extensive literature on the subject. They offer a long list of causes for the problems of interprofessional cooperation, and what follows is a summary of the reasons most often mentioned; various efforts to overcome these obstacles are reviewed in the next main section. As noted earlier, it is hard to disentangle the specifically professional dimensions from those due to agency differences.

- Problems in communication due to separate physical location and difficulties in reaching or meeting one another. Teachers, for instance, cannot be reached in class, and in the limited times when they are free, they probably cannot reach other workers who are often away from their offices. Moreover, school heads or specialist pastoral care staff often act as 'gatekeepers' between the school and outside workers, and the degree to which class teachers are consulted, involved and kept informed will vary from school to school.
- Differences in agency structures, procedures, levels of decision making, catchment area, etc. Examples here are lack of coterminous boundaries, so that a secondary school could be dealing with two or three social work teams; or the probability that a basic grade social worker or EWO will deal directly with the head of a large comprehensive. Mutual ignorance on these matters may make it hard for a worker to identify the appropriate person to deal with and the procedures to follow.
- Ignorance of each other's role, priorities, methods of work, professional language, and the values associated with these. There is a lack of opportunities to learn, whether in initial training, in joint staff development, or informally. Stereotyping abounds. Sometimes the other worker's role and values, even if understood, are not accepted as fully legitimate. Thus, fears are expressed about the use of confidential information; differing views about what is best for the child are not always respected.
- A tendency to emphasise professional distinctiveness. Professional jealousies may take the form of claims to be more 'caring' about a child, or reluctance to share information.
- Differences in status, pay and conditions of service. EWOs and youth workers, for example, may feel they are accorded low status. Multi-disciplinary teams and joint projects are hampered by differences in pay and conditions.

Social workers and teachers

In the light of the literature discussed above, it comes as no surprise to learn that the relationship between teachers and social workers is regarded as the most problematic one. Accounts of joint projects or the placement of social workers in schools have described some persisting difficulties in relationships (Derrick, C239; Francis, C244; Marshall and Rose, C250; Morris, C251; Leggett, C265), so the problems are by no means caused simply by physical separation and lack of contact.

A number of writers have examined the similarities and differences between these two groups to try and account for the problem (Harbert, Kogan, in ADSS, C211; Craft and Craft, C215; Davies, C217; Davie, Evans, Picardie, in Kahan, C221;

Milner, C222; Davies, C237; Musgrave, C252; Packwood, C253; Robinson, C254). What emerges from this literature is that social work and teaching share many common values, and both are concerned with socialisation and social functioning, but their goals and objects of attention are different and they receive dissimilar endorsement from society as to the ultimate value of their activities.

Any differences in initial recruitment are greatly enlarged by separate professional training, and the two professions have evolved distinctive styles of work to achieve their respective goals. Thus, two groups of people emerge whose everyday experiences are different, producing characteristic casts of thought and attitude, though according to Davies (C217), one thing they do share is being fairly powerless in large welfare bureaucracies. The following is a composite description from the literature, which tries to encapsulate the key distinctions.

- Schools represent social authority, written in bricks and mortar, whereas social workers have to cope with society's ambivalent attitudes towards the groups they attempt to help. Social workers are more likely than teachers to see themselves as agents of change trying to promote a fairer distribution of resources in society.
- Teachers are concerned primarily with cognitive development and the acquisition of knowledge; social workers are committed to more intangible and global goals of personal well-being and social functioning.
- Teachers — certainly those at secondary schools — relate principally to the child or young person, while social workers deal more with the family as a whole, perhaps in a wider community context.
- Teachers work mainly in large group settings, with all that implies for management and control, and are more attuned to average needs and achievements, whereas social workers focus on individuals or very small groups, and must be sensitive to what is unique and individual. The teacher's contact with a child is more frequent but less personal.
- Teachers' relationships with young people are heavily influenced by the institutional setting; they have to be aware of the collective sense of purpose within the school yet have a high degree of autonomy in their everyday work, which is largely unsupervised. Social workers often operate outside the safer territory of the office, and while they are bound by agency purposes and mandates, they have considerable autonomy and discretion, even affecting clients' liberty, though this is subject to formal supervision.

Additional distinctions can be drawn from this literature, but a crucial one concerns differences in attitudes towards the process of education in schools. Teachers in mainstream schools are likely to have a strong belief in the importance of school to the child's personal and social development: hence their efforts to involve other agencies in trying to ensure that a child attends school and can benefit from it; hence, too, their concern that the classroom behaviour of a few can jeopardise the educational progress of the majority. Social workers are also likely to place high value on education and learning, but are less likely to see the school as the only possible setting for these, and concern about the school experiences of individual children may lead them to discount the all-embracing demands of the school and its staff.

Routine interaction between agencies and professionals is necessary if existing procedures and arrangements concerning young people are to function at all. There may be particular circumstances, however, in which it is decided that more effort needs to be put into interprofessional and interdepartmental communication and practice. The next section gives examples of different kinds of collaboration and examines their underlying rationale.

V.4 FORMS OF INTERAGENCY AND INTERPROFESSIONAL COLLABORATION

There are signs of growing awareness that individual agencies and professionals in the education and social welfare sectors have not been working together as effectively as they might, and that this has costs, both for the organisations concerned and for the child or family who may be the focus of attention or otherwise. There are also signs that more initiatives are being taken to overcome the obstacles to collaboration.

Commentators who have analysed these obstacles, reviewed in the previous section, have sometimes outlined general strategies for overcoming them. The following are some examples which indicate the range of remedies proposed (Harbert, Kogan, in ADSS, C211; Davies, C217, C218; Davie in Kahan, C221; Davies, C237; Dunn in Dunn et al, C241):

- corporate planning to review and coordinate policies, operations and resources;
- making agency boundaries coterminous;
- local monitoring to identify blocks in communication and the development of local communication systems for sharing basic information;
- careful analysis of working situations in their organisational context, to identify points of friction;
- joint in-service training;
- opportunities to learn and practise the skills of inter-professional work;
- reduction of anomalies in pay and conditions of service;
- the development of interdisciplinary teams and cross-placement of workers;
- combined efforts by professionals in different agencies to change their own bureaucracies and make them more responsive to consumers;
- adequate resourcing of services.

This section reviews the literature on specific initiatives undertaken to improve interagency or interprofessional collaboration, in terms of the kinds of goals sought, which are grouped broadly under three headings — policy and management, interprofessional understanding, and cooperative practice. First, however, it documents the precipitating factors that have stimulated these initiatives.

Where agencies have come together to review their working arrangements, the literature reveals that a variety of factors may provide the initial stimulus. These include: the gradual realisation that distant and inefficient liaison is counter-productive (Price and Briault, C223; Price, C224); a tragedy that highlights inadequacies in existing relationships (Hampshire, C20); an identified problem that requires interagency discussion (Cleveland, C15; Cumbria, C16; Devon, C18; Dorset, C19; Hampshire, C21; Isle of Wight, C23; Liverpool, C24, C25; North Yorkshire, C26; Northants, C27; Staffordshire, C28; Strathclyde, C29; West Glamorgan, C31); or an external request to initiate cooperation (Home Office, C293).

It is a somewhat different situation when an outside body decides to promote interagency and interprofessional communication and convenes groups, seminars and conferences with this aim in view. The South Glamorgan experiment sponsored by the DHSS Social Work Service and the Welsh Office, reported in Kahan (C221), started out in this way but through the establishment of special task groups, had a more enduring influence on the interdepartmental consultative processes in the local authority concerned (Gamble in ADSS, C211). Another initiative established interprofessional task groups within a university setting which discussed school-related problems. Bastiani and Ward (C213) provide detailed process notes on the workings of these interprofessional groups.

Collaboration between agencies or workers may operate at varying degrees of intensity. At the level of liaison, this could amount to keeping each other informed and consulting regularly on matters of policy or practice. At the level of cooperation, this may require each agency or professional to work in such a way that they can attain mutually agreed goals. This may develop into joint action, entailing an actual pooling of resources to reach this objective. Initiatives described in the literature could perhaps be organised along this dimension, but not easily. In the review that follows, the examples are grouped roughly into policy and management initiatives, improving interprofessional understanding, and cooperative practice (including joint projects).

V.4.a Liaison and Cooperation in Policy and Management

Collection and sharing of information

When an issue has been identified, there is need for a common focus which can enable an interagency pooling of knowledge and the collection of opinion, information and statistics to take place. The working party is the usual model for this kind of exercise, which is generally a one-off effort, and many of the local authority working parties cited above had this as one of their purposes.

The SCYPTAR experiment (Study Conference on Young People in Trouble or At Risk, C227) in Hertfordshire, comprising representatives from the Courts, Community Relations, the Church, Education, Police, Social Services and the Youth Service, institutionalised this process. It did this by maintaining a standing group, which met five times a year to: review current thinking on the prevention, diagnosis and treatment of young people at risk or in trouble; provide a focal point for interchange of views; maintain a flow of research and information; and encourage local study groups. This included a study on school non-attendance.

Formulation and coordination of policy and strategy

Agencies may find their work overlapping, conflicting or duplicating if there has not been coordination at departmental level. An example might be the provision of off-site special units by Education and Social Services, with no clear demarcation in terms of remit and acceptable referrals from school.

Price and Briault (C223) and Price (C224) describe coordinating groups set up at divisional level specifically involving Social Services and Education. A Dorset report (C19) recommends a joint planning group of officers designed to investigate optimal methods of providing social work services in schools.

A Home Office Circular (C293) urged the Police to cooperate with other agencies in the prevention of delinquency, and a second one (C294) describes some of the initiatives that resulted. Burton (C214) describes regular meetings between chief officers of Police, Social Services, Education and Probation, producing management statements that could be translated into operational procedures for each department.

Certain types of need may be experienced or identified by individual agencies which require a coordinated approach at local level. In the absence of any such interagency grouping there is no forum in which to express the need and plan the response. Price and Briault (C223) and Price (C224) describe the establishment of joint Social Services/Education committees at local level which parallel the consultations between chief officers at divisional level. The interagency project set up in South Wales, reviewed by Kahan (C221), included a range of working groups established to examine issues of concern to Social Services and Education, resulting in a wide variety of interagency initiatives being set up in local areas.

Clarification of procedures

Within authorities a need for a more precise understanding of legal procedures, agency responsibilities and reciprocal requirements for information and feedback may be indentified. These can be codified into referral procedures, codes of practice and statements of legal obligations, and then disseminated to all concerned (Cumbria, C16; Dorset, C19; West Glamorgan, C31).

V.4.b Improvement of Interprofessional Understanding

Ignorance of another agency's work and stereotyping of a fellow professional's attitudes and capability are often identified as problems hindering effective cooperative work. These may be overcome either as a result of participating in interagency committees or groups, or by setting up special meetings to promote better interprofessional understanding. A Hampshire report (C21) describes a 'care committee' with agency representatives who met termly in each other's offices to discuss their work and their links with other agencies.

The Cumbria report (C16) recommends joint in-service training courses or joint seminars. The South Glamorgan report, (Kahan, C221) and Bastiani and Ward (C213), describe the ways in which these can promote better understanding or bring into clearer focus the barriers which exist to greater interprofessional communication. Bastiani and Ward feel their interprofessional groups might have been more satisfying if they had focused more on an achievable project of practical relevance to participants' everyday work. The importance of joint in-service training has often been stressed, but the literature on this appears to be scant.

V.4.c Cooperative Practice

The literature gives examples of various types of cooperative practice between professionals from different agencies. The models outlined below start with the coordination of casework, which is fairly widely established, and move through to interdisciplinary teams and joint projects which, to be successful, require considerable flexibility on the part of participants.

Coordination of casework

A need strongly identified by agencies is to bring together professionals who are working with the same child. The case conference is the usual model, initially used to decide a suitable course of action and then reconvened to review progress at regular intervals. Other regular meetings with more general functions are recorded by the DES report (B4) on truancy and behavioural problems in school. These are termly meetings bringing together the school, the education department, Social Services personnel and magistrates for broad discussions about children who may have come to the attention of these agencies.

Similar groups are reported in the Pack Report (C5). A regular Dinner Club based at a school in North Wales is reported, consisting of representatives from child health services, Probation, Social Services, Education Welfare Service, Police and School Liaison, who review current work with children (C296). New groupings to meet needs not already covered are recommended by a Hampshire report (C21), and a new panel is proposed, drawn from Area Education, Divisional Social Services, Child Guidance, Area Health and Probation, which is intended to resolve conflicts when Social Services and Education are unable to agree to bring a child or parent to court. A liaison committee of magistrates, teachers, social workers and probation officers is recommended by a Cumbria report (C16) to review the progress of children in care or under supervision.

One-off cooperative exercises

The Police and the Education Welfare Service have a common interest in seeing a reduction in the numbers of children loose on the streets playing truant, and in some cases this has led to special joint initiatives such as truancy patrols, which are conducted over a limited period of time with the aim of returning as many children as possible to school. Rowlands (C299) reports joint patrols on the part of EWOs and police officers, and Reynolds (C298) and North Wales Police (C296) describe police initiatives of this kind which have the support and cooperation of the EWS.

Other examples of short-term collaboration between professionals from different agencies can be found in reports of the social education courses given by outside agencies, which have been provided in schools for fifth year pupils as a counter attraction to absenteeism. Pritchard (C232) describes a course involving Police, Probation and Social Services; Bradford Education Department (C229) brought together a teacher, EWO and social worker; Padmore (C231) describes a social education initiative involving a teacher, probation officer, university lecturer and representative from Nottingham Young Volunteers. A report from Bedfordshire (C228) shows youth workers and IT workers linking up with teachers and social workers.

Consultation services to other professionals

Initiatives within schools which aim to change existing practice or attitudes can be undertaken, with some success, by outside professional workers. The key factors in this case would appear to be the extent to which the workers concerned carry authority. Examples include initiatives by educational psychologists to help teachers understand individual children and manage their classes (Loxley, C124; Ravenette, C127; Wolfendale, C131); and some research experiments which place teams of social welfare professionals in schools, partly to help teachers with classroom management techniques.

Gatekeepers

One approach to interprofessional collaboration is to reduce the need for teachers and social workers to communicate directly with each other, with all the attendant possibilities of misunderstanding, by providing a gatekeeper who is acceptable to both groups. In schools this role is often performed by the school counsellor, who may assume responsibility for all welfare work within the institution and, where necessary, for liaison with the relevant social welfare professionals. Although this is often welcomed by outside agency staff, who feel they have direct access to a kindred spirit (Johnson et al, C220), the literature on counselling reveals this to be an ambiguous and sometimes difficult role to sustain within schools.

Placement of specialist workers in other agencies

The rationale behind this is that the professional on placement can supply skills and knowledge which supplement those of the staff of the host agency and enable them to extend the range of the services they can provide. Examples of this approach include the placement or employment of social welfare professionals in schools (Bond, C236; Dinnage, C240; Saltmarsh, C256; Wolstenholme and Kolvin, C257) and the employment of teachers in IT centres (Leggett, C265; Beresford and Croft, C259).

Because the worker on placement is usually outnumbered by the other professionals, acceptance of the legitimacy of the dominant agency values is usually essential for successful collaboration. Social workers in schools will address the welfare needs of children which may be preventing them taking full advantage of their educational opportunities, but may not feel it appropriate to challenge existing school practices. Teachers in IT centres may be required to develop alternative forms of curriculum and more informal styles of relationship with young people, which represent an implicit criticism of normal practice in schools. If this adjustment cannot be made acceptably, there may be an abrupt termination to the placement (Leggett, C265).

An alternative approach is for the minority professionals on placement to carry out work which they feel is necessary, which may in the process challenge existing teacher assumptions, accept the initial criticism and misunderstanding that this may entail but eventually prove their point by demonstrating the success of the methods adopted. Austin (C52) describes how groupworkers placed in Belfast schools successfully challenged teachers' assessment of pupils' potential.

Multi-disciplinary teams and joint projects

If the placement of professional workers in unfamiliar settings represents a first step towards permanent collaboration, the creation of multi-disciplinary teams and joint projects represents the most fully realised form of this objective.

The multi-disciplinary team consists of relatively equal numbers of workers from different professions engaged in a common task, usually in a neutral setting. This often seems to be one of the few occasions on which professionals can leave behind their agency conflicts and differences and achieve a genuine mutual appreciation of each other's knowledge and skill. The Child Guidance team is the prime example of this concept, bringing together psychiatrists, psychologists and social workers from Health, Social Services and Education (Sampson, C141; Johnson et al, C220). Supporters of the service claim that the benefits stemming from this achievement far outweigh the criticisms which have been levelled at Child Guidance (Barnes, C133; Davie, C135; Mead, C139).

Multi-disciplinary teams may also be a feature of joint projects between agencies but in this case the benefits are not just to the workers in terms of greater interprofessional communication, but also to the senior management of their respective agencies. Joint projects between agencies necessitate common funding, management and objectives and the process involved in deciding these may force a clarification of issues which have previously remained blurred (Vincent, C277).

V.5 CONCLUSION

Two major areas of interagency and interprofessional collaboration in relation to young people in trouble can be discerned. In both cases, fundamental questions can be asked concerning the ultimate goal of such collaboration and the benefits which are likely to accrue to young people from such initiatives. An article by Davies (C218) contains some pertinent observations on this subject.

The first area concerns routine processes and procedures. Children who come to the attention of schools and other agencies may be assessed by one service, referred to another for treatment or subject to court procedures. The smooth operation of this system requires some degree of effective communication between the teachers and other welfare professionals involved.

However, there is not always a consensus among the workers involved as to what procedures should be invoked and whether the care or control of the child is the primary aim. Reports about worker perceptions and interagency liaison indicate that conflicts of value or interest may prevent or hold up certain processes which one party to the relationship feels are desirable. If this is a regular experience it may contribute to a climate of opinion in which poor interagency and interprofessional communication is seen to be a problem — one which chief officers feel could be solved by more explicit codes of practice, more case conferences and more area committees and groups pooling their knowledge and experience of certain young people.

In this case, there is an important issue around the ultimate purpose of such interprofessional liaison — whether it results in more imaginative and sensitive responses to the needs of young people or whether the end result is simply a smoother transfer between the parts of the system, primarily concerned with labelling and controlling children.

A related concern is the extent to which young people can make their views known to such groups which may, after all, be deciding their future. The question of child and parent representation at case conferences is an important issue, with considerable variation in practice.

The second level of cooperation concerns the collaboration of agencies in determining local authority policy on major issues, such as the handling of juvenile delinquency or approaches to school-based problems. A specific issue in this case is whether concern over troublesome adolescents must inevitably be the raison d'être of such groups, or whether a desire to coordinate policy on adolescent provision in general, in which the management of problematic behaviour would be one element, might on occasion be the motivating factor.

Again, the assumption is that interagency cooperation on special committees and groups will further the development of coherent and workable policies. The question of the group's membership and the value system of agencies is again important, as conflicts of approach may develop and may not be capable of effective resolution. Whether the representation of interests from the community outside the welfare network is permitted may also have implications for the overall direction of the policy.

Thus, the fundamental question for all interagency collaboration is for what purpose and for whose benefit? While there continue to be differences of opinion about the best course of action to adopt when confronted with young people in trouble, interagency liaison should perhaps be regarded as the first step to resolving conflict and not as a universal panacea.

Individual and Professional Perspectives

A (i) PUPILS

A1

Truants talking,

BUIST, M,
Scottish Educational Review, vol 12, no 1,
1980, pp 40–51

Summarises previous findings of research on truancy and presents comments from young people attending an off-site unit on their feelings about school, work and teachers. Identifies two groups characterised as rule breakers and drifters.

A2

Schooling the Smash Street Kids,

CORRIGAN, P,
MacMillan Press Ltd, 1979, 158pp

Contains chapters reflecting pupil perceptions on why they play truant and 'muck about' in class. Provides interpretation of this behaviour and models of how and why control is exercised in the classroom.

A3

Hooligans or rebels? An oral history of working class childhood and youth 1889–1939,

HUMPHRIES, S,
Basil Blackwell Ltd, 1981, 279pp

Describes the experience of schooling by working class children in the early part of the century through individual recollections, and records incidents of truancy and disruption in the classroom from this period.

A4

The rules of disorder,

MARSH, P, ROSSER, E, and HARRÉ, R,
Routledge and Kegan Paul, 1978, 140pp

One chapter presents pupil explanations of why classroom disturbance occurs and classifies these according to the notion of offences against pupil expectations.

A5

Talking to truants,

SEABROOK, J, in *Truancy*, Turner, B (ed),
pp 70–8, Ward Lock Educational, 1974

Case studies of four truants illustrating the range of personal, family and school factors which produce this form of behaviour.

A6

The significance of classroom dissent,

SHARP, A,
Scottish Educational Review, vol 13, no 2,
1981, pp 141–151

Describes, through observation and comment from individual pupils, the nature of routine classroom deviance and the relationship this has to more extreme forms of disruptive behaviour.

A7

Black side of school,

SHOSTAK, J,
Times Educational Supplement, 25 June 1982,
p 23

Records pupil comments on their relationships with teachers, which is one of the reasons given for truancy.

A8

On your marks: interviews with truants in East London,

SULLIVAN, R, and RICHES, S,
Youth Social Work Bulletin, vol 3, no 5,
September–October 1976, pp 8–10

Explanations of truancy provided by children interviewed in shopping centres, parks and cafés, mainly focussing on school factors such as lack of interest in the curriculum and relationships with teachers.

A9

Learning to labour: how working class kids get working class jobs,

WILLIS, P E,
Saxon House, 1977, 204pp

Describes through group comment, observation and analysis how working class adolescent culture and styles are expressed in the school setting in the form of a counter school culture. Records the ways in which schools and teachers adapt to, accommodate and control this challenge.

A (ii) PROFESSIONAL ASSOCIATIONS

A10

The disruptive pupil,

Appendix E in *Proceedings of the Assistant Masters Association Council, 4–6 January 1978,*
pp 74–7,
AMA Council, 1978

Statement of the action that teachers need to take when faced with disruptive behaviour in class, which quotes from the AMA's *A guide for teachers.* Recommends a clearly defined procedure for dealing with serious cases of disruption.

A11

The maintenance of order in the school community,

Association of Assistant Mistresses,
AAM, 1975, 30pp

Discussion document recommending procedures designed to enable teachers maintain discipline in schools and outlining the sanctions and supportive services available.

A12

Discipline in schools,

National Association of Schoolmasters/Union of Women Teachers,
NAS/UWT, 1974, 17pp

Overview of the issue of discipline in schools, which sets out some definitions of its nature and scope and provides some guidelines for teachers on action they can take if they feel that pupil behaviour has reached intolerable limits.

A13

Retreat from authority,

National Association of Schoolmasters/Union of Women Teachers,
NAS/UWT, 1976, 5pp

A wide ranging review of factors in society which contribute to pupil indiscipline in school, including permissiveness, the influence of television and other mass media, pop culture, weakness of parents, leniency of courts, the poor quality of a minority of teachers, inappropriate curriculum and inadequate staffing.

A14

Discipline or disorder in schools: a disturbing choice,

National Association of Schoolmasters/Union of Women Teachers,
NAS/UWT, 1981, 5pp

Pamphlet suggesting that disruptive behaviour among school pupils is still a serious problem and any reduction of the sanctions which can be applied within the school must lead to a greater need for provision outside the school setting.

A15

Report on truancy and disruptive behaviour in schools,

National Association of the Teachers of Wales,
NATW, 1975, 13pp

Outlines the situation on truancy and disruptive behaviour in Wales and discusses causal factors. Recommends that a school-based community care service should be established in every secondary school, dealing with every aspect of the welfare of the child.

A16

Discipline in schools,

National Union of Teachers Working Party,
NUT, 1976, 23pp

A contribution to the debate about relationships between teachers and pupils. Suggests procedures designed to deal with disciplinary problems and describes the support services available to teachers.

A (iii) EDUCATIONALISTS

A17

Focus on the disruptive pupil,

BALCHIN, R,
Education Today, vol 29, no 2, Summer 1979,
pp 11–17

Considers classroom disruption from the
teacher's point of view, noting the inadequacy
of some parental child rearing patterns.
Highlights the lack of training for teachers in
education colleges about methods of
maintaining discipline and the limitations of
the sanctions available to teachers. Proposes
an Education Code spelling out the
responsibilities of parents, teachers and
children, which would be underwritten by law.

A18

Children in distress,

CLEGG, A, and MEGSON, B,
Penguin Education, 1973, 176pp

Discusses and gives examples of the kind of
distress experienced by children from difficult
family circumstances which can lead to
truancy and behaviour problems at school.
Describes how schools may help or hinder in
these situations and calls for the provision of
a well organised system of supportive
agencies.

A19

Disruptive Pupils,

EVANS, M,
School Council Programme 4: *Individual
pupils*, Schools Council, 1981, 54pp

Report of a seminar on the needs of
disruptive pupils which examined the nature
of the problem and the ways in which schools
could meet these needs from within their own
resources or in co-operation with others.

A20

**Discipline in primary and secondary
schools today,**

JENNINGS, A (ed),
Ward Lock Educational, 1979, 122pp

Collection of articles by teachers, local
authority inspectors, a college of education
principal and a parent reviewing the nature
and function of discipline in schools.
Contributors suggest that it should be seen as
a factor contributing to a positive experience
of education by the pupil rather than a
coercive force.

A21

Bunking off,

JONES, D,
Teaching London Kids, no 5, 1976, pp 3–8

Wide ranging discussion of the causes of
truancy by a former teacher, drawing on
personal experience and the comments of
truants known to him.

A22

Truancy: a long cool look,

MIDWINTER, E,
Youth in Society, no 11, May–June 1975,
pp 4–6

Review of the schools' attempts to enforce
attendance since education was made
compulsory and the legacy of anti-school
attitudes in society reflected in popular
culture. Suggests that radical changes are
needed in curriculum and attitudes if schools
are to meet the educational needs of present
day young adults.

A23

Discipline and dishonesty,

ROBERTS, J,
Education in the North, vol 12, 1975, pp 48–53

Personal view from a teacher about the
inherent contradictions and potential
dishonesty involved in schools imposing
discipline, overtly in the interests of pupils,
which actually meets the needs of the
institution and the teaching profession.

A24

**Cross'd with adversity: the education of
socially disadvantaged children in
secondary schools,**

Schools Council,
Evans/Methuen Educational, 1973, 157pp

Discussion of the ways in which schools can
meet the needs of socially disadvantaged
children. Presents case studies of children
from deprived backgrounds whose behaviour
constituted a considerable challenge to school
resources.

A25

Discipline – whose problem?

Teachers' Action Collective,
Teachers' Action, no 2 (197-), pp 9–18

Suggests that the problem of discipline in
schools should be examined from the point of
view of whose needs are being met. Self-
discipline is a requirement of life but much
external discipline is coercive.

A (iv) MISCELLANEOUS

A26

Order in school,

GRAY, C,
Where, no 132, October 1977, pp 268–271

Discusses the causes of disruption and ways in
which the frequency of violent incidents in
school can be reduced. Suggests better
training of teachers in disciplinary techniques,
earlier intervention with pupils, better
integration of the school into the life of the
community and the provision of sanctuaries in
schools.

A27

The truant's dilemma,

HARRIS, J,
Community Care, no 80, 8 October 1975
pp 18-19

Discussion of the causes of truancy by a
social worker who is also a school liaison
officer. Presents a case study of a hard-core
truant and suggests that sometimes schools
apply sanctions to enforce the return to
school of truants but demonstrate unaccepting
attitudes when they reappear.

A28

Children at risk in school,

HINTON, N (ed),
National Association for Care and
Resettlement of Offenders, 1975, 30pp

Collection of papers arising out of a one day
conference on crime prevention. Topics
covered include the relationship betweeen
schools and juvenile delinquency rates, police
preventive work with schools, and the liaison
between schools and other welfare agencies.

A29

The truancy problem,

MEDLICOTT, P,
New Society, vol 25, no 573, 27 September
1973, pp 768-770

Survey of the issues involved in non-school
attendance including possible causes and
remedies, with particular attention to the
situation in Manchester.

A30

Absence from school,

TERRY, F,
Youth in Society, no 11, May–June 1975,
pp 7–10

An overview of the issues concerning truancy,
including the role of the EWO, legal
sanctions, the relationship with delinquency,
off-site centres, and the nature of educational
experience in the secondary school.

Research on Disaffection from School

B (i) GENERAL

B1

Partnership in education and social services: some school problems,

DUNN, J (ed),
Joint Occasional Publication no 2, University of Lancaster, 1981, 45pp

Collection of readings on different types of school problems including a review of the literature on absence from school, a strategy for the treatment of school phobia, and a screening process to detect early signs of non school attendance.

B2

Size of school, socio-economic hardship, suspension rates and persistent unjustified absence from school,

GALLOWAY, D,
British Journal of Educational Psychology, vol 46, no 1, February 1976, pp 40–7

Analysis of data from 30 comprehensive schools in Sheffield on children missing 50% of possible attendances in the Autumn term. Found that truancy was only a small proportion of unjustifiable absence. There was no association between size of school and persistent absenteeism, but an association was found with socio-economic hardship in the school catchment area. None of these factors was associated with suspension rates, but the former status of the comprehensive as a selective school was associated with high rate of suspension.

B3

Absence from school and behaviour problems in school (Sheffield school and home project),

GALLOWAY, D, SEYD, R, and BALL, T,
Therapeutic Education, vol 6, no 2, 1978, pp 18–34

Overview of the Sheffield School and Home Project, which is analysing groups of poor attenders in Sheffield schools, interviewing parents, investigating the application of legal sanctions to non-attenders and their parents, and examining the use of exclusion by schools and their resort to special groups within the school setting to meet the needs of disruptive pupils.

B4

Truancy and behavioural problems in some urban schools,

HM Inspectorate of Schools,
Department of Education and Science, 1978, 61pp

Survey of 18 schools which noted the general incidence of behavioural problems and absenteeism and examined ways in which schools were dealing with these issues, through pastoral care provision, interagency liaison, school and legal sanctions, and off- and on-site units.

B5

Aspects of secondary education in England: a survey by HM Inspectors of Schools,

HM Inspectorate of Schools,
HMSO, 1979, 312pp

Report by HMIs covering a 10% sample of maintained secondary schools. Contains a section on pupils' behaviour and schools' assessment of the difficulties they were experiencing.

B (ii) ABSENTEEISM/SCHOOL NON-ATTENDANCE

Types and Associated Characteristics

B6

School refusal and truancy,

BARKER, P,
Practitioner, vol 213, no 1275, September 1974, pp 316–322

Discussion of the distinction between two forms of school non-attendance, school refusal and truancy. Suggests that school refusal is characterised by a neurotic or emotional disorder and the school refuser comes from an over-protective family background. Truancy is characterised as an anti-social or conduct disorder associated with families who show lack of affection and interest in the child.

B7

Absence from school,

BUTLER, B, and DUNN, J, in *Partnership in education and social services: some school problems*, Dunn, J (ed), pp 1–13,
Joint Occasional Publication no 2, University of Lancaster, 1981

Review of the literature on absence from school.

B8

Absenteeism in South Wales: studies of pupils, their homes and their secondary schools,

CARROLL, H C M (ed),
University College Swansea, Faculty of Education, 1977, 87pp

Collection of readings on absenteeism in Wales reviewing research findings, reporting a study of pupil attendance in three comprehensive schools, and examining the role of the school as a factor in the generation of truancy.

B9

Persistent school non-attendance,

CAVEN, N, and HARBISON, J J M, in *A society under stress: children and young people in Northern Ireland*, Harbison, J and J (eds), pp 43–54,
Open Books Publishing Ltd, 1980

Analysis of the categories of school non-attenders using data from schools in Northern Ireland and the framework provided by

Galloway's study in Sheffield. Finds a similar lack of association between absenteeism and size of school, and presents information on the socio-environmental characteristics of absentees.

B10

Truancy and school phobias,

DENNEY, A H,
Priory Press, 1974, 160pp

Some causes of truancy and school phobia and the way in which the educational system is attempting to solve these problems. Services available to help children and their families are also considered.

B11

The attitudes of persistent teenage absentees and regular attenders towards school and home,

EATON, M J, and HOUGHTON, D M,
Irish Journal of Psychology, vol 2, no 3, 1974, pp 159–175

Study of groups of persistent school absentees from schools in Northern Ireland compared with regular attenders regarding their attitudes to and expectations of school. Finds that older boys at grammar schools were most likely to stay away.

B12

A study of some factors associated with the early identification of persistent absenteeism,

EATON, M J,
Educational Review, vol 31, no 3, 1979, pp 233–242

Examination of persistent absenteeism and its association with anxiety and difficulties experienced in relating to other people. The findings suggest that absentees related well to their parents generally but relationships with teachers and peers were important factors in the early identification of persistent absenteeism.

B13

School attendance, attainment and behaviour,

FOGELMAN, K,
British Journal of Educational Psychology, vol 48, no 2, June 1978, pp 148–158

Examines the data from the National Child Development Study and finds a relationship between attendance and attainment which is reduced, but still remains statistically significant, after allowance for related social factors such as class. Finds little relationship between attainment at 16 and attendance rates in the primary school.

B14

Absence from school: findings from the National Child Development Study,

FOGELMAN, K, TIBBENHAM, A, and LAMBERT, L, in *Out of school*, Hersov, L, and Berg, I (eds), pp 25–48
Wiley and Sons, 1980

Report of findings from the National Child Development Study, which presents statistics on truancy based on pupil, parent and teacher estimates, and examines these in relation to individual, family and school variables.

B15

Persistent unjustified absence from school,

GALLOWAY, D,
Trends in Education, no 4, December 1976, pp 22–7

Analysis of absenteeism from schools in Sheffield, which indicated that truancy is a relatively minor cause of unjustifiable absence. Parentally condoned absence and socio-medical reasons constituted a larger proportion of reasons. Size of school seems to have no bearing on either absentee or exclusion rates.

B16

Persistent absence from school,

GALLOWAY, D,
Educational Research, vol 24, no 3, June 1982, pp 188–196

Report on the prevalence of persistent absence from schools in Sheffield LEA over three years. Finds that neither illness nor truancy are adequate explanations for the absences of many pupils, and although absence rates are strongly associated with poverty in the schools' catchment areas, there is evidence of the probable importance of variables within some of the schools.

B17

School attendance, school organisation and the role of the educational psychologist,

GREGORY, R P,
Unpublished paper, Birmingham Psychological Service, (ca 1979), 15pp

Survey of the connection between social disadvantage, poor attendance and school organisation in a Midlands school, on the assumption that there is a case for educational psychologists to be more involved in school attendance issues and not restricted to individual referrals. Found that disadvantaged pupils withdrawn from class attended less well than similar pupils at another school whose remedial classes were organised differently.

B18

Characteristics of a group of persistent non-attenders at school,

HARBISON, J J M, FEE, F, and CAVEN, N, in *A society under stress: children and young people in Northern Ireland*, Harbison, J and J (eds), pp 81–9
Open Books Publishing Ltd, 1980

Analysis of the personal and family characteristics of a group of persistent non-attenders using data from schools in Northern Ireland.

B19

Persistent non-attendance at school,

HERSOV, L A,
Journal of Child Psychology and Psychiatry, vol 1, 1960, pp 130–6

Analysis of the social characteristics and family background of children referred for school refusal or truancy, which confirmed to a large extent the hypothesis that school refusal is one manifestation of underlying psychoneurosis and truancy an indication of a conduct disorder.

B20

Out of school: modern perspectives in truancy and school refusal,

HERSOV, L, and BERG, I (eds),
Wiley, 1980, 377pp

Book of readings on non school attendance and school phobia, discussing possible causes in home and school circumstances, the link between truancy and delinquency, court proceedings and the long term outcome of truancy.

B21

Literacy survey: social background and absenteeism,

Inner London Education Authority Research and Statistics Branch, Document RS 679/77, ILEA, 1977, 21pp

Information from the ILEA literacy survey examining pupil absence rates in relation to socio-economic characteristics, behaviour and attitudes of pupils. Further examines the inter-relationship of these factors and pupil absence.

B22

Literacy survey: educational attainment and absenteeism,

Inner London Education Authority Research and Statistics Branch, Document RS 704/78, ILEA, 1978, 19pp

Information from the survey on literacy conducted in ILEA schools. Finds an association between attendance and attainment for both boys and girls of all social classes, nationalities and backgrounds, and for all pupils whatever their attitudes to teachers, school work and other pupils. It was not possible to show whether poor attendance precedes poor attainment or vice versa.

B23

Non-attendance at school: some research findings,

Inner London Education Authority Research and Statistics Branch, Document RS 760/80, ILEA, 1980, 15pp

Overview of some research findings on school non-attendance including definitions, types and levels of non-attendance, factors associated with absenteeism and its long term effects and implications.

B24

A comparative study of the perceptions of school pupils who are frequent absentees and regular attenders,

JACKSON, D F,
Unpublished M.Ed Dissertation, University of Sheffield, 1978, 108pp

The main conclusions are that absence seems to increase as day, week, term and year progress; girl absentees outnumber boys 2:1, although girls have a more positive attitude towards school; and differences in pupils' perceptions are more likely related to sex differences than to whether pupils are regular attenders or frequent absentees.

B25

Survey on unjustified absenteeism and juvenile delinquency,

Lincolnshire Education Committee, Lincolnshire County Council, 1975, 19pp

Survey of school attendance in Lincolnshire and questionnaire survey of school heads for opinions on whether there had been any significant increase in truancy and delinquency since ROSLA. Replies suggested no increase in unjustified absence in secondary grammar and comprehensives but some in secondary moderns, particularly after examinations. No feeling that juvenile crime had increased.

B26

Truancy, school absenteeism and delinquency,

MAY, D,
Scottish Educational Studies, vol 7, no 2, November 1975, pp 97–106

Comparison of two groups of school non-attenders in Aberdeen, those with poor attendance and those defined as truants. Compares them by social background, IQ, classroom behaviour and juvenile court appearances. Finds that although truants were more disadvantaged and had more court appearances than the others, only a minority of irregular attenders appeared in court and only a minority of delinquents were absentees or truants.

B27

The child who dislikes going to school,

MITCHELL, S, and SHEPHERD, M,
British Journal of Educational Psychology, vol 37, no 1, February 1967, pp 32–40

Analysis of the behaviour and attitude to school of 6,000 children attending primary and secondary schools in Buckinghamshire. Found that dislike of school was associated with poor attainment and signs of anxiety at home. Reaction to school affected attendance among children of secondary school age.

B28

The absentees,

MITCHELL, S,
Education in the North, vol 9, 1972, pp 22–8

Examination of the attitude to school, social characteristics and employment record of groups of absentees from schools in central Scotland.

B29

These we serve: the report of a working party set up to enquire into the causes of absence from school,

National Association of Chief Education Welfare Officers,
NACEWO, 1975, 43pp

Report of a working party enquiring into and attempting to classify and evaluate the main causes of irregular school attendance. Provides statistics from a week's attendance in schools in sample areas throughout the country in 1973 and suggests that 20–40% of all normal absences recorded were avoidable. Collates information on underlying causes from the Health Visitors' Association, the National Association of Schoolmasters, the National Association for Remedial Education, and youth and community workers. Concludes that there is a prime need for better motivation of the parent and the child and in some cases the teacher, the school and the Education Authority.

B30

The children we fail,

PHILLIPS, D,
The author, 1978, 66pp

Privately published study of the causes of school non-attendance amongst children living on a housing estate in Southwark, South London. Includes case studies of four non-attenders and reports of contacts with children and parents on the estate. Analyses the nature of the neighbourhood culture and its attitudes towards school and work, and the way in which children's attitude and behaviour reflect these. (See address list at the back of this Bibliography.)

B31

Persistent school absenteeism: some social, psychological and institutional factors related to persistent school absenteeism,

REID, K C,
Unpublished PhD Thesis, University of Wales, 1980, 700pp

An examination of the differences between some social, psychological and institutional factors related to 128 persistent school absentees and two control groups in two inner-city comprehensive schools in South Wales. Measures used include questionnaires, the Brookover Scale of Academic Self-Concepts, the Coopersmith Scale of General Self-esteem, the Rutter (Scale B) Children's Behaviour Questionnaire, the Cohen Scale of Alienation and selected Repertory Grids.

B32

Alienation and persistent school absenteeism,

REID, K C,
Research in Education, no 26, November 1981, pp 31–40

Analysis of the relationship between alienation and persistent school absenteeism drawing on a research study of a group of persistent absentees and two control groups at two schools in South Wales. Finds that persistent absentees score higher on feelings of alienation from school, on certain measures but not others – these may be related to the quality of school pastoral care organisation.

B33

The self-concept and persistent school absenteeism,

REID, K,
British Journal of Educational Psychology, vol 52, no 2, June 1982, pp 179–187

Studies of the self-concept of a group of persistent absentees and their controls in a comprehensive school in South Wales. Found that the absentees had significantly lower levels of general self-esteem, as measured by standardised tests, than their control group.

B34

Case studies and persistent school absenteeism,

REID, K C,
The Counsellor, vol 3, no 5, 1982, pp 23–30

Presentation of two case studies illustrating two different types of absentee, the truant and the disruptive absentee.

B35

Absent, sir,

REID, K C,
Social Work Today, vol 13, no 42, 13 July 1982, pp 12–13

Summary of the findings from a study of persistent absentees in South Wales. Puts forward 12 major reasons suggested by the absentees as reasons for missing school and classifies absentees into four groups: the traditional truant, the psychological absentee, the institutional absentee (mainly school factors) and the generic absentee (citing several of these reasons).

B36

School non-attendance and delinquency,

TENNENT, T G,
Educational Research, vol 13, no 3, June 1971, pp 185–90

Review of the literature on the relationship between school non-attendance and delinquency. Concludes that the studies suggest that there is a significant correlation but warns against regarding truancy as a single syndrome.

B37

Absent from school,

TYERMAN, M J,
Trends in Education, no 26, April 1972, pp 14–20

Review of the literature on truancy, absence rates and school phobia and discussion on the effect of the Children and Young Persons Act 1969.

Attendance Surveys

B38

Truancy: what the official figures don't show,

Anon,
Where, no 83, August 1973, pp 228–9

Article suggesting that the official figure of 90% attendance in schools which is often quoted may be misleading, since it does not reveal how many children are absent for one session or obtain an attendance mark and then disappear for the rest of the day.

B39

Observations on the report of irregular school attendance survey, March 1979,

BARNES, J A,
North Western Regional Society of Education Officers, 1979, 4pp

Survey of irregular school attendance during a week in March 1979. Makes comparisons with a similar survey in 1975 and finds that the general level of school non-attendance has increased together with truancy as a particular category.

B40

Surveys of absenteeism: a question of timing,

BAUM, T,
Educational Research, vol 20, no 3, June 1978, pp 226–230

Examines research findings on patterns of attendance during the day, week and year, and suggests that a reliable picture of school attendance can only be provided by research studies which take a long term view. A national one day survey such as the one undertaken by the DES must be regarded as methodologically flawed.

B41

Patterns of attendance and truancy: a study of attendance and truancy amongst first-year comprehensive school pupils,

BILLINGTON, B J,
Educational Review, vol 30, no 3, November 1978, pp 221–5

Survey of patterns of attendance of the first year intake at four comprehensive schools in Glamorgan. Found that attendance and truancy rates varied as a function of term and the day of the week.

B42

Survey of absence from secondary and middle schools in England and Wales on Thursday 17 January 1974,

Department of Education and Science,
DES, 1975, 25pp

Report of the findings from the DES national survey of absence from secondary and middle schools in England and Wales on Thursday, 17 January 1974. Examines patterns of absence by age, sex, type of school and region, and analyses unjustified absence by the same criteria.

B43

Years IV and V in comprehensive schools,

HM Inspectorate of Schools,
Welsh Office, 1981, 101pp

HMI report on Welsh schools, which outlines a range of issues, policies and practices relating to years IV and V as a contribution to discussion. Comments on the degree of absenteeism and disruption of classes which emerges from the survey, and notes that there is still a considerable amount of casual non-attendance during these school years, which makes it extremely difficult for teachers to maintain continuity.

B44

Attendance at school,

Inner London Education Authority Schools Sub-committee,
Document ILEA 528, ILEA, 1976, 22pp

Report of the findings from the 1976 ILEA attendance survey in primary and secondary schools, classified by age and sex. Includes an appendix report from a working party reviewing existing links between schools and the Education Welfare Service and suggesting improvement.

B45

Attendance survey, 1980,

Inner London Education Authority Research and Statistics Branch, Document RS 753/80, ILEA, 1980, 11pp

Report of the 1980 annual one day survey of attendance in primary and secondary schools in ILEA, including age and sex patterns of attendance.

B46

Attendance survey, 1981,

Inner London Education Authority Research and Statistics Branch, Document RS 791/81, ILEA, 1981, 10pp

Report of the 1981 annual one day survey of attendance in primary and secondary schools in ILEA, including age and sex patterns of attendance.

B47

Perspectives on attendance,

Inner London Education Authority Research and Statistics Branch, Document RS 749/80, ILEA, 1981, 86pp

Survey of attendance in three ILEA comprehensive schools and examination of the relationship between the absence rates of pupils and their personal, social and educational characteristics. Includes information on reasons for absence and action taken for school non-attendance drawn from interviews with 45 pupils.

B48

Attendance survey, 1977,

North Eastern Education and Library Board, NEELB, 1977, 12pp

Survey of attendance in the North Eastern Education and Library Board area of Northern Ireland. Includes comments from school heads on their individual methods of identifying absentees, responding to them and liaising with services such as Education Welfare.

B49

Absenteeism in three project schools: research report,

Sheffield Metropolitan District Council Education Department,
Sheffield Metropolitan District Council, (ca 1979), 19pp

Examination of the rate of absenteeism of the fourth and fifth years in three schools in Sheffield during the Autumn term 1978/79. Notes the pattern of attendance during the day and the week and sex differences in attendance rates.

B50

Patterns of absenteeism in primary and secondary schools,

WHITE, D J, and PEDDIE, M,
Scottish Educational Review, vol 10, no 2, November 1978, pp 37–44

Examination of the patterns of attendance of first year secondary pupils in a comprehensive school in Ayrshire during a school year up to the end of May. Confirmed through examination of primary school records that potential secondary school truants could be identified at that stage.

School Factors

B51

Social relations in a secondary school,

HARGREAVES, D H,
Routledge and Kegan Paul, 1967, 226pp

Analysis of the way in which a counter school culture was created among boys in the lower stream of a secondary modern school.

B52

Deviance in classrooms,

HARGREAVES, D H, et al,
Routledge and Kegan Paul, 1975, 282pp

Analysis of the rules which operate within classrooms and ways in which routine deviance is expressed by pupils and imputed by teachers. Describes the method of social typing used by teachers to define certain pupils as potential troublemakers and the strategies adopted by them to maintain control in the classroom.

B53

Ten good schools: a secondary school enquiry,

HM Inspectorate of Schools,
Matters for discussion series, HMSO, 1977, 36pp

Highlights the qualities of ten good schools of differing type, size and composition and suggests that the regimes are characterised by good preparation, variety of approach, regular and constructive correction of pupils' work and consistent encouragement.

B54

Literacy survey: attendance rates and school characteristics,

Inner London Education Authority Research and Statistics Division, Document RS 685/77, ILEA, 1977, 21pp

Examination of the relationship between school absence rates and school characteristics such as type, size, streaming and status, drawing on data collected in 1973 as part of the ILEA Literacy Survey.

 Key.

B55

Delinquent Schools?

POWER, M J, et al,
New Society, vol 10, no 264, 19 October 1967, pp 542–3

Research study presenting statistics on juveniles appearing before the courts in Tower Hamlets, which demonstrates that schools differed considerably in the delinquency rate of boys attending them, which did not reflect the overall rate of their neighbourhood catchment areas.

B56

School organisation and persistent school absenteeism: an introduction to a complex problem,

REID, K,
School Organisation, vol 2, no 1, 1982, pp 45–52

Literature review of persistent school absenteeism, which discusses research findings on the role of the school organisation and ethos in the generation of truancy and the effectiveness of various forms of intervention such as school counsellors, off-site units and school attendance monitoring.

B57

When teachers and pupils refuse a truce: the secondary school and the creation of delinquency,

REYNOLDS, D, in *Working class youth culture*, Mungham, G, and Pearson, G (eds), pp 124–137,
Routledge and Kegan Paul, 1975

Review of the findings from the South Wales study which presents figures demonstrating variations in the delinquency rate of pupils attending different schools. Explores the nature of the truce which some schools make with their pupils.

B58

Schools do make a difference,

REYNOLDS, D, JONES, D, and ST LEGER, S,
New Society, vol 37, no 721, 29 July 1976, pp 223–5

Presentation of research findings from a study of secondary modern schools in South Wales that suggests that pupils from similar backgrounds and neighbourhoods have very different experiences in schools, which are reflected in differing delinquency rates, academic achievements, attendance rates and future employment potential.

B59

The delinquent school,

REYNOLDS, D, in *The process of schooling: a sociological reader*, Hammersley, M, and Woods, P (eds), pp 217–229,
Routledge and Kegan Paul, 1976

Review of previous research on the effects of schools on pupils and a detailed examination of the differences in regime and ethos which marked certain schools in South Wales as being highly coercive and relatively unsuccessful in preventing truancy, delinquency and vandalism among their pupils.

B60

The sociology of schooling and the absent pupil: the school as a factor in the generation of truancy,

REYNOLDS, D, and MURGATROYD, S, in *Absenteeism in South Wales: studies of pupils, their homes and their secondary schools*, Carroll, H C M (ed), pp 51–68,
University College Swansea, Faculty of Education, 1977

Examination of previous explanations for truancy, which have largely drawn on psychological models. Advocates a sociological approach which analyses aspects of school management structures and general ethos, and presents findings from a study of nine secondary modern schools in South Wales.

B61

Toward a socio-psychological view of truancy,

REYNOLDS, D, in *Working together for children and their families*, Kahan, B (ed), pp 64–81,
Department of Health and Social Security/Welsh Office, HMSO, 1977

Examination of the basis for certain conventional beliefs about the nature and causes of absence from school and presentation of findings from research in South Wales, suggesting the existence of a truce between certain schools and working class pupils which reduces the amount of conflict and disruption experienced by them.

B62

Education and the prevention of juvenile delinquency,

REYNOLDS, D, and JONES, D, in *Alternative strategies for coping with crime*, Tutt, N (ed), pp 21–44,
Blackwell, 1978

Discussion of the role that has been assigned to education in the prevention of delinquency and the way that previous research findings have assumed individual and family explanations for truancy and delinquency. Reviews theories which link education systems with the generation of adverse experiences for pupils which may lead to delinquency, and suggests possible characteristics of schools which have the potential to do this.

B63

Bringing schools back in,

REYNOLDS, D, and SULLIVAN, M, in *Schools, pupils and deviance*, Barton, L A (ed), pp 43–58
Nafferton Books, 1979

Review of the current theories within the British sociology of education examining the role and purpose of schooling in society. Notes as a major goal the social control of working class pupils during their school years and describes the varying quasi-therapeutic and coercive strategies for achieving this which were revealed by their research study.

B64

School factors and truancy,

REYNOLDS, D, et al, in *Out of school*, Hersov, L, and Berg, I (eds), pp 85–110, Wiley and Sons, 1980

Presentation of the findings from research in South Wales which examines factors in the school regime and ethos associated with high and low attendance.

B65

The effects of school: a radical faith re-stated,

REYNOLDS, D, and SULLIVAN, M, in *Problem behaviour in the secondary school: a systems approach*, Gillham, B (ed), pp 37–59, Croom Helm, 1981

Review of the evidence from British and American research studies on the effects of school and a restatement of belief in the importance of schools as determinants of adolescent ability, behaviour and social development.

B66

Fifteen thousand hours: secondary schools and their effects on children,

RUTTER, M, et al, Open Books Publishing Ltd, 1979, 279pp

Research study comparing the progress of children in twelve secondary schools in inner London, which accumulated data on attendance, exam results, behaviour in school, delinquency rates and aspects of school management and ethos. Draws conclusions concerning the school factors which are associated with the most desirable outcomes for pupils.

B67

Fifteen thousand hours: discussion,

TIZARD, B, et al, University of London, Institute of Education, 1980, 48pp

Collection of papers discussing the findings of *Fifteen thousand hours* and noting aspects of the methodology which may have affected the results.

B68

Schools and deviance,

WOODS, P, *Contemporary issues in education* series, block 4, no 17, Open University Press, 1981, 48pp

Section of Open University Educational Studies course reviewing current research on the interaction between pupils and teachers and the extent to which schools are involved in the creation of deviance among pupils.

Truancy

B69

An examination of truancy and its implications for educational administration,

AVERY, J, Unpublished MA Dissertation, University of London, Institute of Education, 1978, 127pp

Traces the recent development of interest in truancy, the implications of ROSLA, the possible consequences of truancy, and the role of the Education Welfare Service, and concludes with an evaluation of the extent of truancy in an outer London borough. Attempts to show that the existing machinery to monitor and control truancy is unable to cope.

B70

Truants: some personality characteristics,

BILLINGTON, B J, *Durham and Newcastle Research Review*, vol 9, no 43, Autumn 1979, pp 1–6

Analysis of the personality characteristics, as measured by standardised tests, of groups of truants and non-truants in four comprehensive schools in South Wales. Found that truants were significantly less popular than non-truants but personality differences in terms of anxiety and insecurity, although present, were not statistically significant.

B71

Truancy, delinquency, the home, and the school,

FARRINGTON, D, in *Out of school*, Hersov, L, and Berg, I (eds), pp 49–63, Wiley and Sons, 1980

Research findings from the longitudinal Cambridge Study in Delinquent Development, which establishes from teachers' responses a truancy rating for the secondary school age sample, and presents data on the family background, personal characteristics and delinquency rating of truants.

B72

Becoming a truant: the social administrative process applied to pupils absent from school,

GREEN, F L, Unpublished MSc Thesis, Cranfield Institute of Technology, 1980, 118pp

Review of previous research on truancy and school phobia and presentation of case studies of individual children, demonstrating the way in which school attendance or non-attendance can be part of a total life experience of conflicting demands from home and school. Examines the way in which education welfare officers use their discretion in applying official procedures to truants and their families.

B73

Truancy in Glasgow,

Institute for the Study and Treatment of Delinquency, Glasgow Working Party, *British Journal of Criminology*, vol 14, no 3, July 1974, pp 248–255

Survey of attendance rates in Glasgow Corporation schools during two sample weeks. Examines the rates of suspected and definite truancy for primary and secondary schools, and discusses possible causes in home and school circumstances.

B74

London Units truancy survey,

LOWE, M, NORTON, P, and DOWLING, P, *FSU Quarterly*, no 12, Winter 1977, pp 17–21

Survey of the extent of truancy among children in families on the caseloads of Family Service Unit workers in London. Found 40% persistent non attendance, and in many cases no action was being taken by the authorities.

B75

Truancy: data from a self-report survey,

MAWBY, R I, *Durham and Newcastle Research Review*, vol 8, no 39, Autumn 1977, pp 21–33

Analysis of the incidence of self-reported truancy by pupils attending two secondary schools in Sheffield, classified by home estate, sex, school and social class. Finds differences in neighbourhood truancy rates and suggests that the amount of truancy revealed is greater

than official sources have registered. Both findings are seen as significant pointers to new kinds of neighbourhood work which might be undertaken by social workers.

B76

Progress in secondary schools: findings from the National Child Development Study,

STEEDMAN, J, National Children's Bureau, 1980, 265pp

Research data from the National Child Development Study on progress in secondary schools, which includes a section on behaviour related to school including truancy. Found that comprehensive pupils have a higher rate of truancy than other kinds of schools and that their teachers rated them as worse behaved or worse adjusted to school than others.

B77

Housing and truancy,

TIBBENHAM, A, *New Society*, vol 39, no 753, 10 March 1977, pp 501–2

Article using data from the National Child Development Study, which analyses the relationship between school attendance and housing conditions. Finds an association between truancy and overcrowding.

B78

Truancy,

TURNER, B (ed), Ward Lock Educational, 1974, 128pp

Book of readings on the issue of truancy, including a review of attendance surveys, interviews with truants and descriptions of initiatives in London and Liverpool.

B79

A research into truancy,

TYERMAN, M J, *British Journal of Educational Psychology*, vol 28, no 3, 1958, pp 217–225

Comparison of different groups of truants, differentiated by degree of persistence and extent of parental knowledge, with non truants analysed by sex, age, socio-environmental factors and personality traits. Highlights the importance of parental attitudes to school and presents an influential characterisation of truants as lonely, insecure and unhappy.

B80

Truancy,

TYERMAN, M, University of London Press, 1968, 128pp

Mainly concerned with the issue of children avoiding school without parental knowledge and the related problem of school phobia, based on a study in a Welsh town. Suggests that the causes of truancy lie in genetic influences, the neighbourhood, school, home influence and psychological maladjustment.

School Refusal

B81

School phobia: classification and treatment,

BAKER, H, and WILLS, U, *British Journal of Psychiatry*, vol 132, no 26, 1978, pp 492–9

Analysis of the individual and family characteristics of 99 cases of school phobia seen at a child guidance clinic over a period of twelve years.

B82

School refusal in early adolescence,

BERG, I, in *Out of school*, Hersov, L, and Berg, I (eds), pp 231–249,
Wiley, 1980

Discussion of the individual and family characteristics of a group of secondary school age children admitted to a psychiatric in-patient unit for school refusal. Reviews previous research findings on school phobia, including prevalence and responses to treatment.

B83

A detailed strategy for the rapid treatment of school phobics,

BLAGG, N, in *Partnership in education and social services: some school problems*, Dunn, J (ed), pp 27–35,
Joint Occasional Publications, no 2,
University of Lancaster, 1981

Suggested guidelines for treating cases of school refusal, including check lists of background information to be obtained, methods of negotiating with parents and schools, and strategies for reducing the child's anxiety and helping him resume attendance at school.

B84

School refusers: how do they fare?

BOREHAM, J,
ILEA Contact, vol 10, no 7, 19 June 1981, p 6

A follow-up study of 54 young people who had attended St Thomas' Day Hospital Tuition Group for persistent school refusers. 45 had successfully attended school or college or remained in one job for more than one year, 5 were still not capable of steady attendance at school or work.

B85

School phobia,

CHAZAN, M,
British Journal of Educational Psychology, vol 32, November 1962, pp 209–217

Analysis of the individual and family characteristics of 33 cases of school phobia referred to a child guidance centre between 1949 and 1959. Suggests that over-protective parental attitudes, serious mental or physical illness in one or both parents, and the demands of a new situation in school are important precipitating factors.

B86

School refusal: an enquiry into the part played by school and home,

COOPER, M G,
Educational Research, vol 8, no 3, June 1966, pp 223–9

Analysis of the individual and family characteristics of two groups of children, one characterised as possibly school phobic, the other defined as truants. Suggests that both groups presented a common basis of partial withdrawal from social interaction. Suggests that the role of school appears to be minimal.

B87

School phobia as a manifestation of family disturbance: its structure and treatment,

DAVIDSON, S,
Journal of Child Psychology and Psychiatry, vol 1, February 1961, pp 270–287

Discussion of the characteristics of 30 cases of school phobia and suggested methods of treatment.

B88

Out-patient treatment of severe school phobia,

FRAMROSE, R,
Journal of Adolescence, vol 1, no 4, December 1978, pp 353–361

Four case studies illustrating the principles of an out-patient management approach to severe school phobia. The main elements are helping the individual to overcome his anxieties, working with his family and liaising with other agencies.

B89

'The whining schoolboy ... creeping like snail unwillingly to school'.

HAMILTON, W B,
Nursing Mirror, 25 May 1978, pp 12–17

Discussion of the causes of school phobia and methods of treatment, including special units, individual psychotherapy, occupational therapy, drug therapy, and family casework.

B90

Refusal to go to school,

HERSOV, L A,
Journal of Child Psychology and Psychiatry, vol 1, June 1960, pp 137–145

Analysis of the clinical features, type, outcome and follow-up treatment of 50 cases of school refusal. Suggests that refusal to attend school is not a clinical entity but one aspect of behaviour in an affective disorder, often precipitated by a change of school, the death of a relative or a stay in hospital.

B91

Unwillingly to school: school phobia or school refusal – a psychosocial problem,

KAHN, J H, NURSTEN, J P, and CARROLL, H C M,
Pergamon, 1981, 229pp

Gives an overview of the issues concerning truancy and school phobia and looks at school facilities for dealing with school refusal, the support services available, and different methods of treatment.

B92

Dealing with school refusers,

ROCK, E,
Cambridge Journal of Education, vol 10, no 1, Lent Term 1980, pp 13–20

Advocates the early identification and treatment of school refusers and stresses the importance of co-operation between social, psychological and educational agencies. Includes examples of good practice based on case histories.

B (iii) DISRUPTIVE BEHAVIOUR IN SCHOOLS

Prevalence and Incidence of Disruption

B93

Survey of violence, indiscipline and vandalism in schools,

Department of Education and Science, DES, 1975, 23pp

Report of a DES survey of 100 LEAs in 1973, who were asked to send statistics of the number of incidents of violence and classroom disruption reported to them which were serious enough to cause concern. Numbers of children involved in incidents were very low and most authorities felt that there had been no significant increase in misbehaviour.

B94

All you need know about disruption,

DIERENFIELD, R,
Times Educational Supplement, 29 January 1982, p 72

Survey of 465 heads and teachers of schools in 41 LEAs throughout the country, who were questioned on their perception of the seriousness of behaviour problems experienced in class and the techniques they favoured for controlling such behaviour. It was generally felt that disruptive behaviour was a serious but not critical problem, and good teachers employing effective teaching methods with the support of the head and parents should be equal to dealing with it.

B95

Emotionally disturbed children in ordinary schools: concepts, prevalence and management,

JONES, N J,
British Journal of Guidance and Counselling, vol 3, no 2, July 1975, pp 146–159

Discussion of the nature of maladjustment and review of the findings from research studies on the prevalence of maladjustment in school age children. Describes school programmes of treatment and management which can provide support for teachers and enable children to remain in ordinary schools.

B96

Disruptive and violent pupils: the facts and the fallacies,

LASLETT, R,
Educational Review, vol 29, no 3, June 1977, pp 152–162

Review of findings from national and local studies of disruptive behaviour in schools, underlining the methodological shortcomings of the surveys and the difficulty of obtaining reliable definitions of such conduct.

B97

Violent and disruptive behaviour in schools,

LOWENSTEIN, L F,
National Association of Schoolmasters, 1975, 72pp

Survey of 825 primary, 141 middle and 846 secondary schools in England and Wales to ascertain the nature and incidence of violent and disruptive behaviour in schools. Records frequency of incidents by type and size of school and the age and sex of disruptive pupils. Includes comments by teachers on the problems experienced and suggested management techniques.

B98

Education and behaviour problems in Northern Ireland,

WILSON, J R, and IRVINE, S R,
Therapeutic Education, vol 7, no 2, 1979, pp 24–37

Review of research findings on the nature and incidence of behaviour problems in Northern Ireland schools and discussion of the effectiveness of the remedial measures currently available.

Field Studies

B99

Disaffected pupils,

BIRD, C, CHESSUM, R, FURLONG, J, and JOHNSON, D (ed),
Brunel University, Educational Studies Unit, 1980, 134pp

Research study conducted in six schools in two outer London boroughs investigating pupil motivation for disaffected behaviour such as truancy and disruption. Using material from pupil case studies, analyses the experiences at home, in the community and in employment which provide alternative sources of identity for young people and challenge their ascribed pupil status. Describes the different models of pastoral care adopted by schools and their differential use of alternative education units.

B100

Discipline in the classroom: an empirical study,

DAVIE, C A M,
Education in the North, vol 12, 1975, pp 54–9

Observation of teacher–pupil interaction in class, and classification of pupils as high, medium and low deviants according to the number of rebukes they received for misbehaviour. Examines the extent to which this categorisation reflects real differences between children, and the classroom management implications for teachers.

B101

Schools and disruptive pupils,

GALLOWAY, D, et al,
Longman, 1982, 176pp

Summary of findings from a DES sponsored research project on schools and disruptive pupils based in Sheffield. Analyses suspension and exclusion rates, the differences in rates between schools, and the individual and family characteristics of suspended pupils. Describes the provision of special groups within schools for disruptive pupils, their administration and curriculum, and teacher and pupil perceptions of their purpose and effectiveness. Discusses the experience of teacher stress and how this is affected by differing models of discipline and pastoral care, and recommends tackling problem behaviour through the school's policy, organisation and ethos.

B102

The impossible child,

LANE, D A,
Association for Behaviour Modification with Children, vol 3, no 1, 1979, pp 1–8

The 'impossible' child is described as more hostile than other pupils, coming from families with a history of psychiatric or educational disorders, and suffering from health·and related conditions.

B103

Disruptive behaviour in a secondary school,

LAWRENCE, J, STEED, D, and YOUNG, P,
Educational Studies Monograph no 1, University of London, Goldsmiths' College, 1977, 68pp

Analysis of 101 incidents of disruptive behaviour recorded in a multi-racial comprehensive senior high school. Includes comments from teachers and discussion of the nature and meaning of disruptive behaviour within schools.

B104

Dialogue on disruptive behaviour: a study of a secondary school,

LAWRENCE, J, et al,
PJD Press, 1981, 93pp

Report of a research project monitoring incidents of disruptive behaviour and teachers' reactions to them in a multi-racial, mixed, comprehensive secondary school in an outer London Borough. Records pupil behaviour which staff find particularly difficult and stressful, and notes their suggestions for improving school resources and organisation to counter this. Includes case studies of disruptive incidents from teacher and pupil points of view.

B105

Disruptive pupils in schools and units,

TATTUM, D,
John Wiley and Sons, 1982, 329pp

Sociological account of the nature and meaning of disruptive behaviour in schools through detailed examination of the context in which it takes place. Discusses authority relations and school rules and contains explanations of disruptive behaviour provided by a sample of 29 pupils attending a detached unit. Contains descriptions of a school-based unit and an off-site unit, and concludes that disruptive behaviour should not be condemned or condoned but used constructively to examine problematic aspects of school life.

B106

Educational attainment and behaviour at school,

VARLAAM, A,
Greater London Intelligence Quarterly, no 29, December 1974, pp 29–37

Analysis of the extent and nature of the association between behavioural difficulties at school and children's educational difficulties, using data collected in 1971 during the ILEA Literacy Survey. Found that abnormal behaviour, measured by standardised tests, was frequently accompanied by backwardness in verbal reasoning, reading, English and other subjects.

B107

The problem child in schools,

WALL, W D,
London Educational Review, vol 2, no 2, Summer 1973, pp 3–21

Review of research studies demonstrating the incidence of maladjustment, the qualitative differences by sex and social class, and the relationship between learning failure and emotional disturbance. Recommends additional training of teachers so that appropriate learning experiences can be provided for each child in the light of his or her special needs, within the school setting.

Readings

B108

Troublesome children in the class,

CASPARI, I,
Routledge and Kegan Paul, 1976, 144pp

Review of the nature of difficult behaviour in the classroom and discussion concerning the needs of children presenting behaviour problems to teachers. Considers the type of stress experienced by teachers and ways in which they can help the child.

B109

Control and discipline in schools: perspectives and approaches,

DOCKING, J W,
Harper and Row, 1980, 263pp

Review of research findings covering the definition of disruptive behaviour, psychological and sociological explanations of children's behaviour, teacher–pupil relations, the management of classroom behaviour, the curriculum, pastoral care and special provision, and the effectiveness of punishment in schools.

B110

Problem behaviour in the secondary school: a systems approach,

GILLHAM, B (ed),
Croom Helm, 1981, 195pp

Book of readings advocating a systems approach to reducing behaviour problems in schools. Includes papers on systems theory and methods of analysing a school system, the role of withdrawal units and strategies to enable teachers to defuse confrontation situations.

B111

The disruptive pupil in the secondary school,

JONES-DAVIES, C, and CAVE, R (eds),
Ward Lock Educational, 1976, 122pp

Book of readings on disruptive behaviour in school, covering case studies of behaviour, management techniques in schools, disruptive children in community homes, and the role of welfare services.

B112

Behaviour problems in the comprehensive school,

UPTON, G, and GOBELL, A (eds),
University College Cardiff, Faculty of Education, 1980, 177pp

Review of research findings on the nature of behaviour problems in schools, classroom life, teacher-pupil interaction, and different methods of dealing with difficult behaviour.

B113

Behaviour problems in schools,

WEDELL, K (ed),
University of Birmingham, Faculty of Education, *Educational Review*, vol 29, no 3, June 1977, 229pp

Collection of articles on behaviour problems in school, including a review of surveys of disruptive behaviour, research on pupils excluded from school, teacher stress, the typing of pupils by teachers, and methods of managing problem behaviour.

B114

Behaviour problems in school: a source book of readings,

WILLIAMS, P,
Hodder and Stoughton, 1974, 250pp

Psychologically oriented collection of readings describing behaviour problems in school as identified by teachers, methods of identifying and possible causes of maladjusted behaviour in children, and clinical methods of treatment.

Management Techniques

B115

Disruption in schools: the impact of organisational factors on coping strategies,

DAVIES, J A,
Unpublished MA Dissertation, University of London, Institute of Education, 1981, 216pp

Looks at the effects of disruptive behaviour on the organisation of the school, particularly the pastoral care system.

B116

Disruptive pupils and teacher stress,

DUNHAM, J,
Educational Research, vol 23, no 3, June 1981, pp 205–213

Analysis of the sources of teacher stress in the experience of teaching disruptive pupils. Describes staff responses to stress situations and their recommendations for reducing this through group support and good inter-professional communications.

B117

Exploring techniques for coping with disruptive behaviour in schools,

LAWRENCE, J,
Educational Studies Monograph no 2, University of London, Goldsmiths' College, 1982, 74pp

Presentation of findings from three linked studies of techniques for analysing and coping with disruptive behaviour in schools. Lists behaviour found difficult by teachers and the frequency of different kinds of action taken to deal with it. Provides a grid for measuring and analysing the difficulty of different classes and presents a programme for reducing classroom problems through positive behaviour modification techniques.

B118

Dealing with disturbing behaviour in the classroom,

PRESLAND, J,
Journal of the Association of Educational Psychologists, vol 3, no 3, 1973, pp 28–32

Description of a behaviour modification programme with the aim of reducing disruptive behaviour in class and eliminating the rewards for disturbing behaviour.

Policy, Provision and Practice

C (i) LEGISLATION AND COMMITTEE REPORTS

C1

Report of the Children and Young Persons Review Group,

BLACK, Sir H (Chairman),
HMSO, 1979, 62pp

Report of a committee set up to review the legislation and services relating to the care and treatment of children and young persons under the Children and Young Persons Act (Northern Ireland) 1968 and to make recommendations as to changes in the legislation and organisation of these services. Includes recommendations on the legal sanctions to be available in the case of school non-attenders.

C2

Children and Young Persons Act 1969,

Cmnd 6494, HMSO, 1969, 126pp

Legislation currently in force in England and Wales under which non-attendance at school can be one of the grounds for making a supervision or care order on a child if other care and control conditions are met.

C3

Education Act 1981,

HMSO, 1981, 50pp

Legislation implementing some of the recommendations of the Warnock Report, specifically in relation to the responsibility of local education authorities for the identification and assessment of children with special needs and the introduction of new categories for describing special needs.

C4

Report of the Committee on Children and Young Persons (Scotland),

KILBRANDON, C J D, Lord (Chairman),
Cmnd 2306, HMSO, 1964, 123pp

Report of the committee recommending changes in legislation regarding juveniles, which paved the way for the implementation of the Children's Hearings system in Scotland. Includes section suggesting that unreasonable failure to attend school would be one of the grounds on which a child could be brought before the children's panel.

C5

Truancy and indiscipline in schools in Scotland,

PACK, D C (Chairman),
Scottish Education Department, HMSO, 1977, 138pp

Report of a committee enquiring into truancy and indiscipline among primary and secondary school pupils in Scotland. Conducted its own survey of truancy in schools and considered the role of guidance staff, social workers and the Child Guidance Service. Recommends the creation of special day units as an intermediate stage between ordinary schools and List D schools.

C6

The role and training of education welfare officers,

RALPHS, L (Chairman),
Local Government Training Board, HMSO, 1974, 17pp

Report on the role and function of the Education Welfare Service, which concludes that it needs strengthening if it is to continue to provide support for the education system, and that further training is required for education welfare officers to enable them to continue to provide social work services.

C7

West Indian children in our schools: interim report of the Committee of Inquiry into the Education of Children from Ethnic Minority Groups,

RAMPTON, A (Chairman),
Cmnd 8273, Department of Education and Science, HMSO, 1980, 120pp

Discusses the representations which have been made from certain quarters that West Indian children are over represented in ESN schools and a disproportionate number are excluded and suspended from school. Collected some statistics from one LEA but was unable to draw any firm conclusions.

C8

Report of the Committee on Local Authority and Allied Personal Social Services,

SEEBOHM, F (Chairman),
HMSO, 1968, 370pp

This report on the personal social services generally, which led to the creation of social services departments, examines the role of the teacher in the social care of the child and assesses the adequacy of existing school welfare services. Concludes that social work in schools should be the responsibility of the social services department and that education welfare officers should be allowed to transfer to social services departments.

C9

Social Work (Scotland) Act 1968,

HMSO, 1968, 90pp

Contains the legislation currently in force in Scotland under which children can be referred to the Children's Hearings on the grounds of non-attendance at school.

C10

Psychologists in education services,

SUMMERFIELD, A (Chairman),
Department of Education and Science, HMSO, 1968, 186pp

Review of the present numbers, remit, training and future development of educational psychologists in the School Psychological Service.

C11

The law of education (8th Edition),

TAYLOR, G, and SAUNDERS, J B,
Butterworth, 1976, 570pp

Standard work on education law, including notes on the interpretation of various sections of the 1944 Education Act. Contains the legislation under which parents can be prosecuted for the non-attendance at school of their children.

C12

A new partnership for our schools,

TAYLOR, T (Chairman),
Welsh Office/Department of Education and Science, HMSO, 1977, 228pp

A report reviewing the role and functions of school governors. Recommends a tightening up of the definitions of suspension and exclusion from school and greater standardisation of procedures between local education authorities. Suggests that LEAs and not school governors should make the final decision regarding the suspension of a pupil.

C13

Special educational needs: report of the Committee of Enquiry into the Education of Handicapped Children and Young People,

WARNOCK, H M (Chairman),
Department of Education and Science/Welsh Office/Scottish Office, HMSO, 1978, 416pp

Report reviewing educational provision for children and young people with physical and mental handicaps, which recommends the abolition of statutory categories for handicapped pupils and the provision of special education in relation to a child's individual needs as distinct from his disability. Suggests that wherever possible such children should be educated in ordinary schools with special units and classes attached rather than in special schools.

C (ii) LEA SERVICES AND INITIATIVES

Official Reviews of Policy and Provision

C14

Vandalism and indiscipline in schools: report of a working party,

Association of Northern Ireland Education and Library Boards,
ANIELB, 1976, 15pp

Report of a working party surveying the nature and incidence of vandalism and indiscipline in Northern Ireland. Recommendations include the introduction of social education as a specific subject in the curriculum, greater parental involvement in the school, preventive measures to inhibit vandalism, more in-service training for teachers, improved support services, and the establishment of off-site withdrawal units for disruptive pupils.

C15

Disruptive and violent behaviour in schools,

Cleveland Education Authority,
Cleveland Education Authority, 1978, 11pp

Report analysing the type of pupils presenting behaviour problems in Cleveland schools and reviewing the remedial measures and sanctions available to them. Discusses the advantages of off-site units and provides a check list of procedures for head teachers and other staff in dealing with disruptive behaviour.

C16

No small change: the report of the working party on problem children in schools,

Cumbria Education Department,
Cumbria Education Department, 1976, 65pp

Report from a working party on disruptive children in school, whose terms of reference were to define the problem, assess its prevalence and recommend helpful action. Presents statistics on the juvenile crime rate, numbers of children in care, social deprivation indicators and the numbers of 'problem' children in schools. Stresses the need for programmes of educational support for such children at an early stage and the need for schools to examine their curriculum and pastoral care systems. Includes appendices on the work of a special teacher within schools and a counsellor.

C17

Home school links: report of the working party on educational welfare,

Department of Education for Northern Ireland,
HMSO, 1976, 27pp

Report reviewing ways in which schools can promote the general welfare of their pupils and the community as a whole. Includes proposals for improving and extending existing links with parents, making school resources available to the community, developing counselling services in secondary schools, and providing more concentrated help in areas of social disadvantage.

C18

Disruptive and violent behaviour in schools,

Devon County Council Education Department,
Devon County Council, 1975, 63pp

Report on disruptive and violent behaviour in schools, which seeks to establish the limits beyond which schools should not be expected to tolerate extreme misbehaviour. Includes case studies of individual disruptive incidents and comments on how they were handled, and reviews the various sanctions available to schools. Provides an overview of external agencies and the circumstances in which pupils may be referred to them.

C19

Disruptive pupils and their problems: report of the working party,

Dorset Social Services Department,
Dorset County Council, 1976, 65pp

Report of a working party with the brief to investigate the issue of difficult children in schools and the problems associated with them. Discusses the possible causes of disruptive behaviour in the home and school, and reviews preventive measures which can be adopted by schools. Reviews the provision of remedial education, counselling services, home and school liaison, the role of the Education Welfare Service and County Psychological Service, and describes special initiatives taken by schools and off-site centres established by the LEA. Describes the role of external agencies and recommends clarification in liaison and procedures. Includes an appendix setting out a code of practice for liaison between schools and area social services centres.

C20

Pastoral care arrangements in secondary schools: report of the working party,

Hampshire Education Authority,
Hampshire Education Authority, 1975, 104pp

Review of existing pastoral care arrangements in Hampshire schools and recommendations for future inter-professional co-operation. Discusses the existing responsibilities of external agencies such as Education Welfare, School Psychological Service, Social Services, Health Service and the Police, and suggests ways in which liaison could be improved.

C21

Help for difficult pupils: report of a working party of the Hampshire Education Authority,

Hampshire Education Authority,
Hampshire Education Authority, 1979, 41pp

Report of working party established to make recommendations on ways in which schools could provide more effective help for difficult pupils within the school setting. Includes wide ranging discussion of the possible causes of behavioural problems in individual, home, neighbourhood and school circumstances, and concentrates on measures that schools and teachers can adopt to prevent problems arising, defuse them when they occur, and attempt to meet the underlying needs of the child. Discusses co-operation between the Education Service, Social Services and Child Guidance. Recommends clearly defined and agreed policies on disruptive behaviour in schools, regular reviews of organisational patterns and greater involvement of pupils in the life of the school. Includes appendix of information from schools on practices and sanctions which have been found helpful.

C22

Disruptive pupils: report of the Schools Sub-Committee to the Education Committee,

Inner London Education Authority,
ILEA, 1978, 5pp

Report of the Schools Sub-committee of ILEA on provision for disruptive pupils, which analyses the nature of the problem, reviews present methods of dealing with it, and proposes financial support for additional teaching posts to enable schools to make their own arrangements either on or off site. Foresees the likely need for additional school support centres which, it is suggested, may lead to a decrease in the number of pupils suspended from school.

C23

Report of the working party set up to consider the needs of disturbed and disturbing pupils on the Isle of Wight,

Isle of Wight Education Committee,
Isle of Wight Education Committee, 1979, 42pp

Working party report examining the current levels of provision for children exhibiting school phobia, emotional withdrawal, under achievement or disruptive behaviour symptomatic of underlying maladjustment. Examines pastoral care and remedial provision in different types of school, alternative units and the role of external services. Includes information on the nature and extent of the perceived problems from a survey of head teachers, and recommends a range of school-based and interagency initiatives as counter measures. Proposes the establishment of a 'no return' off-site unit for truanting and disruptive pupils.

C24

The suspended child,

Liverpool Education Committee, Teachers Advisory Committee,
Liverpool Education Committee, 1974, 56pp

Report from a teachers' advisory committee reviewing the issues surrounding disciplinary problems in schools, the suspension and exclusion of pupils and alternative provision. Analyses the roots of the problem, which are seen to lie mainly in the family background, and describes existing arrangements within schools and LEAs. Suggests that the sanctions provided by legal action are inadequate and reports experience from other authorities which have established special units on and off site.

C25

Interim report of the Standing Committee for Disruptive Pupils,

Schools and Legal Working Parties,
Liverpool Education Committee, 1979, 68pp

Interim report of a standing committee considering problems arising out of and associated with disruptive behaviour in schools. Two working parties were established to consider the law relating to juveniles and methods of dealing with disruptive pupils in the education system. Legal controls and sanctions were felt to be generally inadequate and the schools working party recommended that the LEA encourage the development of on- and off-site units for disruptive pupils. Contains comments from other LEAs on their experience of on- and off-site provision, and reports from head teachers on the type of problems experienced and school policy in dealing with them.

C26

Report on disruptive pupils,

North Yorkshire Teachers' Associations Consultative Panel,
NYTACP, 1977, 11pp

Report of a teachers' association survey of schools in North Yorkshire designed to obtain information on general standards of behaviour, truancy, the incidence of disruptive behaviour, suspensions and the effectiveness of the supportive services. Found that disruption was generally regarded as a minor problem with very few pupils meriting suspension. Sets out some general guidelines for averting the problem and suggested procedures for liaising with parents and outside agencies.

C27

Report of the Disruptive Pupils Study Group,

Disruptive Pupils Study Group,
Northants Education Department, 1979, 9pp

Short working party report discussing general issues concerning disruptive pupils and reviewing the special provision which might be made for them. Recommends that each school should have a statement of policy concerning disruptive pupils which would note the feasibility of meeting their needs within school and indicate the point at which suspension became necessary.

C28

Disruptive pupils in schools,

Staffordshire Education Committee,
Staffordshire Education Committee, 1977,
120pp

Working party report which examines the
problems presented by and procedures for
dealing with disruptive pupils in schools.
Contains information from a survey of head
teachers detailing the extent of the problem
and their experience of liaison with outside
agencies. Contains substantial contributions
from external agencies such as Social Services,
Probation and Education Welfare on the role
of their services in relation to the school.
Adopts a broadly preventive policy focussing
on early identification of potential difficulties
and good practice within schools.

C29

Report on school attendance

Strathclyde Regional Council Department of
Education,
Strathclyde Regional Council, 1977, 55pp

Working party report examining procedures
for recording and reporting attendance at
school and pursuing non-attendance,
procedures for suspension and exclusion, and
the liaison between schools, parents and
external agencies. Recommends greater
consultation and co-operation between
agencies, and includes statistics on school
attendance in Strathclyde and examples of
systems for monitoring and identifying non-
attendance.

C30

Report of a working party of the Education Service: disruptive pupils in secondary schools,

Suffolk Secondary Education Sub-Committee,
Suffolk County Council, 1976, 15pp

Report of a working party considering what
action should be taken on the treatment of
disruptive pupils in Suffolk secondary schools.
Presents information from a survey of head
teachers on the nature and incidence of
disruptive behaviour and reviews pastoral care
provision, suspension procedures, liaison with
the Social Services Department and external
specialist provision. Suggests the
establishment of on-site units for disruptive
pupils.

C31

Research into non-attendance at school: final report – stage III,

West Glamorgan County Council Education
Committee,
West Glamorgan County Council, 1980, 74pp

Final report of a survey of non-attendance at
schools in West Glamorgan, which discusses
various issues arising out of it. Considers the
role of the education welfare officer in detail
and highlights various problematic areas
concerning liaison with schools and other
agencies and potential role conflict. Examines
liaison with Social Services in a similar way
and reviews the operation of the courts in
respect of prosecutions for school non-
attendance and includes statistics on the
outcomes over a 12 month period. Makes
detailed recommendations on the future
development of the Education Welfare
Service, and draws up procedural guidelines
for consultation between the Education and
Social Services Departments.

C32

Local education authority responses to disruptive behaviour: a research note,

YOUNG, P, LAWRENCE, J, and STEED, D,
Policy and Politics, vol 7, no 4, 1979,
pp 387–393

Review of LEA responses to disruptive
behaviour in schools as revealed in working
party reports and other documents. Suggests
that differences in policy may have their origin
in the way that disruption is defined and
whether it is seen as undesirable behaviour to
be prevented or regarded as stemming from
the characteristics of a group of pupils who
need special provision.

C33

Local education authorities and autonomous off-site units for disruptive pupils in secondary schools,

YOUNG, P, STEED, D, and LAWRENCE, J,
Cambridge Journal of Education, vol 10, no 2,
Easter Term 1980, pp 55–70

Review of LEA policy regarding the
establishment of off-site units as recorded in
working party reports and other papers.
Examines the basis on which the decision is
made, the nature of the proposed unit, the
type of child for which it is intended and the
perceived advantages and disadvantages of
off-site provision.

General Provision

C34

Child care services and the teacher,

FITZHERBERT, K,
Temple Smith, 1977, 226pp

Provides an extensive guide for teachers on
the services available to them in dealing
with children 'at risk', from the assumption
that schools and teachers have primary
responsibility for the child's welfare and for
preventive work. Describes Education
Welfare, health and psychiatric services, social
work services and Child Guidance. Discusses
the overlap and how professional conflicts
may hinder useful work. Suggests how
teachers can make best use of these services
and promote co-operation.

C35

Educational systems for disruptive adolescents,

TOPPING, K J,
Research paper no 13, Calderdale
Psychological Service, 1982, 160pp

Comprehensive literature review drawing on
British and American sources, of educational
provision for disruptive adolescents. Includes
discussion of day and residential special
schools, off-site centres, on-site units/classes,
on-site support teachers and
paraprofessionals, and external personnel
resources.

Provision for Children with Special Needs

C36

The remedial service,

ADAMS, C,
ILEA Contact, vol 7, no 27, 2 March 1979,
pp 8–10

Short article on the remedial service run by
the Schools Psychological Service in Tower
Hamlets, which provides special help to pupils
with a variety of learning difficulties.

C37

Teaching the maladjusted,

Anon,
Education, vol 155, no 6, 8 February 1980,
pp i–iv

Review of the origins of provision for children
with special needs and survey of current levels
of provision in maintained special schools and
day classes. Notes the current debate on
integrated provision and issues of staff
training, and describes the work of support
services such as Child Guidance and the
School Psychology Service.

C38

Special provision for disturbed pupils: a survey,

DAWSON, R L,
Macmillan Educational, 1980, 110pp

Findings from a survey of special schools,
special units and classes for disturbed pupils,
which describes pupil characteristics,
treatment programmes, educational
programmes, and outcomes and evidence of
success. Suggests that the type of programme
adopted may be influenced by the relative
numbers of pupils with conduct or neurotic
disorders.

C39

Educating slow-learning and maladjusted children: integration or segregation?

GALLOWAY, D M, and GOODWIN, C,
Longman, 1979, 163pp

Review of the development of special
education for educationally subnormal and
maladjusted children. Discusses the issues
concerning whether education for such
children should be integrated with, or
segregated from, ordinary schools and
describes innovations in school and classroom
practice.

C40

Children with special difficulties: an ILEA action research project,

Inner London Education Authority,
Educational Research, vol 19, no 1, November
1976, pp 3–12

Report of an initiative by ILEA in which
additional money was allocated to four areas
in London for schools to use to meet the
needs of pupils identified as having special
difficulties. 600 projects were approved
including on- and off-site units, fostering links
between home and school, language
programmes, pastoral care arrangements,
support for teachers, diagnostic and screening
techniques, and improvements in the school
environment. Findings from an evaluation of
some of the projects are included.

C41

Special adjustment units in comprehensive schools. I: Needs and resources,

JONES, N J,
Therapeutic Education, vol 1, no 2, 1973,
pp 23–7

Article providing definitions of maladjustment
and descriptions of possible symptoms which
might aid recognition by teachers. Reviews the
evidence from national surveys of the
incidence of maladjustment in school age
children.

C42

Special adjustment units in comprehensive schools. II: Structure and function,

JONES, N J,
Therapeutic Education, vol 1, no 2, 1973, pp 27–31

Outlines the structure and function of a school-based programme for emotionally disturbed children and describes the work of the Brislington Unit at Bristol, an on-site unit.

C43

Special adjustment units in comprehensive schools. III: Selection of children,

JONES, N J,
Therapeutic Education, vol 2, no 2, 1974, pp 21–6

Describes the methods used to identify and select children for treatment within a special on-site unit at Brislington School, Bristol. Suggests that careful screening and observation at an early age might prevent minor disorders becoming major problems, and discusses the difficulty of providing for a range of children whose overt behaviour might be similar, but whose underlying needs are very different.

C44

Special adjustment units in comprehensive schools. IV: The therapeutic process,

JONES, N J,
Therapeutic Education, vol 3, no 1, 1975, pp 43–9

Describes the treatment methods employed in the Brislington Special Unit and notes that since children's problems vary in severity and complexity, a flexible system of management and treatment is required.

C45

Maladjusted pupils in ordinary schools,

KOLVIN, I, et al,
Special Education Forward Trends, vol 3, no 3, September 1976, pp 15–19

Report on the Newcastle school-based action research project, which aimed to examine ways of preventing and treating symptoms of maladjustment among children in ordinary schools. Specialist professionals such as social workers, psychologists and psychiatrists were redeployed to work in schools, undertaking activities such as parent counselling, teacher consultation, group counselling, nurture work, behaviour modification and training.

C46

Dealing with behaviour problems in school: a new development,

LANE, D A, and MILLAR, R R,
Community Health, vol 8, no 3, January 1977, pp 155–9

Article describing the work of the Hungerford Educational Guidance Centre, which is run on behavioural lines within the framework of contract therapy and provides a means whereby the school and the centre can together provide therapy for the child. Gives examples of behaviour problems which were worked out within school with the aid of the centre.

C47

Day schools for maladjusted children,

LANSDOWN, R,
Association of Workers for Maladjusted Children, 1970, 46pp

Report by a group of head teachers describing their work in day schools for children with special needs. Discusses the operation of the school as a therapeutic community.

C48

The educational guidance centre,

MONGON, D,
ILEA Contact, vol 7, no 28, 9 March 1979, pp 7–9

Description of the work of the education guidance centre run by the School Psychological Service in Hackney. The centre works with pupils who have shown behaviour problems at school and uses behaviourist or psychotherapeutic approaches which are varied to meet the needs of each child.

C49

Day units for children with emotional and behavioural difficulties,

RODWAY, A (ed),
Monograph 1, Association of Workers for Maladjusted Children and Therapeutic Education, 1981, 56pp

Selection of articles describing adjustment groups, tutorial classes and units and a day adjustment centre, located both on and off site for children with special needs.

C50

The tutorial class,

WILLIAMS, A, et al,
ILEA Contact, vol 7, no 30, 23 March 1979, pp 23–5

Description of the tutorial class which provides part-time special educational treatment for the child who is unable to meet the social demands of an ordinary school. Although remedial education is provided, the primary emphasis is on helping children with behavioural problems to learn and develop at their own pace in a small group.

C51

Education of disturbed pupils,

WILSON, M, and EVANS, M,
Schools Council Working Paper no 65, Methuen Educational, 1980, 287pp

Findings from a three year enquiry, sponsored by the Schools Council, into the theory and practice of educational work with disturbed children. Presents examples of good practice from special schools and special units and classes in ordinary schools, and discusses the characteristics of each form of provision which can be matched to the needs of an individual child.

School Support Workers and Teams

C52

To be called stupid,

AUSTIN, S,
Schools Curriculum Project/Northern Ireland Polytechnic, 1975, 260pp

Description of an initiative by the Schools Project in Community Relations in Northern Ireland, which placed a groupworker in four Belfast schools to work with children in the non-academic streams who had apparently gained little from their school careers. The groupworkers developed close relationships with the children and set up special programmes for them involving outside trips, residential sessions, community service and external speakers. One of the workers' main objectives was to sensitise fellow teachers to the needs and potential of lower stream pupils, and their placement within the school setting enabled them to influence teacher attitudes, demonstrate the potential of pupils, challenge the relevance of the school curriculum to their needs, and provide information on individual and family circumstances as an explanation for difficult behaviour at school.

C53

A team approach to disruption,

Barnsley Special Education Team,
Special Education Forward Trends, vol 8, no 1, March 1981, pp 8–10

Description of the work of the Barnsley Special Education Team, consisting of six teachers, who provide a peripatetic support service to teachers who require help with an individual child or groups of children. The circumstances surrounding the referral are fully investigated and appropriate strategies devised, which may take the form of individual work with a child withdrawn part or full time from class, work with a small group withdrawn from class, or work with the class as a whole.

C54

An alternative procedure,

COULBY, D,
ILEA Contact, vol 9, no 32, 6 March 1981, p 5

Report on the work of a peripatetic interprofessional team in an ILEA Division, which provides a support service for schools. The team consists of 12 teachers, an educational psychologist and senior education welfare officer, who provide a variety of interventions with school management staff, individual teachers, parents and children. Includes some individual case studies.

C55

Birmingham home–school liaison officers,

LLEWELYN-DAVIES, et al, in *Educational action projects*, vol 1, pp 1–22, Department of the Environment, 1977

Evaluation of a scheme in Birmingham which appointed two home–school liaison officers, with the objective of providing closer contact between schools and families and developing community service and educational projects on a local basis. The officers were regarded as full members of the school staff with their own teaching responsibilities. The evaluation describes how the original objectives were modified in the light of the head teachers' and individual officers' perception of their role and function.

C56

The answer to disruptives?

STERNE, M,
Education, vol 158, no 9, 28 August 1981, p 180

Description of the Manchester Disruption in Schools Scheme, which assigns teachers to work in schools as full members of staff, to identify ways of dealing with disruptive pupils and assisting the school in providing a more appropriate learning environment for children. Work so far has included a special curriculum for fifth-formers, the design of a programme of tutorial work, analysis of classroom processes, and operating groupwork methods in a withdrawal unit.

Off-site Units

Policy issues

C57

Disruptive units,

Advisory Centre for Education/National Association for Multiracial Education, ACE/NAME factsheet, *Where*, no 170, July 1981, pp 19–24

Summarises the case against off-site units on the following grounds: they may be used as a first resort when reform of the school structure and curriculum might be more appropriate; reasons for referral are inconsistent and unclear; concern about possible racial discrimination; no choice for parents and students; labelling effects on children; limited curriculum; and use of problematic techniques such as behaviour modification.

C58

Separate development,

ALHADEFF, G, et al,
Times Educational Supplement, 9 July 1982, p 17

Discussion of the rationale for the development of special units, which underlines their contribution to good practice but argues against regarding them as anything other than experimental.

C59

The establishment of school support units for disruptive pupils: a study of social control in urban education,

BASINI, A J C,
Unpublished MA Thesis, University of London, King's College, 1980, 242pp

Investigates the establishment of off-site units in one division of ILEA, demonstrates the divergence of attitudes towards units on the part of teachers, headmasters and heads of units: units are variously seen as instruments of social control exercising covert racism, providing compensatory education, or providing inadequate education in comparison to the mainstream. Concludes that the units were not needed and should never have been established, and that disruptive pupils should be catered for within ordinary schools.

C60

Urban schools and 'disruptive pupils': a study of some ILEA support units,

BASINI, A,
Educational Review, vol 33, no 3, 1981, pp 191–206

Article based on a thesis outlining the findings from an empirical study which investigated the establishment of off-site school support units for disruptive pupils in one division of ILEA. Presents material from interviews, with mainstream teachers and unit teachers demonstrating differences in perspective regarding the nature and purpose of the units.

C61

ESN revisited,

BUTLER, C,
Issues in Race and Education, no 22, September–October 1979, pp 1–2

Discussion of the controversy surrounding the placement of Black children in off-site units. Discounts the suggestion that this is an expression of overt racism, but suggests that the structural disadvantage and discrimination experienced by Blacks makes it more likely that they will express their alienation in ways defined by the school as disruptive, and thus be regarded as eligible for alternative education away from the mainstream.

C62

Units for disruptives: a behavioural approach to management,

CROWTHER, G,
ILEA Contact, vol 7, no 24, 26 January 1979, pp 10–11

Discusses the use of a behavioural approach in off-site units for disruptive children.

C63

Disruptive pupils: labelling a new generation,

FRANCIS, M,
Name, vol 8, no 1, Autumn 1979, pp 6–9

Sustained criticism of the practice of off-site provision for disruptive pupils, which questions current definitions of disruptive behaviour, outlines the development of off-site units and discusses contentious issues of programming, philosophy and functions.

C64

Special units: some educational issues,

GOLBY, M,
Socialism and Education, vol 6, no 2, Summer 1979, pp 6–9

Discusses the relationship between special units and mainstream education and sees a role for units in influencing practice in mainstream schools and contributing to the educational attainment of pupils who might be disadvantaged elsewhere. Argues, however, that a common curriculum meeting the needs of all pupils within the comprehensive school must be the major objective and any departures from this can only be justified on individual grounds. There is also the potential danger of idiosyncratic curricula springing up around specialised and possibly outmoded concepts of education.

C65

Education outside schools in London: an overview,

GRUNSELL, A,
Unpublished paper, available from the author, Centre for Urban Educational Studies, London, 1979, 9pp

Describes the growth of alternative education provision outside schools in London under the auspices of Education, Social Services or voluntary bodies and the cross-fertilisation of professional styles and practice which has resulted. Includes guidelines on the organisational preconditions which are necessary for satisfactory work off site.

C66

The meaning of special units,

LLOYD-SMITH, M,
Socialism and Education, vol 6, no 2, Summer 1979, pp 10–11

Discusses some of the underlying reasons for the growth of off-site provision and advances two additional possible causes for the apparent increase in disruptive behaviour among pupils. These are seen as the downturn in the economy and consequent bleak job prospects which robbed schools of their traditional justification for advocating co-operative conduct, and the reduced willingness of teachers to tolerate 'bad' behaviour.

C67

Dumping grounds: ILEA's exclusion policies,

National Association for Multiracial Education,
Issues in Race and Education, no 19, March–April 1979, pp 1–3

Criticises ILEA's exclusion policies, which result in many children from minority ethnic groups being placed in off-site units. Suggests that the schools are not prepared to make sufficient adjustments to accommodate them, and the education they receive in units is too narrow and lacks the activities and opportunities provided by mainstream school life.

C68

Lifting the lid off sin bins,

National Association for Multiracial Education,
Issues in Race and Education, no 26, May–June 1980, pp 1–4

Article in a news sheet produced by the National Association for Multiracial Education which records concern about the growth of disruptive units. Specific issues raised include: the over-representation of pupils from ethnic minorities, the lack of liaison between teachers in units and teachers in contributory schools, the referral procedures, the inadequacy of the curriculum, and the treatment philosophies of some units.

C69

Sin-bins: the integration argument,

NEWELL, P,
Where, no 160, July–August 1980, pp 8–11

Criticism of the growth of off-site provision for disruptive pupils, which is seen as particularly divisive in the context of the debate currently underway concerning the integration of children with special needs into mainstream education.

C70

Sinbin to sanctuary: saving the system,

Teachers' Action Collective,
Teachers' Action, no 12, June 1979, pp 22–6

Criticises ILEA policy on provision for disruptive pupils and contrasts the amounts of money which have been spent on setting up off-site centres, with the lack of support for a Free School run on collective lines with the participation of parents and children.

C71

Teething troubles: questions about the early days of units for disruptive children,

WEBB, S,
Unpublished paper, available from the author, at ILEA, Division 9, Education Welfare Service, 1980, 5pp

Raises some issues on the role of disruptive units based on first-hand experience in ILEA. Suggests there should be more formal procedures for assessing and referring children, recording their progress and reintegrating them into their original schools.

C72

The off-site centre role,

WRIGHT, T,
ILEA Contact, vol 26, no 8, 29 February 1980, pp 19 and 28

Discusses the advantages of off-site centres, which include the opportunity to re-examine the nature of the child's problem, relief from peer group pressure, closer pupil–teacher contact and relevant curriculum, which all help to produce a more positive attitude towards learning and facilitate re-entry into the original school.

National and local provision

C73

Disruptive units: ACE survey,

Advisory Centre for Education,
Where, no 158, May 1980, pp 6–7

Results of a nationwide survey of special units revealing a substantial increase in this kind of provision across the country. Found that 89% of unit students remain on the register of feeder schools so that referral is seen as a 'within institution' change.

C74

Behavioural units: a survey of special units for pupils with behavioural problems,

HM Inspectorate of Schools,
Department of Education and Science, 1978, 52pp

National survey of on- and off-site units recording number and distribution of units, provision of equipment, pupil characteristics, referral and admission criteria, record keeping, and links between units and parents. Notes that procedures for returning pupils to school were often less well developed than those for referral to units. Philosophies varied, emphasising different approaches such as social adjustment, remedial work in basic skills and general enrichment for deprived pupils.

C75

Disruptive Pupils Programme: progress report,

Inner London Education Authority Schools Sub-Committee,
Document ILEA 8394, ILEA, 1978, 20pp

Progress report on the implementation of the ILEA Disruptive Pupils Programme, describing the type of schemes which have been approved to date and seeking approval for additional funding.

C76

Disruptive Pupils Programme,

Inner London Education Authority Schools Sub-Committee,
Document ILEA 9215, ILEA, 1979, 41pp

Progress report on the Disruptive Pupils Programme under which a variety of on- and off-site projects were set up to assist ILEA schools in meeting the educational needs of pupils with severe behavioural problems. Describes the different kinds of projects which were approved and includes statistics from each Division.

C77

Disruptive Pupils Programme,

Inner London Education Authority Schools Sub-Committee,
Document ILEA 0379, ILEA, 1980, 5pp

Brief progress report on the implementation of the Disruptive Pupils Programme.

C78

Support Centres Programme monitoring study: first annual report,

Inner London Education Authority Research and Statistics Division,
Document RS 744/80, ILEA, 1980, 39pp

Report by the Research and Statistics Division on the centre, pupil and programme characteristics of units funded under the ILEA Support Centres Programme. Found that most centres had all the necessary components for providing a complete educational programme, appeared to have qualified staff and good pupil/teacher ratios, and that approximately one third of the pupils who left centres during the year returned to parent schools.

C79

Support Centres Programme: monitoring and evaluation report no 2,

Inner London Education Authority Research and Statistics Division,
Document RS 788/81, ILEA, 1981, 6pp

Second stage of the monitoring and evaluation study of support centres, mounted by the ILEA Research and Statistics Division. This focussed on the organisation and work of a representative sample of 32 on-site and off-site voluntary agency, intermediate treatment, and educational guidance centres. Five out of the nine voluntary agency and IT centres studied did not expect to return any of their pupils to their parent schools because of the pupils' age and the degree of their alienation from school.

C80

Ethnic census of school support centres and educational guidance centres,

Inner London Education Authority Research and Statistics Divisions,
Document RS 748/81, ILEA, 1981, 6pp

Short report describing the ethnic origin of children attending ILEA off-site school support centres and educational guidance centres.

C81

Out of site, out of mind?

NEUSTATTER, A,
Times Educational Supplement, 27 February 1981, p 19

Overview of the development of truancy centres in different parts of the country which considers their rationale and philosophy.

C82

Disruptive units in a local authority,

PAYNE, J,
Unpublished MA Dissertation, University of London, Institute of Education, 1980, 205pp

Examines the Disruptive Pupils Programme established by ILEA in 1978 and compares provision within each division of ILEA.

C83

Out of site: alternative provision,

ROCK, D, and TAYLOR, N,
Teaching London Kids, no 15, 1980, pp 17–19

Overview of the nature and function of different kinds of off-site centres in London including school support units, special units run by the School Psychological Service, home tuition centres and IT centres.

C84

What should schools do with their problem children?

ST-JOHN BROOKS, C,
New Society, vol 55, no 947, 8 January 1981, pp 44–7

Overview of current philosophy and policy concerning provision for children regarded as problematic in schools. Describes some current practice in centres on and off site and a scheme providing support for teachers in the classroom.

C85

Special units and classes for children with behaviour problems: an informal survey of LEA practice,

TOPPING, K J, and QUELCH, T,
Psychological Service Research Paper no 6,
Calderdale Education Department,
Metropolitan Borough of Calderdale, 1976, 17pp

Overview of the provision of special units and classes for children with behavioural problems from information provided by local authorities. Discusses the aims of units, admission criteria, management techniques, duration of stay, administrative structures and problems encountered.

Unit Reports and pupil reactions

C86

School's out! ✓

BALL, C and M, in *Community works 1: aspects of three innovatory projects*, Dungate, M (ed), pp 3–57,
Community Projects Foundation, 1980

Description of the work of the 149 Centre in Reading, which caters for children referred for disruptive behaviour, truancy and school refusal. The centre tends to be used as a last resort by the local schools so its role is largely seen as providing alternative education up to school leaving age for referred pupils. Includes accounts of discussion with staff and case studies of individual children.

C87

The Hanworth Road Centre,

Brunel Institute of Organisation and Social Studies, Educational Studies Unit,
Brunel Institute, 1976, 9pp

Report of the work of a unit attached to two secondary schools in Hounslow to provide for the educational and social needs of persistent non-attenders. The centre does not have a policy of automatically returning children to school, although some may feel able to do so, but provides an alternative education until school leaving age.

C88

Disruptive children and the Key Centre,

DAIN, P,
Remedial Education, vol 12, no 4, November 1977, pp 163–7

Description of the work of the Key Centre, which caters mainly for disruptive children. Pupils are accepted on the basis that they will eventually be reintegrated back into their schools, and while they are at the centre they continue to attend school for one day a week where their behaviour is monitored by teachers. Drama sessions and open-ended group meetings are held, which enable children to talk and act out their individual concerns. Parents meetings are held every month and there are good relations with local schools.

C89

Newlands Centre,

DAVIES, G,
Baseline – Journal of the Birmingham Association of Social Education Centres, no 2, Spring 1982, pp 19–20

Report of the work of an off-site educational guidance centre which has a policy of reintegrating children back into school and a programme that uses behavioural modification techniques.

C90

What pupils think of special units,

GALWAY, J,
Comprehensive Education, no 39, Winter 1979,
pp 18–20

Includes comments from pupils on their experiences at school prior to being placed in on- and off-site units, and discusses the implications for schools and teachers of the educational and emotional needs of children revealed by units.

C91

Absent from school: the story of a truancy centre,

GRUNSELL, R,
Writers and Readers, 1980, 117pp

Account of the establishment and operation of a truancy centre in Islington. Describes negotiations with schools to initiate the first referrals and subsequent problems of reintegration, and gives a realistic picture of the rewards and trials of day to day work with difficult, disadvantaged children.

C92

Some aspects of disruptive behaviour in secondary schools with particular reference to special units,

JOHNSON, M A,
Unpublished MSc Dissertation, University of London, Institute of Education, 1978, 85pp

Discusses the causes of and responses to disruptive behaviour and surveys the provision of special units in one large urban education authority. Examines the conflicts between sectors of the Education Service following the establishment of units and suggests that they are not an adequate solution to the problem of disruption.

C93

Punishment or cure?

LING, R,
Times Educational Supplement, 9 July 1982,
p 19

Case study of a pupil suspended from school at age 13 and placed in an off-site unit, illustrating the problems involved in demonstrating effectiveness and reconciling unit philosophy with pupil expectations which have been formed in mainstream schooling.

C94

Deviance in schools: an appraisal of behavioural units and their pupils,

MABON, D,
Unpublished MA Thesis, University of Keele, 1980, 400pp

Study of 23 children referred to three off-site units in Liverpool for non-attendance at school and disruptive behaviour. Standard tests of self-concept, verbal ability, alienation and maladjustment, among others, were administered when they first arrived at the unit and then three months later. Significant improvements were found on all measures.

C95

Disruptive pupils,

MACK, J,
New Society, vol 37, no 722, 5 August 1975,
pp 289–290

Report on two off-site centres in Leeds catering for disruptive pupils, some of whom may return to school while others stay until school leaving age. Counselling and group therapy is central to the philosophy of one of the units.

C96

Day care and education at St John's Community Home School, Birmingham,

McKAIL, C R, et al,
Community Homes Gazette, vol 74, no 6,
September 1980, pp 204–210

Description of a day care unit at a community home with education, which provides education for children who are not accepted by schools following their discharge from CHE, detention centres, observation and assessment centres and residential education placements. Suggests that this maximises the use of an expensive resource and provides a service for a number of children whose emotional, social and academic needs are not being met elsewhere.

C97

Journal for workers in social education centres,

National Organisation for Initiatives in Social Education (NOISE),
Issue no 1, NOISE, June 1981, 36pp

Contains short reports of the work of off-site units around the country and two longer articles on the nature of the problems facing schools and the differing responses of local education authorities.

C98

The Argyle Street Project,

PALFREY, C F,
Community Home Schools Gazette, vol 73, no 5, August 1979, pp 203–212

Description of a project in South Wales catering for school non-attenders who attend the centre for one term before returning to their school. Educational attainment was reported to have improved and children attended regularly and became involved in their school work.

C99

Safe haven for truants,

ROBINSON, T J,
Community Care, no 9, 29 May 1974,
pp 10–12

Described the work of the Adelaide Centre in London, which caters for children who refuse to attend school. Provides an alternative education up to school leaving age and attempts to equip pupils for independence in the adult world.

C100

Short-term sanctuary,

ROWAN, P,
Times Educational Supplement, 2 April 1976,
pp 21–4

Overview of the development of off-site provision and description of the work of the Reading Day Unit, an on-site adjustment unit at Brislington School, Greensfield Remedial Centre in Gateshead, a therapeutic educational guidance centre in Hoxton, and the Hungerford Centre, which is run on the basis of behavioural contract therapy.

C101

Back to school,

SPENCER, D,
Times Educational Supplement, 9 July 1982,
p 18

Description of the work of two units in Sunderland and Ilfracombe catering for disruptive pupils, which both use behaviour modification techniques.

C102

Experiment at Parkhead Centre,

SWAILES, A,
Special Education Forward Trends, vol 6, no 1, March 1979, pp 23–5

Description of the work of an off-site centre accepting children suspended for disruptive behaviour. The programme aims to be outward looking, individualised and flexible, introducing young people to as many useful experiences as possible. Rules are kept to a minimum and behaviourist techniques are apparently not used. Roughly half the pupils accepted since the start have been reintegrated into their original schools.

C103

The off-site unit,

TAYLOR, M, MILLER, J, and OLIVEIRA, M,
Comprehensive Education, no 39, winter 1979,
pp 13–17

Report of the work of an off-site unit which is a voluntary project, grant-aided by ILEA. Children are referred for non-attendance at school and where possible they will be reintegrated back into school, although some are too close to the leaving age to make this worthwhile. The article describes the programme provided for them.

C104

Broadway School: report on a special unit – Spring term 1980,

THOMAS, H,
Baseline – Journal of the Birmingham Association of Social Education Centres, no 2, Spring 1982, pp 15–18

Report of the work of an on-site unit within a school, catering for disruptive pupils, school refusers and school non-attenders. Includes case studies of individual pupils.

C105

Croydon learns to span the education gap,

VERNON, B,
Municipal Review, vol 4, no 77, April 1977,
pp 8-10

Describes the work of two separate but allied units in the London Borough of Croydon, which cater for disruptive, absentee or school refusing pupils. Discusses some of the underlying causes of the behaviour.

C106

Absent with cause: lessons of truancy,

WHITE, R,
Routledge and Kegan Paul, 1980, 285pp

Report of the work of the Bayswater Centre in Bristol, which provides full-time alternative education for adolescents who have stopped attending ordinary schools and for whom the alternative might be residential care or assessment centre. Describes a year in the life of the centre and reflects on the shortcomings of mainstream education as revealed and highlighted by the positive experiences of pupils in the centre. Includes individual case studies and a description of a similar centre in Denmark.

Education Welfare Service

C107

Education welfare: the patchwork service,

DAVIS, L F,
Community Care, no 98, 18 February 1976,
pp 16–17

Report of a survey of the Education Welfare
Service in England and Wales which in
general reveals an undermanned and underdeveloped service, with EWOs carrying
unmanageable case loads and often denied
proper supervision.

C108

**Education welfare in the Borough of
Hillingdon,**

Educational Studies Unit,
Brunel University, Institute of Organisation
and Social Studies, (ca 1976), 10pp

A composite report by five EWOs in
Hillingdon, outlining their duties and working
relationships, and drawing attention to the
factors which they consider influence the
provision of education welfare services within
the Borough. Concludes with their suggestions
for some desirable future developments.

C109

**The Education Welfare Service, Borough
of Hounslow,**

Educational Studies Unit,
Brunel University, Institute of Organisation
and Social Studies, (ca 1976), 7pp

Outlines the duties and working relationships
of the Education Welfare Service in Hounslow
and draws attention to the factors which
influence the provision of education welfare
services at a national, borough and area level.
Includes suggestions on some desirable future
developments.

C110

**The task of the senior in the supervision of
EWOs in their work with families where a
child has been referred for non-attendance
at school,**

GOLDSCHMIED, E, and HICKIE, H,
*News and Views . . . . Social Work in
Education*, no 4, 1979, pp 22–6

Article discussing ways in which senior
education welfare officers can help improve
the quality and effectiveness of the EWO's
work with referred children and their families
through analysing the interplay between all
members of the family.

C111

**An evaluation of the effectiveness of home
visits by an education welfare officer in
treating school attendance problems,**

GREGORY, R P, et al,
City of Birmingham Education Department,
1981, 19pp

Findings from a research study investigating
the effectiveness of home visits by an EWO to
the parents of children referred to him by
secondary schools for non-attendance.
Compares the subsequent attendance of two
groups of children who had or had not
received home visits and finds no significant
difference between them. Suggests there is
need for improvements in the schools'
methods of recording attendance and their
liaison with EWOs.

C112

Education welfare: strategy and structure,

MacMILLAN, K,
Longman, 1977, 165pp

A comprehensive study of all aspects of the
Education Welfare Service and the role of the
education welfare officer, drawing on data
obtained from a national survey.

C113

Are EWOs a vanishing species?

MILNER, J,
Community Care, no 321, 7 August 1980,
pp 20–1

Discussion of the role of EWOs and their
training needs. Suggests that the CQSW,
which is regarded as the appropriate
qualification for EWOs, will only become
relevant when there is some agreement on the
nature of the social work aspects of the job,
which is lacking at present.

C114

Beyond the truant,

PEDLEY, F,
New Society, vol 31, no 650, 20 March 1975,
pp 723–4

Discussion of the past history and present role
of the EWO in the light of the
recommendations of the Ralphs Report on the
Education Welfare Service. Suggests that the
attendance enforcement aspects of their role
will continue to make relations with social
workers difficult, as they will often have a
different perspective.

C115

The Education Welfare Service,

Society of Education Officers,
SEO, 1979, 9pp

Response to the Association of Directors of
Social Service paper which suggested that
EWOs should transfer from Education
Departments to Social Services. The Society
of Education Officers finds this unacceptable
and responds to the individual points made by
clarifying and detailing the work currently
being done by EWOs.

C116

Getting it together,

WEBB, S,
Unpublished paper, available from the author,
at ILEA Division 9, Education Welfare
Service, 1980, 11pp

Description of the case loads, work methods,
liaison work and future plans of a team of
EWOs set up in Lambeth to work with
disruptive children and their families, children
suspended from school, children with
behaviour problems and children placed in
off-site units.

C117

**Named person and the Education Welfare
Service,**

WEBB, S,
Unpublished paper available from the author,
at ILEA Division 9, Education Welfare
Service, 1981, 5pp

Discusses the suitability of the EWO to act as
the 'named person' suggested by the Warnock
Report, who would have responsibility for
identifying, recording and monitoring children
with special needs. Discusses the knowledge,
contacts and skills already possessed by
EWOs, which could be brought to the task,
and includes suggestions on how the job
might best be done.

C118

**The behavioural approach to non-
attendance cases,**

WOOD, J,
ILEA, Division 7, Education Welfare Service,
1981, 10pp

Description of a treatment strategy which can
be used by EWOs when working with cases of
school non-attendance, involving a complete
diagnosis of all the individual, environmental
and school factors impinging on the problem
and the identification of specific tasks which
could help to alleviate difficulties experienced
in all three areas.

School Psychological Service

C119

The practice of educational psychology,

CHAZAN, M, et al,
Longman, 1974, 422pp

Textbook on the nature and practice of
educational psychology.

C120

**The School Psychological Service,
Education Department, London Borough
of Hounslow,**

Educational Studies Unit,
Brunel University, Institute of Organisation
and Social Studies, 1976, 19pp

Report on the work and organisation of the
School Psychology Service in the London
Borough of Hounslow and its links with the
Child Guidance Team, schools, parents and
other agencies.

C121

Reconstructing educational psychology,

GILLHAM, B (ed),
Croom Helm, 1978, 197pp

Book of readings discussing the new
directions being taken by school psychological
services and individual educational
psychologists, which represent a move away
from exclusive reliance on psychological
testing of individual children.

C122

**The proper study of educational
psychology,**

HARGREAVES, D,
*Journal of the Association of Educational
Psychologists*, vol 4, no 9, 1978, pp 3–8

Discusses the relationship of educational
psychology to mainstream academic
psychology and educational practice in
schools and classrooms. Suggests that the
subject lacks self-confidence because of its
status as an applied, rather than pure, science
and as a consequence is over-reliant on
academic psychology theory, which may have
little relevance to the needs of education.
Educational psychology needs to have a
thorough understanding of what goes on in
the classroom.

C123

**Community psychology: an alternative
perspective,**

LOXLEY, D,
Unpublished paper, Sheffield Education
Department Psychological Service, 1976, 16pp

Literature review on the subject of community
psychology, which discusses the shape and
direction it could take including intervention
in schools.

C124

Community psychology and education,

LOXLEY, D,
Psychology and Education Conference,
Keele Educational Research Association,
1979, 20pp

Discussion of the nature of educational
psychology and the contribution it can make
to the quality of life for different groups
throughout the community. Describes the new
work that educational psychologists are doing
in schools but warns against conniving with
the existing system in order to gain some
influence in the school.

C125

**Discipline in schools: supportive roles of
psychiatric and social services,**

National Association of Schoolmasters/
Union of Women Teachers,
NAS/UWT, 1978, 4pp

Discussion of the role of the School
Psychological Service and Child Guidance in
providing support to schools faced with
disruptive behaviour. Warns against the
isolation from classroom practice which can
limit the practical value of the advice
proffered and calls for greater liaison between
classroom teachers and representatives of
other agencies.

C126

**Working it out together: an objectives and
priorities exercise,**

PRESLAND, J, et al,
*Journal of the Association of Educational
Psychologists*, vol 5, no 2, 1979, pp 3–10

Presentation of the findings from an exercise
undertaken by a team of educational
psychologists who looked systematically at
their work in an attempt to identify objectives
and establish priorities. As an addition to
maintaining individual referral work, they
looked at ways of extending psychological
services to a wider range of children.

C127

**Psychologists, teachers and children: how
many ways to understand?**

RAVENETTE, A T,
*Journal of the Association of Educational
Psychologists*, vol 3, no 2, 1972, pp 41–7

Discussion of techniques of working with
children and teachers which enable the child
to make sense of his experience and
communicate feelings and allow the teacher to
analyse her perceptions of the child and gain
new insights.

C128

**The role and function of the educational
psychologist: the way forward?**

TOPPING, K,
*Journal of the Association of Educational
Psychologists*, vol 4, no 5, 1977, pp 20–9

Literature review covering the development of
educational psychology as a profession and
noting the recent change in orientation
towards structural intervention in
organisations.

C129

**Consumer confusion and professional
conflict in educational psychology,**

TOPPING, K J,
Bulletin of the British Psychological Society,
vol 31, July 1978, pp 265–7

Survey of headteachers, classroom teachers
and educational psychologists in a northern
city to establish the relative priorities they
placed on various aspects of the work of the
School Psychological Service. Found that
headteachers favoured the assessment and
treatment of individual children, but class
teachers did not perceive psychologists as
being effective in facilitating changes in pupil
behaviour.

C130

**Psychological services for children in
England and Wales,**

WEDELL, K, and LAMBOURNE, R,
Occasional Papers, vol 4, nos 1 & 2, Division
of Educational and Child Psychology, British
Psychological Society, 1980, 84pp

Overview of the current provision of
psychological services for children in England
and Wales using data from a national survey,
which includes information on the current
pattern of work of psychologists, their views
on the way these services should be organised
and comments on appropriate methods of
training.

C131

Working with teachers,

WOLFENDALE, S,
*Journal of the Association of Educational
Psychologists*, vol 4, no 2, 1976, pp 20–4

Review of the literature on ways in which
educational psychologists are working with
teachers, and discussion of the factors which
need to be taken into consideration in order
to evolve new methods of work.

C132

**An evaluation of a school psychological
service: the Portsmouth pattern,**

WRIGHT, H J, and PAYNE, T A N,
Hampshire Education Department, March
1979, 69pp

Substantial study of the Portsmouth School
Psychological Service which describes the
priorities and objectives of the service, and the
general activities and individual casework of
the educational psychologists. Includes a
survey of user reactions to the service, with
comments from class and head teachers.

Child Guidance Service

C133

Child guidance: a reply to George Rehin,

BARNES, G,
Social Work Today, vol 3, no 5, 1 June 1972,
pp 3–5

Response to the Rehin article on the future of
the Child Guidance Service, which suggests
that current practice in certain child guidance
teams may be closer to the community-based
ideal than the writer recognises. Suggests that
child guidance units provide a valuable
meeting place for the exchange of ideas on
how work with disturbed parents and children
can best be developed, extended and
improved.

C134

Child Guidance Service: report 1977–1979,

Central Regional Council, Education
Department,
Central Regional Council, 1980, 49pp

Describes the work of the Child Guidance
Service of the Education Department of the
Central Regional Council of Scotland.
Demonstrates the wide variety of work with
different institutions undertaken by the
Service, which includes a specialist
consultancy service to children's homes, an
advisory remedial service to children in special
schools, and group therapy in association with
other professionals in day IT units for school
non-attenders.

C135

**Seven answers to Professor Wall and
Professor Tizard,**

DAVIE, R, et al,
London Educational Review, vol 2, no 2,
Summer 1973, pp 38–60

Collection of articles in response to the Tizard
criticisms of the Child Guidance Service,
offering both defence against and support for
the original article and suggesting possible
improvements to current practice.

C136

**The family and child guidance clinic,
Hounslow,**

Educational Studies Unit,
Brunel University, Institute of Organisation
and Social Studies, 1977, 21pp

Research report on the work of the family
and child guidance clinic in Hounslow,
covering the work of the child guidance team
and their relationships with schools, the
Education Department, School Psychological
Service and the Social Services Department.

C137

**The educational psychologist and child
guidance,**

FAWCETT, R,
*Journal of the Association of Educational
Psychologists*, vol 5, no 1, 1979, pp 8–11

Discussion of the role of educational
psychologists in child guidance teams, which
reviews the literature on the practice and
effectiveness of child guidance. Suggests that
the traditional child guidance model is
professionally unrewarding for educational
psychologists and more can be achieved by
adopting an advisory role viz-à-viz teachers
and parents than retaining an exclusively
clinical role.

C138

**Child guidance and delinquency in a
London borough,**

GATH, D, et al,
Oxford University Press, 1977, 190pp

Research study examining variations in child
guidance referral rates and juvenile
delinquency rates between different schools
and neighbourhoods in the London Borough
of Croydon. Found that child guidance and
delinquency rates co-varied according to
demographic and socio-economic variables in
different neighbourhoods and co-varied
between different Croydon schools, which
apparently exercised an independent effect.

C139

Treatment opportunities in child guidance clinics,

MEAD, S and D,
Social Work Today, vol 5, no 24, 6 March 1975, pp 734–740

Comparison of the working experience of social workers in a child guidance clinic and a social services department, which demonstrates the higher rate of direct contact with clients achieved by the child guidance clinic social workers. The authors argue for the continuation of the Child Guidance Service on the grounds that the autonomy of the clinic allows it to develop in a wide variety of ways to meet the assessed needs of children and families and the preferences of workers.

C140

Child guidance at the end of the road,

REHIN, G F,
Social Work Today, vol 2, no 24, 23 March 1972, pp 21–4

Criticism of the Child Guidance Service, which questions whether it is more effective in dealing with children referred by GPs, schools and parents than those who cope on their own. Suggests that the child guidance teams should be abolished and the various psychology and psychiatry professionals freed to develop new practices within the community.

C141

A dream that is dying,

SAMPSON, O C,
Bulletin of the British Psychological Society, vol 28, September 1975, pp 380–2

Article reviewing the historical development of the child guidance team, which acknowledges that current practice has fallen short of the original ideal.

C142

Maladjusted children and the Child Guidance Service,

TIZARD, J,
London Educational Review, vol 2, no 2, Summer 1973, pp 22–37

Influential article reviewing the development of the Child Guidance Service and criticising its current practice on the grounds of ineffectiveness, isolation from school practice and restricted coverage.

C143

Which way for child guidance?

WHITTAM, H,
Social Work Today, vol 8, no 21, 1 March 1977, pp 9–11

Article reviewing different perspectives on the role of child guidance, which concludes that there is a lack of knowledge outside the service concerning its role and functions, and that individual clinics could act as centres for more preventive and community-based work.

C (iii) SCHOOL SERVICES, INITIATIVES AND SANCTIONS

Pastoral care

C144

Perspectives on pastoral care,

BEST, R, JARVIS, C, and RIBBINS, P,
Heinemann Educational, 1980, 292pp

Critical collection of readings on the subject of pastoral care, which examines the relationship between pastoral care and authority and sets the concept within its historical context and other school welfare roles and networks. Examines strategies for care and analyses the extent to which the roles of counsellor and teacher can or should be separated.

C145

Education for personal autonomy: an inquiry into the school's resources for furthering the personal development of pupils,

BLACKHAM, H J (ed),
Bedford Square Press, 1978, 211pp

Book of readings on methods of organising pastoral care and ways in which staff can be supported in their work.

C146

Teaching and counselling: pastoral care in primary and secondary schools,

GALLOWAY, D,
Longman, 1981, 168pp

A series of case studies drawn from primary and secondary schools illustrating important themes in the practice of pastoral care, including the school's disciplinary policy, liaison with and support for teachers, parents and outside agencies, handling disruptive behaviour and providing remedial teaching.

C147

The teacher and pastoral care,

HAMBLIN, D H,
Basil Blackwell, 1978, 287pp

Discussion of the basic objectives of pastoral care and guidance within secondary schools and the application of certain models and techniques to key issues such as induction to school, examination skills, aggressive behaviour, truancy and self-inflicted injury.

C148

Problems and practice of pastoral care,

HAMBLIN, D H (ed),
Basil Blackwell, 1981, 306pp

Book of readings discussing the knowledge and skills required for the exercise of pastoral care and possible methods of evaluation. Includes chapters on issues such as the integration of handicapped pupils into the school and working with disruptive pupils.

C149

Pastoral care,

MARLAND, M,
Heinemann, 1974, 248pp

Book of readings on different aspects of pastoral care and counselling, which examines different organisational structures and presents some case studies.

C150

Planned pastoral care: a guide for teachers,

McGUINESS, J B,
McGraw-Hill, 1982, 152pp

Book on pastoral care, which outlines a structure within which teachers can offer guidance to young people. Suggests strategies and techniques that can be used and discusses issues around the early identification and management of pupils with difficulties.

C151

Pastoral care: the system of control,

Teachers' Action Collective,
Teachers' Action, no 5, 1976, pp 22–7

Discussion of the realities of pastoral care, which suggests that a necessary controlling and disciplining function lies beneath the caring rhetoric. The provision of pastoral staff and special units diverts financial resources away from basic education, removes responsibility from the classroom teacher and is ultimately untenable because of the range and number of problems involved.

Counselling

C152

A comparison of the effect of behavioural counselling and teacher support on the attendance of truants,

BEAUMONT, G R,
Unpublished Thesis for Diploma in School Counselling, University College Swansea, 1976, 192pp

Compares the effectiveness of group behavioural counselling and teacher support methods, in reinforcing appropriate behaviour. Concludes that counselling produces a more positive attitude towards school and better attendance than the teacher support method.

C153

The teacher and counselling,

HAMBLIN, D H,
Basil Blackwell, 1974, 346pp

Discussion of the different aspects of counselling within the school setting, including relationship with the teacher, possible models of practice within school, group counselling and guidance, and vocational and education counselling.

C154

The counsellor and strategies for the treatment of disturbed children in the secondary school,

HAMBLIN, D H,
British Journal of Guidance and Counselling, vol 3, no 2, July 1975, pp 172–189

Argues in favour of special units in which disturbed pupils can follow individual programmes which develop such skills as standpoint-taking, decision-making, co-operation and self-control. The counsellor's skills are especially relevant in the construction of these individual programmes and in facilitating a successful transition from the unit back to the ordinary classroom.

C155

Teachers as counsellors,

HOLDEN, A,
Constable and Co Ltd, 1969, 211pp

Discussion of the personal qualities, organisation and administration which would be needed by teachers wishing to undertake a counselling role in schools. Considers selection and training and the various moral issues which are likely to arise.

C156

Counselling in secondary schools,

HOLDEN, A,
Constable and Co Ltd, 1971, 190pp

Analysis of some of the practicalities of counselling within school, including the conflicting roles of teachers and counsellors, managing referrals and the relationship of counselling to the school authority system.

C157

Pupil perceptions of counselling: a response to Murgatroyd,

HOOPER, R,
British Journal of Guidance and Counselling,
vol 6, no 2, July 1978, pp 198–203

Analysis of pupil perceptions of counselling in a school in South West England, which challenges Murgatroyd's research by finding that children in this establishment were quite willing to approach the counsellor with personal problems and others arising out of the school setting. Suggests that research on the orientation of counsellors is significant in this context and the individual in this case was more client centred than the institution-centred counsellors reported from other schools.

C158

Counselling adolescents in school,

JONES, A,
Kogan Page, 1977, 200pp

Analyses the need for counselling services for adolescents in school and outlines the problems of setting up a counselling scheme, integrating it into the organisation of the school, winning the trust of pupils and securing the co-operation of school staff. Includes some case studies of pupils and describes some of the problems encountered.

C159

The professionalisation of counselling in education and its legal implications,

LEWIS, D G, and MURGATROYD, S J,
British Journal of Guidance and Counselling,
vol 4, no 1, January 1976, pp 2–15

An examination of the position of counsellors within schools in relation to the processes and organisation which usually accompany the establishment of professions. Suggests that as far as the secondary schools are concerned, contractual recognition of competence, training and expertise does not yet seem to have taken place. Suggests there is a need for collective action on the part of counsellors to secure their position.

C160

Guidance and counselling in British schools: a discussion of current issues,

LYTTON, H, and CRAFT, M (eds),
Edward Arnold, 1974, 189pp

Collection of readings on different aspects of guidance and counselling in schools, including the social and philosophical context of the work, practical issues of working within schools, and relationships with external agencies such as Child Guidance and Social Services.

C161

Guidance in comprehensive schools: a study of five systems,

MOORE, B M,
National Foundation for Educational Research, 1970, 101pp

Overview of the development of guidance systems in five different schools. Notes that, to a considerable degree, the achievement of educational and guidance objectives is dependent upon major factors within the environment and school setting.

C162

Ethical issues in secondary school counselling,

MURGATROYD, S,
Journal of Moral Education, vol 4, no 1, 1974, pp 27–37

Discussion of ethical issues which need to be considered by counsellors working in school settings, focussing on how confidential client-counsellor relationships need to be, how clients should be referred to counsellors and whether counsellors are institutional or client-based agents.

C163

Pupil perceptions of counselling: a case study,

MURGATROYD, S J,
British Journal of Guidance and Counselling, vol 5, no 1, January 1977, pp 73–8

Survey of pupil perceptions of counselling in a school with a highly developed counselling service. Found that counsellors were regarded by pupils as senior teachers with considerable administrative duties, including major responsibility for checking attendance registers for truancy and reporting truants to the education welfare officer. They were not seen as major sources of help with personal problems.

C164

Counselling the disaffected,

WILLIAMS, K,
The New Era, vol 54, no 6, July–August 1973, pp 134–8

Discussion of the limitations of counselling disaffected pupils who have already experienced the range of sanctions offered by school and society. Suggests that behaviour modification techniques might be effective as a last resort.

Curriculum Initiatives

C165

School by beginners,

DRINKWATER, C,
New Society, vol 57, no 982, 10 September 1981, p 428

Description of an initiative in which fifth form boys and girls in a school in Wales who might otherwise play truant, act as tutors to primary school children in a neighbouring school providing help with reading and spelling.

C166

In and out of school: the ROSLA Community Education Project,

WHITE, R, and BROCKINGTON, D,
Routledge and Kegan Paul, 1978, 200pp

Report of a project providing a social education curriculum once a week outside school for a group of pupils in their last year of compulsory schooling. Describes the content of the programme and the type of children involved and discusses the implications for mainstream education.

On-site and School-sponsored Units

C167

Guidance notes for teachers in withdrawal centres in ordinary schools,

DAIN, P,
City of Birmingham Education Department, (197–), 4pp

Notes for teachers in withdrawal units, which discuss criteria for referring children to units, general ethos, programme, involving classroom teachers, assessment and evaluation, and procedures for returning children to the main school.

C168

The on-site unit,

HOLMAN, P, and LIBRETTO, G,
Comprehensive Education, no 39, Winter 1979, pp 10–12

Description of the nature and functions of on-site units, which discusses some of the problems encountered in devising aims and objectives, providing effective teaching, and reconciling the needs of the school and the needs of the pupil.

C169

The Hermitage Adjustment Unit, Ilfracombe School,

HUNKIN, J, and ALHADEFF, G,
Therapeutic Education, vol 6, no 1, 1978, pp 13–18

Description of a unit for disruptive pupils linked to a school in Devon, which uses a behaviour modification token economy system as a means of improving pupil motivation. The unit originally contained senior pupils who stayed for the remainder of their school careers but attempts are now made to identify pupils who may need placements at an earlier stage.

C170

A continuing approach: Fairfax House and Group 4 at Sidney Stringer School,

JONES, A R, and FORREST, R,
Sidney Stringer School and Community College, 1977, 46pp

Description of two groups operating within the framework of Sidney Stringer School and Community College in Coventry. These cater for pupils experiencing difficulties with attendance, performance in class and relationships with adults and peers, and provide remedial education, community service placements and work experience courses. Provides information on the philosophy and administration of the service and contacts with external agencies.

C171

Care, control, and the urban school: a study of Downtown Sanctuary,

LEAVOLD, J M,
Unpublished MA Dissertation, University of London, King's College, 1977, 152pp

Considers contrasting theories of deviancy and interpretations of the sanctuary movement as variously a liberal and caring aspect of the schools pastoral care system or as a means of exercising control over rebels against the system. After examining a specific London sanctuary the author concludes that care and control are inextricably linked and it is the size of the school which prevents teachers from forming effective relationships with pupils.

C172

Intermediate treatment in school,

WITTER, F, and POSTLETHWAITE, N,
Youth in Society, no 35, June 1979, pp 25–7

Description of the work of the IT unit, which is an integral part of Paddington School in Liverpool. Presents a case study of a pupil referred for school non-attendance, which illustrates the working methods of the unit. These include a client-centred approach, a flexible and varied programme, small groups with stable staff membership, and activities which extend the individual experience of pupils.

Suspension and Exclusion

C173

Suspension: ACE suspensions survey,

Advisory Centre for Education,
Where, no 166, March 1981, pp 20–6

Survey of LEA suspension procedures, which reveals extensive variations in the way such procedures are interpreted at local level and the extent to which parental rights of appeal are safeguarded.

C174

Children excluded from school: the results of a survey,

DAVIS, L F,
British Association of Social Workers and Association of Directors of Social Services, 1977, 18pp

Report of a survey of social services departments to determine the extent of the difficulties created by children being excluded from school and subsequently referred to Social Services for care, supervision or 'treatment'. Found that over half of the 66 authorities contacted did not experience a problem, but comments from the remainder revealed substantial problems of liaison and communication with schools, with social workers often required to get involved at a late stage.

C175

Exclusion and suspension from school,

GALLOWAY, D,
Trends in Education, no 2, Summer 1980, pp 33–8

Findings from a retrospective study of the statistics of exclusion and suspension from Sheffield schools over a four year period. Notes that the cause of exclusion was usually a slow increase in tension leading to a precipitating incident, and that exclusion rates and referral rates for special education were idiosyncratic to each school and not related in any obvious way to social disadvantage in the catchment area.

C176

A study of pupils suspended from schools,

GALLOWAY, D,
British Journal of Educational Psychology, vol 52, June 1982, pp 205–212

Survey of a sample of children suspended from schools in Sheffield, which provides information on individual characteristics, family background, medical history, involvement with social work agencies and the Police, and social and educational adjustment. Suggests that pupils at risk of suspension have educational and possibly constitutional problems which would cause concern at any school, but schools apparently differ in the degree to which they are able to handle these problems internally.

C177

Suspensions and the sin bin boom: soft option for schools,

GRUNSELL, R,
Where, no 153, November–December 1979, pp 307–9

Discussion of the growth of suspension as a sanction employed by schools, which underlines the fact that there is little consensus on the meaning and definition of disruptive behaviour and suspension statistics are often unreliable. Suggests that more resources should be channelled into enabling schools to identify and deal with their own problems than setting up off-site units.

C178

Beyond control? Schools and suspension,

GRUNSELL, R,
Writers and Readers, 1980, 132pp

Looks in depth at how and why children get suspended from school in one London borough. Includes statistics on suspension rates and case studies of individual pupils.

C179

The suspension of pupils from school: an aspect of juvenile justice?

JENNINGS, R,
Howard Journal, vol 19, no 3, 1980, pp 156–165

Discussion of the legal aspects of suspension from school, which highlights the inconsistency of procedure between local authorities and the lack of safeguards for the legal rights of parents and pupils in the informality of the processes.

C180

The relationship of personality and behaviour to school exclusion,

LONGWORTH-DAMES, S M,
Educational Review, vol 29, no 3, June 1977, pp 163–177

Comparison of the personality and behaviour of children excluded from school with peers who had not been excluded, as measured by standardised tests. Found that there was no significant difference in personality, but excluded children scored higher on certain maladjusted behaviour tests. Suggests that disruptive children may be behaving in a socially precise way to maintain their position in their sub-culture.

C181

The suspension of pupils from school,

National Association of Governors and Managers,
Paper no 12, NAGM, 1980, 4pp

Statement by the National Association of Governors and Managers of their policy on suspension and the rights and responsibilities of schools, governors, parents and pupils, which takes account of the recommendations of the Taylor Report.

C182

The school system's response to bad behaviour,

NEWSAM, P A,
Howard Journal, vol 18, no 2, 1979, pp 108–113

Discussion of LEA responses to disruptive behaviour, which notes that powerful pressures are driving schools to remove pupils who threaten the viability of the institution, but sees initiatives such as the school support centres as essentially providing pupils with a second chance.

C183

Suspension,

TAYLOR, F,
ACE information sheet, *Where*, no 154, January 1980, pp 23–5

Information sheet from the Advisory Centre for Education, which sets out the law on suspension and itemises the steps that parents can take to ensure that their interests and those of their child are safeguarded at every point of the proceedings.

C184

Exclusion from school,

YORK, R, HERON, J, and WOLFF, S,
Journal of Child Psychology and Psychiatry, vol 13, 1972, pp 259–266

Research study of 41 children excluded from schools in Edinburgh. Examines the personal characteristics of the children, their family backgrounds, IQs and behaviour as measured by standardised tests. Suggests that exclusion is the culmination of a series of aggressive acts by a seriously disturbed child from an exceptionally stressful and socially deprived background.

C (iv) COURT PROCEEDINGS AND OUTCOMES

C185

From 'List D' to day school,

ANDERSON, R R,
Dundee College of Education, 1980, 149pp

Investigation of the process of returning pupils from residential List D schools to ordinary schools, which provides information on school perceptions of the problems involved and the degree of readiness of the pupil. Includes extensive reports of the difficulties pupils experienced in their original schools and their views on List D schools and the return placement. Follow-up data appeared to show a relatively low success rate.

C186

The use and significance of school reports in juvenile court criminal proceedings: a research note,

BALL, C,
British Journal of Social Work, vol 11, no 4, Winter 1981, pp 479–483

Short research note describing an unexpected finding from a study of the factors influencing magistrates in making care orders in criminal proceedings, which revealed the importance of school reports to the decision making process.

C187

School reports for the juvenile court: a review of practice and procedure,

BALL, C,
British Journal of Social Work, Spring 1983 (forthcoming)

Survey of the practice within juvenile courts regarding the disclosure of the contents of school reports to defendants, which finds a wide variation in procedure with the bias toward reports not being shown to parents and children. Practice within individual courts appears to be idiosyncratic and influenced by the personal preferences of justices' clerks, headteachers and juvenile panel members.

C188

Truancy and the courts: research note,

BERG, I, et al,
Journal of Child Psychology and Psychiatry, vol 18, 1977, pp 359–365

Pilot study of the relative effect on subsequent school attendance of two court disposals, adjournment and supervision orders, using data from juvenile court statistics in Leeds. Found that the adjourned group attended school more satisfactorily than the supervised group during the six months following their first appearance in court.

C189

The effect of two randomly allocated court procedures on truancy,

BERG, I, et al,
British Journal of Criminology, vol 18, no 3, July 1978, pp 232–244

Report of the subsequent attendance of 96 children brought to the juvenile court under care proceedings because of school non-attendance, who were randomly allocated by magistrates to two possible court disposals without the knowledge of social welfare officials. Found that the adjourned group, who were repeatedly brought back to court to assess progress on school attendance, achieved a more satisfactory level of attendance than the group made the subject of supervision orders.

C190

Features of children taken to juvenile court for failure to attend school,

BERG, I, et al,
Psychological Medicine, vol 8, 1978, pp 447–453

Examination of the characteristics of 84 children taken to court for failure to attend school. Identifies three different components of the problem, described as clinical truancy, school withdrawal and school refusal, and suggests that all three kinds of absenteeism tend to affect most children to some extent.

C191

Girls will be girls: sexism and juvenile justice in a London borough,

CASBURN, M,
Explorations in feminism, no 6, Women's Research and Resources Centre Publications, 1979, 25pp

Description of the processing of girls by the juvenile court in a London borough. Suggests that care orders are frequently invoked in the case of non school attendance as a way for courts to exercise control over the behaviour of girls which deviates too far from the accepted female norm.

C192

Children appearing before juvenile courts: a framework of consultation. Report of the working party on co-operation and communication between agencies concerned with children and young persons appearing before juvenile courts in Wales,

DAVIE, PROFESSOR R (Chairman),
Clwyd County Council, 1977, 23pp

Reviews some of the existing shortcomings of interagency co-operation and communication regarding children coming before the courts in Wales and recommends improvements in consultation and the exchange of information between agencies.

C193

Some characteristics of school non-attenders assessed at Lisnevin School,

ELLIOTT, R,
Community Home Schools Gazette, vol 69, no 8, November 1975, pp 400–3

Short report on the characteristics of boys, referred to Lisnevin School in Northern Ireland for assessment, who have previously appeared in court for non-attendance at school. In some cases the boys are being assessed prior to committal to training school, in others the aim is to provide reports to the juvenile court for boys on remand. Finds an inconsistency of policy among Library and Education Boards regarding the numbers committed to training school or referred for assessment.

C194

Administrative and legal procedures available to local education authorities in cases of poor school attendance,

GALLOWAY, D, BALL, T, and SEYD, R,
Durham and Newcastle Research Review, vol 9, no 46, Spring 1981, pp 201–9

Description of the legal sanctions against parents and children available to local education authorities in the case of school non-attendance and analysis of the actual legal action taken by one LEA during two school years. Provides statistics on juvenile and magistrate court outcomes and identifies some of the factors influencing LEA decisions about the use of formal procedures.

C195

The selection of parents and children for legal action in connection with unauthorised absence from school,

GALLOWAY, D, BALL, T, and SEYD, R,
British Journal of Social Work, vol 11, no 4, Winter 1981, pp 445–461

Examination of selection processes involved in the differential treatment by EWOs of parents of poor school attenders, in which one group was invited to attend a meeting of the LEA's School Attendance Section. A second group of parents were prosecuted in the magistrates' court, the children of the third group were brought before the juvenile court and no

formal action was taken against a fourth group. Concluded that there appeared to be no clear and consistent principles governing the selection of cases for formal action.

C196

School attendance following legal or administrative action for unauthorised absence,

GALLOWAY, D, BALL, T, and SEYD, R,
Educational Review, vol 33, no 1, 1981, pp 53–65

Analysis of the individual, family and neighbourhood characteristics of groups of absentee pupils in Sheffield. Comparisons were made between the levels of attendance achieved by different groups of pupils who were subject to different forms of intervention for school non-attendance, or against whom no formal action was taken. Found that children who received no formal intervention for absenteeism or who changed schools achieved a higher level of attendance over the same period of time than children brought before the juvenile court, or children whose parents were prosecuted in the magistrates' court. There was insufficient evidence however to make any causal connections between different types of intervention and patterns of attendance.

C197

Finding a way back for reluctant children,

GALLOWAY, D, BALL, T, and SEYD, R,
Social Work Today, vol 12, no 33, 28 April 1981, pp 15–17

Overview of the findings from a series of studies in Sheffield investigating the nature of the formal procedures available to education authorities in the case of school non-attendance, the methods by which EWOs select pupils and/or their parents for prosecution and the subsequent attendance of pupils who have been subject to these procedures. Concludes that absenteeism develops as part of a wider pattern of behaviour associated with multiply disadvantaged conditions, and legal proceedings do not appear to be an effective technique in reducing the incidence of this behaviour. They might, however, have a role in securing parental co-operation in a carefully planned programme designed to meet the child's educational needs.

C198

Care and discretion: social workers' decisions with delinquents,

GILLER, H, and MORRIS, A,
Burnett Books Ltd, 1981, 127pp

Examination of the nature of social worker decision making and the criteria used to type a case and determine whether a child should be made the subject of a care order. Includes discussion on the varying ways in which truancy can be interpreted to provide supporting evidence for the decision that has already been made.

C199

Court reports: facts or fantasies?

GILLER, H,
Paper presented at the NACRO conference 'Could do better? School reports in the juvenile court', 21 May 1982, National Association for Care and Resettlement of Offenders, 1982, 9pp

Overview of the issues concerning the use of social enquiry reports with special attention to the role of the school report in court decisions. Includes a review of the research findings, which indicate that schools may have some influence on the production of delinquent behaviour.

C200

Study of children on care orders and supervision orders made under section 1(2)e – C & Y P Act 1969 in a metropolitan district,

HIRST, S, et al,
Clearing House for Local Authority Social Services Research, no 2, 28 March 1980, pp 57–112

Investigation of the characteristics of children committed to care and placed under supervision primarily for school non-attendance in Bradford, and the extent to which magistrates followed social worker recommendations. Found that the care order was the main outcome of court proceedings and social worker recommendations for both care orders and supervision orders were largely followed by magistrates. Intermediate treatment was not regarded by social workers as a viable alternative to a care order.

C201

School non-attendance,

JOHNSON, S F,
Community Home Schools Gazette, vol 70, no 6, September 1976, pp 263–9

Presents statistics on 350 adolescents in six Birmingham observation and assessment centres relating to age, sex, type of court order and type of offence. Finds that over half the children going through observation and assessment centres during the period covered were involved in truancy at a reportable level and there was a tendency for truants to be absconders and have problems of aggression and violence.

C202

Children out of court,

MARTIN, F M, FOX, S J, and MURRAY, K,
Scottish Academic Press, 1981, 331pp

Comprehensive research study of the Children's Hearings system in Scotland, which analyses referral statistics, the role of the Reporter, the process of the Hearings and the views and attitudes of parents, children, social workers and panel members. Includes statistics on the numbers of children referred for truancy and the eventual outcomes from the Hearings.

C203

Children in trouble,

MILLHAM, S,
Paper presented at All-Party Parliamentary Group for Children, Meeting of 6 May 1981, All-Party Parliamentary Group for Children, 1981, 24pp

Discusses the role of schools in providing the adverse experiences which may help to precipitate children into delinquency and subsequent processing through various institutions. Notes the considerable influence that school reports for court have on magistrates and suggests that schools may be unaware of the impact which their recommendations are likely to have on a child's subsequent career.

C204

Education cases and the juvenile court,

RATHBONE, R,
Justice for Children, 1979, 6pp

Overview of the issues involved in the use of legal proceedings for school non-attendance. Suggests that the enforcement of school attendance by the courts is an example of the treatment of symptoms rather than the disease.

C205

Truants under suspended sentence,

REYNOLDS, D,
Community Care, no 215, 31 May 1978, pp 20–2

Description of the experiment in Leeds comparing the outcomes of two randomly allocated court procedures and the subsequent reactions of social welfare professionals who had not been notified of the research.

C206

Executing 'decisions' in the children's hearings,

SMITH, G, and MAY, D,
Sociology, vol 14, no 4, November 1980, pp 581–601

Description of the process of decision making within the Children's Hearings system, using case studies, some of which involved non-attendance at school. Illustrates the difficulty experienced by panel members in reaching clear cut decisions when aspects of the case do not readily fit the theories and explanations available to them or when their interpretation of the facts is challenged by parents.

C207

In whose best interests? The unjust treatment of children in courts and institutions,

TAYLOR, L, LACEY, R, and BRACKEN, D,
The Cobden Trust/MIND, 1979, 109pp

As part of a review of the treatment of children in courts and institutions, includes statistics and discussion on the numbers of children committed to care under Section 1(2)(e) of the 1969 Children and Young Persons Act for persistent truancy in 1977.

C208

Truancy and stealing: a comparative study of Education Act cases and property offenders,

TENNENT, T G,
British Journal of Psychiatry, vol 116, no 535, June 1970, pp 587–592

Comparison of two groups of boys brought before the juvenile court for truancy or stealing. Suggests that they share similar family and environmental backgrounds and show similar levels of educational attainment. The Education Act group were significantly more often found to be the youngest members of their family.

C209

The use of Section 40 of the Education Act by the London Juvenile Court,

TENNENT, T G,
British Journal of Criminology, vol 10, no 2, 1970, pp 175–180

Survey of children prosecuted for school non-attendance in London, which found that this represented 0.2% of all pupils and 0.7% of 14 year olds.

C210

Care proceedings for school non-attendance and their outcomes,

THOMAS, J,
Information sheet, National Youth Bureau, 1982, 6pp

Collates national figures from official sources on the number of care proceedings for school non-attendance and their outcomes, including information on care orders and children in care. Also includes some figures on prosecution of parents under the 1944 Education Act.

C (v) INTERAGENCY AND INTERPROFESSIONAL LIAISON AND PERCEPTIONS

C211

Co-operation between education and the personal social services: report of proceedings, Social Services Conference 1978,

Association of Directors of Social Services, ADSS. 1979. 108pp

Report of a conference on the theme of co-operation between Education and the personal Social Services in which contributors identified possible strains in the relationship between departments and individual workers and areas of practice in which fruitful collaboration might be possible.

C212

Co-operative care: a school counsellor's experience of liaison between school and welfare agencies,

BARTLETT, G,
Centre for Information and Advice on Educational Disadvantage, 1976, 9pp

Describes the establishment of a counselling post within a community school in Halifax and the establishment of working relationships with the Police, Social Services, Education Welfare and the School Psychological Service.

C213

Inter-professional groups: lessons from a trial scheme,

BASTIANI, J, and WARD, D,
University of Nottingham, School of Education, 1979, 50pp

Report of two pilot schemes bringing together teachers, social workers, probation officers, youth workers and education welfare officers as an in-service training exercise sponsored by the University of Nottingham. Groups were established to examine the problems generated by truancy and absenteeism and community development issues. A detailed record was kept of the process of each group, which revealed the characteristic strains and difficulties of interprofessional collaborative work. The authors discuss the implications for interagency co-operation of this exercise and provide short profiles of six contrasting styles of interprofessional groups.

C214

Who's afraid of the police?

BURTON, D,
Social Work Today, vol 13, no 3, 22 September 1981, pp 12–13

Discussion of the advantages experienced by Police, Probation, Social Services and Education through close liaison and co-operation. Discusses the regular liaison meetings of chief officers from all four services in Lincolnshire, which are said to enable clear management statements to emerge that can be translated into operational procedures for each department. Notes that individual relationships between professionals can be difficult at local level and describes the exchange schemes in which workers from each agency can gain a better understanding of each other's work.

C215

The inter-professional perspectives of teachers and social workers: a pilot inquiry,

CRAFT, M and A,
Social and Economic Administration, vol 5, no 1, 1971, pp 19–28

Survey of the interprofessional attitudes of teachers and social workers attending an in-service course in North Devon. Found that there was a high degree of consensus in their views.

C216

Linking home and school: a new review (3rd edition),

CRAFT, M, et al (eds),
Harper and Row, 1980, 397pp

Book of readings on methods of strengthening the links between home and school, which includes sections on the relationship of schools to external agencies. Reviews the work of support services such as the Education Welfare Service, discusses the advantages and disadvantages of certain people such as counsellors and head teachers acting as the link between schools and external agencies, considers the professional differences and similarities between teachers and social workers, and identifies future areas for co-operation between the two services.

C217

Relations between social worker and teacher,

DAVIES, B,
Social Work Today, vol 8, no 8, 23 November 1976, pp 9–11

Examination of the nature of interprofessional relations between teachers and social workers, which suggests that the differences that actually separate the two groups are often less important than what they believe separates them. Notes that the new bureaucracies in Education and Social Services make it difficult for field level practitioners to preserve personal and professional autonomy, and that each may criticise the other for failings which they recognise in their own organisation. Suggests there is scope for interprofessional co-operation to change their own agencies.

C218

Agency collaboration or worker control? Alternative models for more integrated services to young people,

DAVIES, B,
Youth in Society, no 22, March–April 1977, pp 3–6

Article questioning the uncritical acceptance of interagency collaboration as a good thing in itself, which seeks to establish the ultimate objectives of such collaboration and the ultimate beneficiaries. Suggests that other models of co-operation between agency workers are possible involving work together to tackle institutional inadequacies and structural weaknesses and failings.

C219

Getting on with intermediate treatment: a report of the plenary sessions of the conference held at the City Hall, Sheffield 9–11 July 1979,

Department of Health and Social Security, DHSS, 1980, 41pp

Collection of the main conference papers on the theme of community-based activities for young people at risk or in trouble, emphasising the need for liaison between agencies such as Education, Social Services, Probation and the Youth Service. Includes a contribution from Mark Carlisle, as Secretary of State for Education and Science, on the relationship between education and intermediate treatment.

C220

Secondary schools and the welfare network,

JOHNSON, D, et al,
Allen and Unwin, 1980, 207pp

Research report based on collaborative interviews and discussions with teachers and agency workers, which provides an account of their roles in relation to pupils and clients and their limits of accountability, co-operation and coexistance with other institutions and groups. Includes sections on the Education Department, Social Services, Education Welfare, School Psychological Service, Child Guidance and Juvenile Bureau in two outer London boroughs, and includes some evaluative comments from teachers and other professionals on their experiences of working relationships with each other. In a wide ranging report there is also coverage of models of school counselling and pastoral systems and the establishment and operation of an off-site unit.

C221

Working together for children and their families,

KAHAN, B (ed),
Department of Health and Social Security/ Welsh Office, HMSO, 1977, 207pp

Influential initiative by the Welsh Office and the Social Work Service Development Group of the DHSS, which brought representatives together from the schools and welfare services in South Glamorgan for residential seminars and conferences which explored the points of strain and conflict in the co-operation between different departments and professions. Interagency working groups were established to tackle identified problems of liaison and collaboration, and the booklet reports on their achievements and includes papers on the professional stances of teachers and social workers and research on truancy.

C222

Out of bounds,

MILNER, J,
Social Work Today, vol 13, no 32, 27 April 1982, pp 16–17

Examination of the underlying reasons for differing attitudes of teachers and social workers to truancy, which suggests that teachers' attitudes may vary according to their position in the primary, junior, middle and senior school levels where academic work assumes greater or less importance.

C223

Non-attendance at school,

PRICE, J R, and BRIAULT, E W H,
Inner London Education Authority, 1976, 7pp

Joint statement by an ILEA/Inner London Social Services working party, which discusses the involvement of both services and the schools in the prevention of non-attendance. Reviews initiatives currently being taken by schools and recommends the widening of current arrangements for liaison between the two departments at area level. Notes that the work of social service departments is not always understood within schools and recommends greater dissemination of illustrative case studies.

C224

Can the gladiator and our soldiers co-exist?

PRICE, J R,
Health and Social Service Journal, 8 July 1977, pp 1022–4

Description of an initiative taken in Islington to improve communication between Education and Social Services, which had previously existed on a very low level. Closer liaison at policy level between officers from the two departments was paralleled by meetings between staff of area teams and local schools to develop joint strategies for their neighbourhoods and identify shortcomings in their existing working relationships. Provides examples of co-operative work in intermediate treatment.

C225

Working together for children in trouble: report of a seminar on intermediate treatment,

Social Work Service Group,
Scottish Education Department, May 1980, 44pp

Seminar on the theme of co-operative work on behalf of children in trouble reviewing the current provision of IT in Scotland. Includes contributions from the Director of Social Work of Lothian Region and the Deputy Director of Education of Strathclyde Region, setting out the areas in which greater co-operation between the two departments is needed. Booklet contains short reports from individual IT projects, which often provides a grassroots view of the existing state of liaison between education and social work departments at local level.

C226

Collision courses: interdepartmental policy conflicts over young people in trouble,

SCRUTTON, S,
Youth in Society, no 48, November 1980, pp 11–12

Case study of a juvenile on placement at an IT centre with a history of difficult and disturbed behaviour and the problems encountered attempting to reintegrate him back into school. The author discusses the implications for similar young people of Social Services and Education policy at a local level, where economic cuts are reducing the amount of resources available within schools to deal with disaffected young people and also limiting the number of places available within special education and off-site facilities. In many cases children may be suspended for considerable periods of time and at risk of committing further offences.

C227

Co-operative care: an experimental inquiry in Hertfordshire,

WATKINS, R,
Disadvantage in Education, vol 1, no 1, November 1976, pp 21–3

Description of the work of the Study Conference on Young People in Trouble and at Risk (SCYPTAR) in Hertfordshire, which brings together representatives from Education, Social Services, Police, Magistrates, Youth Service, Area Health, Community Relations and Diocesan Youth Chaplaincy. The Conference meets on average five times a year and has received papers on crime prevention panels, intermediate treatment, and practice and procedures in the juvenile court. Two exploratory projects based in secondary schools examined procedures for dealing with children in trouble and examined retrospective case histories. The recommendations underlined the need for good interagency liaison, particularly on the occasion of the first court appearance.

C (vi) INTERAGENCY CO-OPERATIVE PRACTICE

Multi-professional

C228

The Tuesday project,

Bedford Social Services Department, 1981, 9pp

Description of an IT programme provided as part of an integrated studies period for fifth year pupils in school, by an interprofessional team of youth leaders, social workers, teachers, education welfare officers and the intermediate treatment officer.

C229

A Bradford groupwork project, Spring 1982,

Bradford Education Services, Education Welfare Service, July 1982, 20pp

Account of two evening groups meeting at school with disadvantaged children referred for irregular attendance. Staffing consisted of one teacher, two EWOs and one social worker on placement. A 2½ day residential component was provided by the Save The Children Fund Project at Hilltop in Ilkley. Includes individual case histories of the children and forms for assessment.

C230

Co-operative care: practice and information profiles,

DERRICK, D, and WATKINS, R, Centre for Information and Advice on Educational Disadvantage, 1977, 73pp

Case studies of a range of interagency co-operative exercises including school social workers, the Liverpool social education team, community and home link teams, interagency working parties, research projects and special interest groups.

C231

Social education in a secondary school,

PADMORE, K, Nottingham Young Volunteers, 1981, 19pp

Description of a social education project involving regular weekly sessions for a term in Glaisdale Comprehensive School Nottingham, for fifth form pupils viewed as truants, disruptives and underachievers by the school. The team of workers included teachers, a probation officer, a university lecturer and the Nottingham Young Volunteers Organiser. The report describes the programme devised for the group and discusses the implications of this approach.

C232

Untapped source,

PRITCHARD, J, *Times Educational Supplement*, 16 October 1981, p 20

Report of the Caldicot School Socialisation Project in Gwent, providing a social education course for fifth year pupils with the participation of a social worker, probation officer, a policeman and teachers.

School Social Work

C233

Social work in relation to schools,

ANDREWS, C, *Social Work Today*, vol 4, no 25, 7 March 1974, pp 797–801

Discussion paper from a BASW working party on social work in relation to schools. Identifies areas of need where there is scope for co-operation between Education and Social Services, such as children with behavioural problems, family need for material aid and welfare benefits, and non-attendance at school. Reviews the current ways that social work services are being provided and discusses the pros and cons of locating these services in the school or in the community.

C234

Social work services for children in school,

Association of Directors of Social Services, ADSS, 1978, 45pp

Statement from the ADSS highlighting the need for social work services in school and describing some of the possible tasks. Reviews the current state of the Education Welfare Service and suggests that it would be in a better position to undertake this work if its functions were transferred from Education to Social Services.

C235

School social work and crime prevention,

AVERY, P, and ADAMSON, R F, *Howard Journal*, vol 12, no 4, 1969, pp 264–270

Account of the work and role of school social workers and the way in which they help other staff members become more aware of the children's problems. Discusses casework and the relationships with outside social work agencies, and gives some attention to the role of the school in the prevention of delinquency.

C236

Partnership in practice: a study of the pastoral care system and its interaction with a school social worker in a Haringey comprehensive school,

BOND, C M, Polytechnic of North London, Survey Research Unit, Research Report no 10, 1981, 154pp

Research study of the operation of a pastoral care system in a Haringey comprehensive school and the relationship of pastoral care staff with a school social worker. Discusses the various models of pastoral care used in schools and notes possible points of conflict between teachers and social workers. In general the school social worker was seen as a valued member of the team whose role was complementary to that of pastoral care staff.

C237

Social workers: providing a service for children in school,

DAVIES, C, *News and Views . . . Social Work in Education*, no 4, 1979, pp 15–21

Sets out some of the current problems in teacher-social worker relationships, including mistrust, ignorance of each other's role, and stereotyping. Highlights how communications between schools and various other caring agencies can often break down, resulting in neglect of the child. Suggests that difficulties can be overcome by effective communication, consultation machinery, democratic management and professional support.

C238

Social work in education,

DAVIS, L F, *Ideas*, no 32, February 1976, pp 72–6

Examination of the possible roles for social workers within education, including diagnosing principal areas of inadequacy, conflict and personal distress within the family, initiating remedial measures, mediating between home and school, and monitoring the effectiveness of the action taken.

C239

Social work support team: Grange County Comprehensive School,

DERRICK, D (ed), Centre for Information and Advice on Educational Disadvantage, 1977, 12pp

Description of an initiative at Grange Comprehensive School, Ellesmere Port, through the creation of a special social work support team, consisting of a social worker, teacher/counsellor and education welfare officer. The objective was to provide a full range of counselling and social work facilities to groups of schools for the benefit of school staff, children and parents, and to enable the school to undertake more preventive work. Benefits have included greater understanding of a problem, greater accessibility, speed of response and effectiveness. Liaison with classroom teachers remained problematic in some cases however.

C240

Social work in a school setting,

DINNAGE, R, *Social Work Today*, vol 10, no 2, 5 September 1978, pp 12–14

Description of the work of a part-time social worker within a comprehensive school, seeing boys individually and in groups and acting as advisor to pastoral care staff.

C241

Education and social services: a partnership,

DUNN, J, et al, Joint Occasional Publication no 1, University of Lancaster, 1981, 37pp

Collection of readings on various aspects of the partnership between Education and Social Services. Provides an overview of various existing models of co-operation and discusses systems of pastoral care, the role of school counsellors as links between schools and other agencies, and examples of school social work.

C242

Education and Social Services: models of partnership,

DUNN, J (ed), Joint Occasional Publication no 3, University of Lancaster, 1982, 30pp

Collection of papers on social work support for schools, including descriptions of the Haringey school-based social work scheme, the pyramid model of social work support to schools using a team of counsellors, education welfare officer and social worker, an off-site residential unit in Scotland, and a groupwork project with second year pupils in a secondary school.

C243

Hillhead Junior High School Services Truancy Project,

FIRTH, R,
Centre for Information and Advice on Educational Disadvantage, 1977, 12pp

Short report on a Gateshead project in which an extra teacher was appointed to visit the families of children with a record of poor school attendance. Close liaison was established with Social Services to provide follow-up in the case of substantial family difficulties. A group of children were identified as possibly benefitting from special intervention, who attended a youth centre each morning where they followed a remedial education and personal development programme before returning to school in the afternoon.

C244

Working in no man's land,

FRANCIS, N,
Times Educational Supplement, 11 March 1977, pp 20–1

Examination of the role of liaison teachers, based on the experience of the new posts created in West Yorkshire. Highlights the important work they were able to do providing support to families and school staff, but does not minimise the difficulties experienced in establishing a distinctive role in relation to teachers and education welfare officers.

C245

Towards a more effective use of social workers in schools (Parts one and two),

HARDING, R,
Association for Counselling and Social Care Bulletin, no 2, August 1975, pp 9–13, and no 3, December 1975, pp 3–8

Two articles, the first of which highlights the division between the teacher/counsellor/ pastoral care staff dealing with children in their school context and the social worker/ liaison officer who is concerned with the child's home environment and the network of external agencies. The second article sets out a possible job description for a school-based worker who would be a combination of school counsellor, liaison officer and family therapist and thus provide a unified service for pupils.

C246

Introducing a school social worker into schools,

HARVEY, L, et al,
British Journal of Guidance and Counselling, vol 5, no 1, January 1977, pp 26–40

A DES sponsored school-based social work programme in Gateshead and Newcastle, which placed social workers in secondary schools to collaborate with teachers in work with at risk and maladjusted pupils. The principal components of the scheme included teacher–social worker consultation, attempts to increase parent–teacher understanding, and a casework approach with the families. Specific help was given to teachers to work out problems of classroom management.

C247

School-based social workers in Haringey,

JOHNSTON, S,
Centre for Information and Advice on Educational Disadvantage, 1977, 8pp

Report of the work of the school-based social workers in Haringey. Social workers receive referrals from teachers, liaise with pastoral care staff, visit the family, see children at school and complete referrals within social work area teams, keeping their files up to date. Report lists the advantages of the scheme and the ways in which other roles such as the EWO have been altered by it and notes still unresolved problems.

C248

Developmental groupwork in the secondary school: an experimental programme for pupils at risk, including irregular attenders,

JORDAN, J (ed),
University College Swansea, Department of Education, Occasional Paper no 6, 1977, 17pp

Report on a six-week full-time personal development programme for children with poor school attendance and some behavioural difficulties. The project was staffed by a teacher and a social worker and used developmental groupwork as a way of helping young people to examine their personal positions and needs and to devise strategies for their own growth. Describes the content of the programmes and the improvement noted in the pupils and discusses how such a programme might be incorporated into the pastoral work of the school.

C249

Social work and the school,

LYONS, K H,
HMSO, 1973, 54pp

Reviews the role of social work in schools. Suggests that the welfare work of schools is best carried out by social workers rather than teachers because of the nature of the work and the value of an independent opinion from another profession. Education social work is an effective tool for prevention work because of the close links which can be developed between schools, parents, pupils and health and welfare services.

C250

An experimental evaluation of school social work,

MARSHALL, T F, and ROSE, G,
British Journal of Guidance and Counselling, vol 3, no 1, January 1975, pp 2–14

Findings from the Central Lancashire Family and Community Project, which attempted to determine experimentally the value of social work undertaken in secondary schools. Five workers with varying social work, youth work, medical and counselling backgrounds were placed in schools with the brief to help children and their families solve or adjust to personal and social problems. Comparisons of groups of children sent to court or referred to the school social worker found that the latter group showed sustained improvement in behaviour and in test measures of social adjustment. Some problems of working in schools and liaising with teachers were encountered but the setting did aid the early identification of potential difficulties.

C251

Teacher with a foot in both camps,

MORRIS, P,
Community Care, no 238, 8 November 1978, pp 20–1

Description of the work of a teacher–social worker in a Liverpool comprehensive. The post has mainly involved providing support for families at an early stage when the pupil first starts school and later on, when specific problems have been identified. Truancy cases are dealt with in conjunction with the local EWO. Some initial hostility and suspicion was experienced from teaching staff but this was eventually overcome.

C252

The place of social work in schools,

MUSGRAVE, P W,
Community Development Journal, vol 10, no 1, January 1975, pp 50–6

Clarifies some of the issues involved in establishing closer relationships between schools and social work agencies. Notes the clear differences of role expectations between teachers and social workers and argues against trying to combine the two. Notes the establishment of social education teams within schools, which is seen as a possible way of providing social work services that avoids some of the administrative problems.

C253

Social workers in schools,

PACKWOOD, T,
Health and Social Service Journal, 3 July 1976, pp 1210–1211

Analyses some of the differences between teachers and social workers that hinder collaboration and suggests there is a case for attaching social workers to schools who might work with children on an individual basis or in association with other teaching staff.

C254

Schools and social work,

ROBINSON, M,
Routledge and Kegan Paul, 1978, 268pp

Overview of the inter-relationship of schools and social work. The first part considers the tasks of education and social work in relation to schools, children and their families, and presents a model of the process of social breakdown as it affects these three participants. Later sections deal with methods of intervention. the role and function of the Education Welfare Service and relationships between teachers and social workers.

C255

Counselling and school social work,

ROSE, G, and MARSHALL, T F,
John Wiley, 1974, 347pp

Report of the findings of the Central Lancashire Family and Community Project, which looked at the effect on the social adjustment of pupils of appointing social workers and counsellors to schools. Through the use of standardised tests it presents results on the effect of various kinds of intervention with the pupils, families and schools on delinquency rates and social adjustment.

C256

Misalliance or a working partnership? Social work in the school setting,

SALTMARSH, M,
Social Work Today, vol 4, no 6, 14 June 1973, pp 161–4

Argues for the placement of social workers within comprehensive schools and describes the contribution they can make. Acknowledges that there can be some difficulties in relating to teaching staff.

C257

Social workers in schools: the teachers' response,

WOLSTENHOLME, F, and KOLVIN, I,
British Journal of Guidance and Counselling, vol 8, no 1, January 1980, pp 44–56

Survey of teachers who participated in a school-based social work scheme and were questioned about their attitudes to the programme. Findings suggest that the teachers valued most of all the support of the social workers and the information about families which the social workers provided. They were less impressed by the social workers' skills in helping them to clarify problems and in assisting them to think of alternative pupil management procedures.

Day Care

C258

Day care in intermediate treatment: a report on the school year 1977–78,

ADDISON, C,
Wandsworth Social Services Department, 1980, 43pp

Report of a research project reviewing the day care programme provided by Wandsworth IT centres during its first year, 1977–78. Notes some difficulty in overall relationships with the Education authority, particularly regarding arrangements for reintegrating children into schools. Identifies certain children who had rejected school but made good progress at the centres and eventually found work when they left.

C259

Intermediate treatment: radical alternative, palliative or extension of social control?

BERESFORD, P, and CROFT, S,
Battersea Community Action, 1982, 25pp

Critical presentation of the work of an IT centre, particularly regarding its role as a source of alternative education for children excluded from school. Notes that the project leaders have given up trying to influence practice within local schools and are attempting to provide compensatory academic and social experiences within the centre. Suggests, as a result of conversations with young people in the community, that disaffection from school is a common experience and the IT centre is providing a numerically and educationally limited, individualised response to a major problem, which distracts attention from the prime need to achieve educational reform within schools.

C260

Hammersmith Teenage Project Annual Report 1981/82,

Hammersmith Teenage Project, 1983

Current report of the work of the Hammersmith Teenage Project, including descriptions of the day care programme and examples of rewards and sanctions and contracts used by the project.

C261

Filling a gap in the arm of care,

HARBRIDGE, E,
Community Care, no 346, 5 February 1981, pp 18–20

Account of the work of the Junior Intermediate Treatment Centre in Islington, in which teachers and social workers co-operate to provide a preventive service for children exhibiting educational and social problems in junior schools. The children return to their schools in the afternoon and will eventually be reintegrated completely.

C262

Intermediate treatment: review of policies and practices in the London Boroughs,

KENNY, D,
Central Policy Unit, Greater London Council, 1981, 55pp

Review of IT policies and practices in London boroughs, commissioned by the London Boroughs' Children's Regional Planning Committee. It notes that underachievement and attendance and behavioural problems at school were common criteria for selection of children for IT projects, particularly those with education programmes. Includes a section on IT relations with Education authorities, which reveals considerable variation between those authorities in the extent to which they were prepared to co-operate with other agencies such as Social Services in the provision of alternative education. A common problem reported was the late referral of children close to school leaving age, who were unlikely to be reintegrated back into the classroom.

C263

The Harvey Centre,

Kensington and Chelsea Social Services Department, (197–), 3pp

Short description of the work of the Harvey Centre, which provides day care for children during the first two years of secondary school. Children may attend the Centre for up to two terms but will continue to attend school for part of the week to maintain links and will eventually return full time.

C264

North Lambeth intermediate treatment, Salamanca project – school-age scheme,

Lambeth Social Services Department, 1980, 19pp

Report of the work of the Salamanca project, which provides day care for young offenders and school refusers. Young people attend the courses and activities under a contract for an academic year, but remain on the roll of their former school. The report includes examples of the contracts used, conditions of referral and the basic education programme provided.

C265

Wandsworth: a multi-disciplinary approach to intermediate treatment,

LEGGETT, E (ed),
National Youth Bureau, 1979, 39pp

Primarily an overview of the development of day care work in Wandsworth, which describes the day care programme provided, models of social groupwork, the involvement of volunteers and work with families. The philosophy of the programme ensures that referrals are not limited just to identified offenders, but include many children viewed as underachieving or disaffected from school. There is some discussion of the relative responsibilities of Social Services and Education for meeting the needs of these children and the practicalities of negotiating with schools regarding eventual reintegration.

C266

Intermediate treatment centres,

LOCKE, T L,
Information sheet, National Youth Bureau, 1980, 3pp

Short analysis of a 1979 survey of 50 IT centres, covering purposes, size, funding, etc. About half had day programmes, including education, and the paper briefly notes the role of LEAs, links with schools, and truants or school refusers as target group.

C267

Day assessment and short-term treatment for juveniles in trouble,

McAULAY, M, and CUNNINGHAM, G,
Community Homes Gazette, vol 74, no 6, September 1980, pp 196–203

Includes description of the work of the persistent non-attenders team at Whitefield House, Belfast, who provide a day care programme for young people referred to them and liaise closely with school to ensure that reintegration takes place satisfactorily. Work undertaken with the families aims to help them with practical everyday organisation.

C268

Lost on the way to school,

McCARRICK, D,
Community Care, no 345, 29 January 1981, pp 16–17

Article discussing the role of IT day care in relation to school non-attendance. Suggests that effective intervention for absenteeism needs to take place at a much earlier stage, but if the point is reached when day care is seen to be appropriate, this should function as a real alternative to school and not seek to reintegrate the child.

C269

Report on the progress of the Markhouse Centre project including reports submitted to the Committee for Community Welfare and the Committee for Education and the Arts, Dec. 1980,

Markhouse Centre, 1980, 19pp

Research report providing information on children attending the Markhouse Centre in Waltham Forest during 1979, giving details of individual and family characteristics, school attendance and offences. Five appendices provide additional material on the special problems exhibited by children, the facilities and services offered by the Centre and case histories of individual children.

C270

Report on the development of the Markhouse Centre,

Markhouse Centre, 1981, 14pp

An overview of the work of a centre in Waltham Forest which provides a range of day care and evening groups for children and young people of different age groups with varying needs. The education programme for children referred from school with attendance and behaviour difficulties can take the form of school-based groups providing support and counselling services for non-attenders, an intensive programme providing half-day care, social skills and community placement schemes on a session basis, and school leavers work experience schemes. Markhouse staff act as link people between the Centre and the schools, visiting them once a week, and also provide individual help to pupils in the school setting.

C271

The Grenville Centre,

London Borough of Merton, Education Department, 1980, 2pp

Short report of the work of the Grenville Centre, which provides day care for pupils referred for disruption and general indiscipline in school. The programme is geared to the individual following a pattern of academic work, crafts and mixed activities in the afternoon. The aim is to reintegrate children into school, although some remain at the Centre until school leaving age.

C272

Report of educational development at Penybryn Intermediate Treatment Centre,

Mid Glamorgan Education Authority, Cynon Valley District, 1980, 3pp

Short report of the Penybryn Intermediate Centre, which provides day care during the course of one term for pupils referred for delinquency and/or truancy. Close links are retained with the school and results so far seem to suggest that attendance improves once the pupil returns to school.

C273

The Hammersmith Teenage Project: an experiment in the community care of young offenders,

National Association for Care and Resettlement of Offenders, Barry Rose (Publishers) Ltd, 1978, 56pp

Report of the establishment and initial operation of the Hammersmith Teenage Project between 1975–77. The project catered for young people who had offended and been cautioned by the police and for teenagers referred from local schools for disruptive behaviour. Provided a flexible and individually-designed day care programme and liaised closely with schools in arranging for young people to be reintegrated on a part-time basis. Describes interagency co-operation with the courts, Police, Education authority and Social Services.

C274

Developing day-care,

PICKLES, T,
Youth in Society, no 52, March 1981, pp 20–1

Discussion of the role of IT day care, which warns against its use as alternative education or as a means whereby schools can dispose of their unwanted or troublesome pupils. Reaffirms that one of the main objectives of day care should be the intention to return the pupil to some form of continuing education within the community, which applies equally to suspended pupils, poor school attenders or disruptive pupils.

C275

The first twelve months: report of the Youth Liaison Tutor Project,

QUIERY, G,
Liverpool Education Committee, 1980, 15pp

Report of a project set up in Liverpool under the Inner City Partnership scheme, in which youth liaison tutors work with young people known to a range of social welfare agencies for persistent absenteeism or serious behaviour difficulties. After extensive liaison with a variety of community agencies, a programme was worked out for individual pupils consisting of tutorial work, community service placements and work experience placements, which was intended to occupy them for the entire week.

C276

Osmond House IT Centre Report,

TAYLOR, R,
Osmond House IT Centre, 1982, 7pp

Report of a Barnado's IT centre in Birmingham. Includes discussion of the day care programme, which offers educational input, social work support, activity-based options and work preparation for young people. The work is undertaken on a medium-to long-term contractual basis with young people who have become irretrievably disenchanted with mainstream education and are highly unlikely to return to normal day school.

C277

Collaboration in action: three IT projects run jointly by Education and Social Services,

VINCENT, J, in *Planning resources for community based treatment of juvenile offenders*, Vincent J, vol 4, pp 38–65, Social Policy Research Ltd, 1980

Description of the organisation, staffing and activities of three IT centres and some general conclusions on the lessons to be learnt from such initiatives. Highlights the problems of establishing a satisfactory identity, building effective relationships with referring agencies, clarifying internal relationships and coping with isolation.

C278

Curriculum planning within day care,

WHITE, R, et al, in *Practice development papers*, Whitlam, M R (ed), pp 143–152, National Intermediate Treatment Federation, 1981

Guidelines for curriculum planning within day care, which asks the kind of questions which would help projects determine what kind of programme they intended to provide and what role they were assuming in relation to schools and the education department.

IT Group Work with Schools

C279

Pilot scheme for school leavers,

BIETZK, M,
Northants Social Services/Southwood Upper School, 1982, 7pp

Six week discussion group held in school with fifth form pupils who had underachieved during their school career, exhibited disruptive behaviour in class and were at risk of being suspended. The group aimed to discuss problems the pupils had encountered during their school careers and used self-assessment questionnaires, role play exercises and modelling. Staff comprised an EWO, two social workers and a teacher.

C280

Starting blocks,

BURLEY, D,
National Youth Bureau, 1982, 24pp

Detailed account of a social education group for young people not attending school, referred by teachers, probation officers and social workers, sponsored by Nottingham Young Volunteers. The approach adopted focussed on enabling young people to take collective action to meet their identified needs and describes their experiences in organising various events and the process within the group. Includes a series of guidelines to enable workers to plan, take part in and evaluate similar groups.

C281

Sandwell Intermediate Treatment Centre, Smethwick: an evaluation of the Centre's work September 1980 to May 1982,

CRUTCHER, M,
Sandwell Social Services Department, 1982, 113pp

Independent research report of the work of the Centre, which provides an intensive evening programme for young people on care and supervision orders and those at risk. Describes the work with children referred for school non-attendance and provides statistics on the subsequent attendance at school of all participants in the programme for the period covered.

C282

Devising a treatment model based on 'girls only' method,

GROVES, I,
Social Work Today, vol 11, no 48, 19 August 1980, pp 12–13

Description of a six week evening IT programme for girls referred for non school attendance, which included a teacher as a staff member and a number of volunteers. The programme was based on discussion and included some role play exercises.

C283

The Ynys Mon Intermediate Treatment Project,

HUTCHINGS, J, et al,
International Journal of Behavioural Social Work and Abstracts, vol 1, no 3, 1981, pp 187–198

Weekly IT group with eight boys from the same community who were experiencing problems at school, identified as low achievers and at risk of residential care. They were released from school to attend at a community centre for afternoon sessions which focussed on analysing their behaviour in and out of school and setting targets for improving their interaction with specified individuals. Results suggested that when planning for changes in behaviour at school, pupil record keeping and reporting back to the group can lead to positive behaviour changes recognised by teachers.

C284

The Thursday Club,

Leeds Social Services Department, 1981, 11pp

Evening IT group for children at risk of court appearance for school non-attendance. Used a mixed programme of creative activities, developmental games and discussion, and achieved improvements in school attendance and personal development.

C285

Getting IT at school,

MORE, W,
Community Care, no 175, 17 August 1977, pp 20–1

Highlights the importance of school in the lives of young people and the key role of the teacher in identifying potential pressure points, and proposes a mutually supportive partnership between teachers and IT specialists in meeting the needs of children.

C286

Turf Lodge Teenage Project: intermediate treatment group report,

MULHOLLAND, M, et al,
Save The Children Fund, November 1980, 12pp

Report of a Belfast evening IT group containing children referred from school for non-attendance. The programme included interaction games, a residential weekend and trips out and some improvement in attendance was obtained.

C287

Preventive work in the school,

PITTS, J,
Youth Social Work Bulletin, vol 1, no 2, January–February 1974, pp 3–8

Description of two school-based IT groups in Lewisham, one held in and one out of school, based on discussion and activities. Suggests that the group experience can offer the underachieving child who has low status within the school an opportunity of succeeding in one area of his school life and using the skills he possesses in a creative way.

C288

Moat Project,

STAINES, L, et al,
Leicestershire Social Services Department,
August 1981, 5pp

Account of a nine week school-based
programme with a group of six fourth-year
girls referred for behavioural problems. The
programme consisted of a mixture of
discussion and activity sessions and involved a
teacher and two social workers with an IT
worker as consultant.

C289

Breaking down the professional barriers,

WARD, D, and PEARCE, J,
Social Work Today, vol 10, no 36, 15 May
1979, pp 19–21

Description of a school-based after hours
group for seven boys on supervision. Involved
the collaboration of a teacher and probation
officer and provided a useful framework for
discussing school-related problems.

C290

IT truants group,

WEISS, I,
Durham Social Services Department, 1981,
11pp

Fortnightly IT group for school non-attenders
covering discussion, craft activities and trips.
Achieved improved school attendance, more
self-awareness and greater articulation of
school-related problems.

C291

Report on Cheetham IT group,

WESTLEY, K,
Manchester Social Services Department,
August 1979, 7pp

Evening activity-based IT group for children
referred by EWOs at risk of local authority
care because of non-attendance at school. The
programme mainly involved physical activities
and sports such as swimming, ten pin
bowling, ice skating and horse riding, and was
successful in arousing and developing some
legitimate interests available to boys on their
own.

Police

C292

The school bobby,

BOURNE, R,
New Society, vol 38, no 735, 4 November
1976, pp 257–8

Article on the work of the Community
Involvement Unit based at Basildon in Essex.
The school liaison officers attempt to build
attitudes of law-abiding citizenship in school
children of all ages and divert potential young
offenders. Activities include participation in a
timetabled course on legal and police history,
work in youth clubs and a combination of
supervision and befriending of young people
who have been cautioned.

C293

**Juveniles: co-operation between the Police
and other agencies,**

Home Office Circular 211/1978, Home
Office/DHSS/DES/Welsh Office, 1978, 4pp

Joint circular, addressed to chief officers of
Police, Probation, Education and Social
Services, urging interagency co-operation,
with Police involvement, in activities to
prevent juvenile delinquency. Gives some

examples, including Police-school liaison,
suggests that chief officers review their
interagency co-operation, and calls on chief
constables to initiate these reviews and report
back to Home Office, with examples.

C294

**Juveniles: co-operation between the police
and other agencies,**

Home Office Circular 83/1980, Home Office,
1980, 7pp
Circular illustrating Police co-operation with
other agencies in work with juveniles, based
on Police responses to an earlier circular.
Includes a section on Police involvement with
schools describing preventive classroom work
and truancy patrols.

C295

Police juvenile liaison and schools,

Merseyside Police, 1982, 13pp

Description of a wide-ranging series of Police
initiatives taking the form of sporting, social
and educational activities designed to promote
good relations between schools, young people
and the Police. Includes a section on a
community relations course involving Police,
Social Services, Probation and Education
Welfare.

C296

**Missing school – missing out? Review of
the Police school liaison officers' scheme
operated in North Wales from its
introduction in Sept 1976,**

North Wales Police, 1979, 18pp

Description of the work of Police school
liaison officers in North Wales, who have
been based in education offices working
closely with Education Welfare Officers and
other education social workers. Their primary
function has been carrying out truancy patrols
but they have gradually extended into other
areas of work, such as home visiting, lecturing
and exhibiting films to schools and IT groups.
They have also taken part in the regular
interagency meetings held at one school.

C297

Police school liaison scheme,

PHILLIPS, K, and HOCKING, C,
Devon and Cornwall Constabulary, Police
Juvenile Bureaux, Plymouth, 1982, 7pp

Description of the preventive programme with
schools carried out by Police school liaison
staff, including films, discussion, sports and
visits.

C298

Children through the net,

REYNOLDS, D,
Community Care, no 289, 8 November 1979,
pp 27–9

Discusses the use of Police truancy patrols as
a means of enforcing attendance and
highlights some of the problems created by
this approach. Also considers some proposals
from the Magistrates' Association to the effect
that the courts should have the power to
impose sanctions on children who fail to
observe a court order requiring them to return
to school.

C299

**An example of co-operation and good
practice between the Sussex Police
Community Relations Department and the
East Sussex County Education Welfare
Service,**

ROWLANDS, G,
East Sussex County Council, 1979, 9pp

Paper presented to the annual conference of
the National Association of Chief Education
Welfare Officers. Describes a co-operative
exercise between the Police and EWOs
conducting truancy patrols in Hastings,
Eastbourne, Brighton and Hove. Presents
statistics suggesting that just over half of the
juveniles checked were condoned absentees or
truants. Warning letters were sent to parents
and some were later prosecuted.

C300

Community policing,

SCHAFFER, E B,
Croom Helm, 1980, 145pp

Contains a chapter on Police work with
schools, which highlights in particular the
work of the Sussex Police school liaison
officers, and measures undertaken to combat
truancy in Strathclyde. Notes the early
recognition by the Police that they needed to
make a special appeal to the non-academic
child, with the result that most courses,
lessons and special projects are practical in
nature.

C301

Police community involvement in Scotland,

SHANKS, N J,
Central Research Unit, Scottish Office, 1980,
34pp

Overview of Police community involvement in
Scotland, which includes a section on work
with schools. Notes the variation between
different forces in their degree of enthusiasm
for the work and coverage of primary and
secondary schools, but highlights some of the
useful teaching packages that have been
developed and the comprehensive and coordinated programme evolved by Tayside
Region. Refers in passing to difficulties
encountered in selecting appropriate parts of
the curriculum for Police courses.

C302

Police preventive work with juveniles,

SHARP, L,
Education Social Worker, no 179, June 1979,
pp 22–8

Discusses the importance of reducing the
current level of truancy because of the link
with delinquency, and describes the objectives
of Police/school liaison, which are seen as
diverting potential juvenile law breakers,
creating trust and understanding between
Police and the young, and providing support
to pupils, teachers and parents.

C303

Police, propaganda and pedagogy,

Teachers' Action Collective,
Teachers' Action, no 14, Spring 1981, pp 9–13

Critical review of Police work in schools,
which suggests that the neutrality of schools is
being infringed and challenged by this
intervention. Notes that in many cases
classroom teachers have little participation in
decision making concerning the desirability of
a Police contribution to the curriculum.

C (vii) ONE-TO-ONE
VOLUNTARY WORK

C304

Called before the panel,

CARDWELL, M,
Rapport, vol 4, no 5, May 1979, p 17

Report on the work of the Volunteer Tutors
Organisation in Glasgow, an independent
charity, which attempts to tackle the
underlying problem of illiteracy and
educational failure among young people,
which often manifests itself in the form of
truancy and delinquency. Adult volunteers are
paired with children who have been referred
to the Children's Hearing and spend time in
their homes, helping with school work and
providing information and encouragement on
any other subject in which they express an
interest.

C305

'I can't read, in fact I'm illegitimate',

HOLMAN, B,
Times Educational Supplement, 28 March 1980,
pp 22–3

Description of individual work with absentee
and at risk children on a West Country estate,
as part of a neighbourhood project sponsored
by the Church of England Children's Society.
Since project workers live on the estate and
have close liaison with schools, they are able
to befriend children and offer practical help in
getting them to school, and also mediate on
their behalf with individual teachers.

C306

**Burleigh College's tutor-mother scheme
for students with learning difficulties,**

MARSHALL, M,
Burleigh Community College, 1981, 13pp

Report of a scheme run by Burleigh
Community College, Loughborough, in which
groups of fourth year pupils with learning
difficulties and associated personality and
behaviour problems take part in the tutor-
mother scheme for one term. Pupils spend all
of one day with a volunteer who has young
children at home and share in the running of
the home and care of the family. Initial results
have indicated considerable gains in self
confidence and independence on the part of
pupils, and the establishment of close
relationships with tutors.

C307

Have you thought of involving volunteers?

PLOUVIEZ, M,
News and Views . . . Social Work in Education,
no 4, 1979, pp 7–11

Discussion of the way in which volunteers can
be used to complement the work of teachers
and social workers helping children with
learning or behavioural difficulties at school.
Describes one scheme in which volunteers
were recruited to act as counsellors to
disturbed children who were underachieving
at school. Each volunteer spent one session a
week with the child during school time
engaging in activities designed to develop
trusting relationships and increase self-
confidence.

Area/Agency/Project/Source Index

For local authority reports, see under geographical area

Aberdeen
B26

ACE
C57,C73,C173,C183

Adelaide Centre
C99

Advisory Centre for Education
See 'ACE'

All-Party Parliamentary Group for Children
C203

Argyle Street Project
C98

Assistant Masters Association
A10

Association for Behaviour Modification with Children
B102

Association for Counselling and Social Care Bulletin
C245

Association of Assistant Mistresses
A11

Association of Directors of Social Services
C115,C174,C211,C234

Association of Northern Ireland Education and Library Boards
C14

Association of Workers for Maladjusted Children
C47,C49

Ayrshire
B50

Barnardo's
C276

Barnsley Special Education Team
C53

Baseline
C89,C104

Basildon
C292

Battersea Community Action
C259

Bayswater Centre
C106,C166

Bedford
C228

Belfast
C52,C267,C286

Berkshire
C46,C86,C100

Birmingham
B12,B17,C55,C88,C89,C96,C104,C111, C167,C201,C276

Birmingham Association of Social Education Centres
C89,C104

Birmingham, University of
B113

Bradford
C200, C229

Brislington School
C42-C44,C100

Bristol
C42-C44,C84,C100,C106,C166

British Association of Social Workers
C174,C233

British Journal of Criminology
B73,C189,C209

British Journal of Educational Psychology
B2,B13,B27,B33,B79,B85,C176

British Journal of Guidance and Counselling
B95,C154,C157,C159,C163,C246,C250, C257

British Journal of Psychiatry
B81,C208

British Journal of Social Work
C186,C187,C195

British Psychological Society
C129,C130,C141

Broadway School
C104

Brunel Institute of Organisation and Social Studies/University
B99,C87,C108,C109,C120,C136,C220

Buckinghamshire
B27

Bulletin of the British Psychological Society
C129,C141

Burleigh College
C306

Calderdale
C35,C85,C212

Caldicot School Socialization Project
C232

Cambridge Journal of Education
B29,C33

Cambridge Study in Delinquent Development
B71

Cardiff, University College of
B112

CED
C212,C230,C239,C243,C247

Central Lancashire Family and Community Project
C250,C255

Central Region
C134

Centre for Educational Research and Development
B1,B7,B83,C241,C242

Centre for Information and Advice on Educational Disadvantage
See 'CED'

Centre of Youth, Crime and Community
B1,B7,B83,C241,C242

Cheetham IT Group
C291

Cheshire
C239

Church of England Children's Society
C305

Clearing House for Local Authority Social Services Research
C200

Cleveland
C15

Clwyd
C192

Cobden Trust
C207

Community Care
A27,C99,C107,C113,C205,C251,C261, C268,C285,C298

Community Development Journal
C252

Community Health
C46

Community Home Schools Gazette
C98,C193,C201

Community Homes Gazette
C96,C267

Community Projects Foundation
C86

Comprehensive Education
C90,C103,C168

Contact
See 'ILEA Contact'

Counsellor
B34

Coventry
C170

Cranfield Institute of Technology
B72

Croydon
C105,C138

Cumbria
C16

Department of Education and Science
B4,B42,B93,C7,C10,C12,C13,C74,C293

Department of Education for Northern Ireland
C17

Department of Health and Social Security
B61,C219,C221,C293

London, Outer
B69,B99,B104,C87,C220

London Boroughs' Children's Regional
Planning Committee
C262

London Educational Review
B107,C135,C142

London, University of
**B67,B69,B103,B115,B117,C59,C82,C92,
C171**

Lothian
C184,C225

Loughborough
C306

Magistrates' Association
C298

Manchester
A29,C56,C291

Markhouse Centre
C269,C270,C277

Merseyside Police
C295

Merton
C271

MIND
C207

Moat Project
C288

Municipal Review
C105

NACRO
A28,C199,C273

NAME/NAME
C57,C63,C67,C68

National Association for Care and
Resettlement of Offenders
See 'NACRO'

National Association for Multiracial
Education
See 'NAME'

National Association of Chief Education
Welfare Officers
B29

National Association of Governors and
Managers
C181

National Association of Schoolmasters
A12-A14,B97,C125

National Association of the Teachers of
Wales
A15

National Child Development Study
B13,B14,B76,B77

National Children's Bureau
B76

National Foundation for Educational
Research
C161

National Intermediate Treatment
Federation
C278

National Organisation for Initiatives in
Social Education
C97

National Union of Teachers
A16

National Youth Bureau
C210,C265,C266,C280

New Era
C164

New Society
**A29,B55,B58,B77,C84,C95,C114,C165,
C292**

Newcastle
C45,C246,C257

Newham
A8

Newlands Centre
C89

*News and Views . . . Social Work in
Education*
C110,C237,C307

NOISE
C97

North Eastern Education and Library
Board
B48

North London, Polytechnic of
C236

North Western Regional Society of
Education Officers
B39

North Yorkshire Teachers' Association
C26

Northamptonshire
C27,C279

Northern Ireland
**B9,B11,B18,B48,B98,C1,C14,C17,C52,
C193,C267,C286**

Northern Ireland Polytechnic
C52

Northumberland
C102

Nottingham, University of
C213

Nottingham Young Volunteers
C231,C280

Nursing Mirror
B89

149 Centre
C86

Open University
B68

Osmond House IT Centre
C276

Paddington School
C172

Parkhead Centre
C102

Penybryn Centre
C272

Plymouth
C297

Policy and Politics
C32

Portsmouth
C132

Practitioner
B6

Psychological Medicine
C190

Rapport
C304

Reading
C86,C100

Remedial Education
C88

Research in Education
B32

RoSLA Community Education Project
C166

Salamanca House
C264

Sandwell IT Centre
C281

Save the Children Fund
C286

School and Home Project
B3

School Organisation
B56

Schools Council
A19,A24,C51

Schools Curriculum Project in
Community Relations
C52

Scotland
**A1,B28,C4,C5,C9,C185,C202,C206,C225,
C242,C301 (See also separate cities and
regions)**

Scottish Education Department
C5,C225

Scottish Educational Review
A1,A6,B50

Scottish Educational Studies
B26

Scottish Office
C13,C225,C301

SCYPTAR
C227

Sheffield
**B2,B3,B15,B16,B49,B75,B101,C124,
C175,C176,C194-C197,C219**

Sheffield, University of
B24

Sidney Stringer School
C170

Smethwick
C281

Social and Economic Administration
C215

Social Policy Research Ltd
C277

Social Work Today
**B35,C133,C139,C140,C143,C197,C214,
C217,C222,C233,C240,C256,C282,C289**

Socialism and Education
C64,C66

Society of Education Officers
B39,C115

Sociology
C206

Author Index

Figures in **bold** type are the reference numbers of items in the Bibliography. Figures in Roman type refer to page numbers of the Literature Review.

Presland, J
B118,C126

Price, J R
29,31,32   C223,C224

Pritchard, J
12,32   C232

Quelch, T
23   C85

Quiery, G
C275

Ralphs, L
29   C6

Rampton, A
23   C7

Rathbone, R
19   C204

Ravenette, A T
14,33   C127

Rehin, G F
13   C140

Reid, K C
4,5   B31-B35, B56

Reynolds, D
4,6-8,10,11,16   B57,B58,B60-B65

Reynolds, D
5,19,28,32   C205,C298

Ribbins, P
11,13   C144

Riches, S
4,5,10   A8

Roberts, J
3   A23

Robinson, M
28,29,31   C254

Robinson, T J
10,24   C99

Rock, D
23   C83

Rock, E
4   B92

Rodway, A
23   C49

Rose, G
12,30   C250,C255

Rosser, E
7,8   A4

Rowan, P
24   C100

Rowland, G
28,32   C299

Rutter, M
4,7,8,16   B66

Saltmarsh, M
28,33   C256

Sampson, O C
13,33   C141

Saunders, J B
3,17   C11

Schaffer, E B
27   C300

Scrutton, S
28   C226

Seabrook, J
4-6   A5

Seebohm, F
28-30   C8

Seyd, R
17-18   B3,C194-C197

Shanks, N J
27   C301

Sharp, A
3,6,7   A6

Sharp, L
C302

Shepherd, M
4   B27

Shostak, J
7   A7

Smith, G
C206

Spencer, D
24,25   C101

St-John Brooks, C
23   C84

St Leger, S
4,7,8,16   B58

Staines, L
12   C288

Steed, D
5-7,10,13   B103,C32,C33

Steedman, J
B76

Sterne, M
13   C56

Sullivan, M
4,7,16   B63,B65

Sullivan, R
4,5,10   A8

Summerfield, A
13   C10

Swailes, A
23-25   C102

Tattum, D
3,5-8,22-25   B105

Taylor, F
15,16   C183

Taylor, G
3,17   C11

Taylor, L
18   C207

Taylor, M
10,22,24   C103

Taylor, N
23   C83

Taylor, R
25   C276

Taylor, T
C12

Tennent, T G
4,18   B36,C208,C209

Terry, F
A30

Thomas, H
C104

Thomas, J
18,19   C210

Tibbenham, A
4   B14,B77

Tizard, B
B67

Tizard, J
13   C142

Topping, K J
13,23,27,29,30   C35,C85,C128,C129

Turner, B
4,5,6   A5,B78

Tutt, N
4,7,16   B62

Tyerman, M J
3,4,18   B37,B79,B80

Upton, G
13   B112

Varlaam, A
7   B106

Vernon, B
24   C105

Vincent, J
22,25,28,33   C277

Wall, W D
B107

Ward, D
12,30-32   C213,C289

Warnock, H M
10,21,22,30   C13

Watkins, R
32   C227,C230

Webb, S
13,25   C71,C116,C117

Wedell, K
13   B113,C130

Weiss, I
13   C290

Westley, K
13   C291

White, D J
3,4   B50

White, R
12,22-25   C106,C166,C278

Whitlam, M R
C278

Whittam, H
13   C143

Williams, A
23   C50

Williams, K
C164

Subject Index

Address List

All Party Parliamentary Group for Children,

c/o Houses of Parliament, London SW1A 0AA. **C203**

Association of Directors of Social Services (ADSS).

For current officers, see most recent edition of Social Services Year Book — section 'Local Authority Associations'. **C174,C211**

Association of Northern Ireland Education and Library Boards (ANIELB).

For current officers see most recent edition of Education Year Book — section 'Associations of Local Education Committees and of Officers'. **C14**

Association of Workers for Maladjusted Children and Therapeutic Education

Monograph available from: Treasurer John G Visser, Dept of Education, University College, P.O. Box 78, Cardiff CF1 1XL. **C47,C49**

Battersea Community Action,

27 Winders Road, Battersea, London SW11. **C259**

British Association of Social Workers (BASW),

16 Kent Street, Birmingham B5 6RD. **C174**

British Psychological Society,

St Andrews House, 48 Princess Road East, Leicester LE1 7DR. **C130**

Burleigh Community College,

Thorpe Hill, Loughborough, Leicestershire. **C306**

Centre for Educational Disadvantage (CED).

Centre has now been disbanded. Publications may possibly be available from Institute of Education Library, 11-13 Ridgemont Street, London WC1 or contact National Youth Bureau, 17-23 Albion Street, Leicester LE1 6GD. **C212,C230,C239,C243,C247**

Hammersmith Teenage Project,

58a Buliver Street, Shepherd's Bush, London W12. **C260**

Justice for Children,

35 Wellington Street, London WC2E 7BN. **C204**

Markhouse Centre,

Markhouse Road, Walthamstow, London E17 8BD. **C270**

National Association of Chief Education Welfare Officers (NACEWO), *now* **National Association of Chief Education Social Workers.**

For current officers see most recent edition of Education Year Book — section 'Educational and Allied Organisations'. **B29**

National Association of Governors and Managers (NAGM).

For current officers see most recent edition of Education Year Book section — 'Educational and Allied Organisations'. **C181**

National Association of the Teachers of Wales,

Ty'r Cymry, 11 Gordon Road, Caerdydd CF2 3AJ. **A15**

National Foundation for Educational Research in England and Wales (NFER),

The Mere, Upton Park, Slough, Berks SL1 2DQ. **C161**

National Intermediate Treatment Federation (NITFED),

Secretary, Ken Hunnybun, Leicester Social Services Dept, County Hall, Glenfield, Leicester LE3 8RL. Pack also available from NYB. **C278**

National Organisation for Initiatives in Social Education (NOISE),

c/o Social Education Research Project, Centre for Advanced Studies in Education, 9 Westbourne Road, Edgbaston, Birmingham 15. **C97**

North West Regional Society of Education Officers.

For current officers see most recent edition of Education Year Book — section 'Associations of Local Education Committees and of Officers'. **B39**

North Yorkshire Teachers' Association's Consultative Panel,

c/o North Yorkshire Education Department, County Hall, Northallerton, North Yorkshire DL7 8AE. **C26**

Nottingham Young Volunteers,

33 Mansfield Road, Nottingham. **C231**

Osmond House Youth and Intermediate Treatment Centre,

78 Alcester Road, Moseley, Birmingham B13 8BB. **C276**

Daphne Phillips,

260 Wendover, Thurlow Street, London SE17 2UW. **B30**

Save the Children Fund (SCF),

Mary Datchelor House, 17 Grove Lane, London SE5 8RD. **C286**

Sidney Stringer School and Community College,

Cox Street, Coventry CV1 5NL. **C170**

Social Policy Research,

1-2 Berners Street, London W1P 3AG. **C277**

Society of Education Officers,

5 Bentinck Street, London W1M 5RN. **C115**